THE LANGUAGE OF DEFENDANTS IN THE 17TH-CENTURY ENGLISH COURTROOM

ELISABETTA CECCONI

THE LANGUAGE OF DEFENDANTS IN THE 17TH-CENTURY ENGLISH COURTROOM

A SOCIO-PRAGMATIC ANALYSIS OF THE PRISONERS' INTERACTIONAL ROLE AND REPRESENTATION

PETER LANG
Bern · Berlin · Bruxelles · Frankfurt am Main · New York · Oxford · Wien

Bibliographic information published by die Deutsche Nationalbibliothek
Die Deutsche Nationalbibliothek lists this publication in the Deutsche Nationalbibliografie; detailed bibliographic data is available on the Internet at ‹http://dnb.d-nb.de›.

British Library Cataloguing-in-Publication Data: A catalogue record for this book is available from The British Library, Great Britain

Library of Congress Cataloging-in-Publication Data

Cecconi, Elisabetta
The language of defendants in the 17th-century English courtroom : a socio-pragmatic analysis of the prisoners' interactional role and representation / Elisabetta Cecconi.
p. cm.
Includes bibliographical references and index.
ISBN 978-3-0343-1110-6
1. Criminal procedure–England–Language–History–17th century. 2. Trials (Political crimes and offenses)–England–History–17th century. 3. Defense (Criminal procedure)–England–History–17th century. 4. Discourse analysis. I. Title.
KD8330.C43 2012
347.42'509032–dc23

2012006505

'Parliament sentencing Thomas Wentworth, 1st Earl of Strafford'
(Thomas Wentworth, 1st Earl of Strafford)
Credit line: © National Portrait Gallery, London

ISBN 978-3-0343-1110-6

Hochfeldstrasse 32, CH-3012 Bern, Switzerland
info@peterlang.com, www.peterlang.com

Printed in Switzerland

To my father, Maurizio

Table of contents

Acknowledgements

The present work is based on a number of studies presented at national and international conferences over the last four years. My thanks go to the conference participants who offered valuable criticism at different stages of my research. I am also grateful to the anonymous reviewer for accepting my manuscript for publication and Katrin Forrer and the team at Peter Lang.

Portions of chapter 2 of this book appeared in print: "Power confrontation and verbal duelling in the arraignment section of XVII century trials", in *Impoliteness and facework across legal contexts – Special Edition of the Journal of Politeness Research*, vol. 7, 101–121 (2011). I offer thanks to this journal for allowing this material to reappear in the present volume.

Chapter 1

The 17th-century English courtroom

1.1 Objects of analysis and the approach taken

Commenting on the defendant's role in contemporary English trials, Goodrich (1988) notices that "in criminal cases ... the defendant's day is seldom a voluble one, their hearing is brief and their processing swift". Such a marginality in present-day trials has been commonly ascribed to the presence of the opposing lawyers and to the supremacy of bureaucracy over personal voices (Gibbons 2003). Quite a different picture, on the other hand, emerges when we go back to the analysis of 17th-century trials. At the time, in fact, the absence of defence counsels made prisoners responsible for their own defence and ascribed to them – at least in principle – a more active role in the courtroom. In 1721 Serjeant Hawkins argued that any defendant "of Common Understanding may as properly [defend himself] as if he were the best Lawyer" (1721: 400). How prisoners practically dealt with their right of cross-examining prosecution witnesses and constructing evidence is one of the basic objectives of the present study. The analysis of the defendant's interactional behaviour will also contribute to highlighting socio-cultural aspects of early modern English (henceforth EmodE) courtroom procedure, thus enabling a better understanding of the historical evolution of the Law system.

The study has a twofold object of inquiry: 1) the interactional role of defendants in 17th-century English trial proceedings (1616–1693) and 2) the ideologically-charged representation of their verbal and non-verbal behaviour in the text, at the author-readership discourse level. The book is therefore divided into two main sections.

The first one focuses on the prisoners' discourse strategies when interacting with judges, lawyers and witnesses in the arraignment section and in the evidence phase of the trial. The second one moves from the consideration that any court record constitutes a communicative act in its own right and focuses on the narrative techniques adopted by the author (be it a third person or first person recording) in order to forge a positive image of the prisoner.

This study forms part of the emerging field of historical courtroom discourse (Archer 2002, 2005, 2006, 2008; Kryk-Kastovsky 2006) where historical information on judicial practice is complemented by a systematic investigation of linguistic factors which reflect the power dynamics in and outside the courtroom. To this purpose, I shall draw on a number of sources in order to show how defendants confronted the reified power of judges in the arraignment section of the trial. The results will reveal to what extent the common assumption according to which an exercise of power is co-extensive with the status of the defendant needs to be rethought in light of the several examples in which low-status prisoners resist and challenge the court's authority for long periods before submitting.

With regard to the defendants' role as examiners, a quantitative and qualitative investigation will suggest that prisoners were quite reluctant to make use of their questioning rights in the first half of the century. It is only from 1650 onwards that data register an increase in the number of examining questions which formally resemble those used by professionals. This kind of 'imitation of professionals' may be explained by the fact that defendants arrived at the bar almost totally unprepared to manage witness-examination. As a result 'borrowing through direct observation' appeared as the only way to construct their defence. Despite the formal similarities between professionals' and defendants' speech acts, however, the analysis will document a considerable difference in terms of their perlocutionary effects. In fact, although defendants were given the right to ask questions of witnesses, they lacked the institutionally recognised position of authority which would allow them to coerce witnesses' answers as professionals did (Archer 2005: 154).

Finally, at the author-readership discourse level, an examination of the authorial voice will show how the recorder relies on a stock of evaluative markers and forms of speech-representation (e.g. omission, slipping from showing to telling, interlacement of voices) in order to assume and construct ideological consensus around the figure of the defendant. This is particularly the case with those political trials which marked the history of England at the eve of the Civil War. In this respect, it will be interesting to see how the author's discourse construction echoes features of that 17th-century propaganda literature which flourished in connection with the increasing tension between Royalists and Parliamentarians and which was so voraciously consumed by the public[1].

Crucial to my analysis is the notion of context in its socio-cultural and historical dimension. Lingusitic factors are in fact understood as related to aspects of their local context of use. In this sense, the book adopts a historical socio-pragmatic perspective whose primary aim is to "investigate examples of local language use from a specific time in the past that takes account of the

1 In the decades before the English Civil War the regimes of the early modern period, as well as individual political grandees, had exploited print media for political purposes, giving rise to a proliferation of political tracts, pamphlets, broadsides, newsbooks subsumed under the term "pamphleteering" (Peacey 2004). For an analysis of how printed culture contributed to the shaping of public opinion, see R. Cust (1986) "News and politics in early seventeenth century England", J. Raymond, *The Invention of the Newspaper*, J. Raymond (ed.) (1999) *News, Newspapers and Society in Early Modern Britain;* D. Zaret (2000) *Origins of Democratic Culture*; J. Raymond (2003) *Pamphlets and Pamphleteering in Early Modern Britain;* N. Brownlees (2005) "Spoken English in Early English Newspapers", (2006) "Gerrard Winstanley and Radical Political Discourse in Cromwellian England", (2011) *The Language of Periodical News in Seventeenth-Century England*; E. Cecconi (2009) "'Ye Tories round the nation': an analysis of markers of *interactive-involved* discourse in 17th century political broadside ballads".

cognitive, social and cultural contexts influencing the interaction" (Archer 2005: 7). Historical socio-pragmatics is a sub-branch of historical pragmatics and as such it shares some of its features and goals as well as some of its problems of data availability and methodology. Below I shall provide a brief overview of historical pragmatics and the methodological challenges it has to face. The description will also be useful for a deeper understanding of the difficulties met by historical socio-pragmaticians.

1.2 An outline of historical pragmatics and socio-pragmatics

Historical pragmatics developed in the 1980s (Stein 1985) but received its full accreditation only ten years later thanks to Jacobs and Jucker's theorisation of this research area in the volume *Historical Pragmatics: Pragmatic developments in the history of English* (1995). As the name suggests, the significance of the new discipline in the field of text and discourse analysis derives from the successful as much as debated combination of historical linguistics and pragmatics. After decades of mutual perplexities about the relevance of an integrated approach of this kind, historical linguists have begun to ask questions which go beyond the structural level of the sentence to include aspects of the socio-cultural context while pragmatics has extended its scope of research to encompass not only the study of the spoken word but also the analysis of historical written texts as communicative acts in their own right.

As a discipline concerned with "chang[es] in traditions of language use resulting from changes in the situational context" (Jacobs and Jucker 1995: 6), the primary aims of historical pragmatics are:

1) the description and the understanding of conventions of language use in communities that once existed and that are no longer accessible for direct observation;
2) The description and explanation of the development of speech conventions in the course of time.

(Jacobs and Jucker 1995: 6)

Such aims have determined the development of two approaches within historical pragmatics: pragmaphilology and diachronic pragmatics. The former describes the contextual aspects of historical texts, including the addresser and the addressee, their social and personal relationships and the goals of the text (Jacobs and Jucker 1995: 11). The latter focuses on the linguistic inventory and its communicative use across different historical stages of the same language (Jacobs and Jucker 1995: 13). Diachronic pragmatic analysis can be conducted in two different ways: either by taking a linguistic form as point of departure and studying the changing discourse meanings of the chosen element *(form-to-function mapping)* or by starting with a speech function and investigating its changing realisation across time *(function-to-form-mapping)*. Analysing speech functions of the past is often a very difficult task since speech-acts are fuzzy concepts which show both synchronic and diachronic variation (see Jucker 2000; Bertuccelli Papi 2000). I shall return to this point below when discussing the methodological problems of historical pragmaticians. My socio-pragmatic investigation of 17th-century trials is closer to pragmaphilology, though in chapter 3 I shall be commenting on diachronic changes occurring in my dataset in relation to defence strategies.

1.3 Problems of data and methodology in historical pragmatics

The problems of methodology are strictly dependent on the data issue. Many of the research tools of contemporary pragmaticians, in fact, are not available to pragmaticians working with the language of the past. While the former can rely on interview techniques, introspection, questionnaire and electronic devices as a basis for their research, the latter can only draw on written records as appropriate evidence for their claims on spoken language (Culpeper and Kytö 2000, Jucker 2000). This dependence on written records for a pragmatic investigation of historical language use was originally seen as problematic for various reasons:

> 1) the assumption – based on the acknowledgement of the traditional dichotomy between spoken and written language – that only spoken data could be a legitimate source for pragmatics
> 2) The scarcity of appropriate data (e.g. spoken data).
>
> (Archer 2005: 10)

However, thanks to the refinement of modern research on spoken/written texts (Biber 1988; Biber and Finegan 1992; Koch 1999) the two models of discourse are no longer seen as mutually exclusive. Studies have shown that written texts of the past can capture a large variety of communicative practices ranging from the language of distance (typically associated with the graphic code) to the language of immediacy (typically associated with the phonic code) (Koch 1999, Jucker 2000)[2]. The former includes the dimensions of physical distance, publicness, lack of acquaintance, independent setting, referential distance, monologue, communi-

2 Many studies have been conducted on orality in EmodE, among them: Biber and Finegan (1992), Taavitsainen (1995), Kryk-Kastovsky (2000), Culpeper and Kytö (2000a, 2000b), Suhr (2002), Brownlees (2005, 2006), Cecconi (2009).

cative independence of partners, prescribed topic development and formality. The latter includes the parameters of physical immediacy, privacy, intimacy of partners, high emotionality, setting in context of action, referential immediacy, dialogue, communicative cooperation of the partners, free topic development, spontaneity (Koch 1999: 400–401). Obviously some written texts entail more features of communicative immediacy than others. These are speech-related genres which have been recently classified in terms of speech-like, speech-based and speech-purposed genres (Culpeper and Kytö 2010: 17). Speech-like text-types are those which contain features of 'communicative immediacy'; they are not based on nor designed to be like speech and their claim to being oral is solely due to the occurrence of features which are speech-like. An example of this category is personal correspondence which has received large attention from researchers at the University of Helsinki (e.g. Nevelainen and Raumolin-Brunberg 2003). Speech-based genres are those based on actual 'real life' speech events and trial texts are an example, whereas speech-purposed genres are those designed to be articulated orally. They include play-texts, which are written to be performed and which strive to achieve a certain degree of approximation to authentic spoken interaction. Culpeper and Kytö interestingly account for different degrees of overlap among the three categories, taking trial texts as an example:

> In principle there is no reason why a text could not be speech-like, speech-based and speech-purposed. It is conceivable, for example, that some Trial proceedings, particularly those which were published in pamphlets and sold for commercial gain are based on speech and are obviously speech-like, but are also speech-purposed in that they have been revised to look more speech-like, thereby creating not only a (possibly) more authentic version of the courtroom interaction but also a more dramatic one.
>
> (2010: 17–18)

As written texts based on authentic courtroom interaction, trial proceedings contain a complex mixture of immediate and distant language as well as of private and public communicative practices. Jucker (2000) was the first to account for the hybrid character of the genre:

> The original interaction of the courtroom is characterised by a certain amount of formality because of the formal and institutionalised situation, but it is also a situation in which some features of the language of communicative immediacy are prevalent. The interactants share a physical surrounding and thus [a] spatial and temporal deictic orientation. The communication may to some extent be embedded in the context; it is dialogic and partly spontaneous. During this interaction the participants may talk about an earlier communicative event, which may indeed be the cause of the interaction in the courtroom, if, for instance, the defendant is accused of having insulted the plaintiff. In that case, the court record will contain embedded in its account of the conversation an account of a conversation outside the courtroom. This original conversation will typically be characterised by communicative immediacy. [...] A court clerk, who is a witness [...] of this second interaction, composes a written document. He becomes the author [...] of a third interaction and addresses a future reader [...] The court record, which basically is an example of the language of communicative distance [...], thus contains a report of a spoken interaction in the courtroom.
>
> (2000: 24–25)

In the course of the analysis attention will be given to the combination of mimetic and diegetic discourse practices and in particular to the way in which the inner dialogism between the direct report of the courtroom participants' voices and the author's comments is responsible for the construction of ideological agreement with respect to the innocence of the defendant. In this sense I will attempt to show the strong relationship which exists between representation strategies and the wider socio-historical context of text-production and text-consumption.

Another methodological issue in historical pragmatics concerns speech functions. The identification of speech acts in a historical perspective is particularly controversial for a number of reasons. First of all speech acts undergo synchronic variation in the sense that they may differ according to the genre in which they occur or their illocutionary force can be indeterminate and change in relation to the situational context of production and reception.

Bertuccelli Papi (2000) explains the fuzziness of the category in terms of consistent theoretical divergencies subsumed under the following headings: propositional meaning vs illocutionary meaning, standard vs occasional meaning, directness vs indirectness, universality vs culture-boundedness, conventionality vs referentiality, society vs cognition, the relation between utterance form and illocutionary structure, the role of context and speech-act typology. Besides synchronic variation, there is also the problem of diachronic variation. As Jucker makes clear, modern speech acts may be a misleading guide for the analysis of the speech acts of earlier stages of the same language: "the differences are not restricted to the realisation of the speech-act but also to its function, to the situation in which it is appropriate and to the social evaluation that is attached to its performance or to its absence" (Jucker 2000: 29). Although a diachronic analysis of insults suggests that there is a direct line of development from the older to the more recent occurrences of a speech act, in some cases it is not possible to trace its linear evolution as the few examples of the item contained in the data available are often too far apart to allow an analysis of all the intervening stages (Jucker and Taavitsainen 2000). A related problem concerns the difficulty of identifying speech acts that focus on the perlocutionary effect rather than on the illocutionary force. In fact, if the data do not record the reaction of the addressee it is hard to say how the utterance would have been construed by the receiver. Finally although speech act verbs can be used as a valid tool to identify speech acts, it is also true that in some cases they may be an unreliable guide to the existence of the speech act they label. In this regard, Jucker (2000) reports the example of the verb "to insult" which is recorded in the *Oxford English Dictionary* as appearing for the first time in 1620 but whose illocutionary force was much older. What is more, even if an appropriate speech act verb exists, it does not occur in its performative force, that is to say, a speaker who wants to insult an addressee does not preface the utterance with "I hereby insult you" (Jucker 2000: 30, see also Jucker and Taavitsainen 2000). In the last decade diachronic speech act studies have proliferated testifying to the need to establish a model for the investigation of speech-functions in historical contexts. A very illuminating contribution in this regard has been the 2008 volume *Speech-Acts in the history of English,* edited by Jucker and Taavitsainen. This collection of papers offers description of specific speech acts (directives, commissives, expressives and assertives) and discusses methodological issues with special attention to the problem of speech-act retrieval in historical data.

1.4 Primary objectives of my study

Fowler claims that power relations in asymmetrical contexts are neither natural nor objective: "they are artificial, socially constructed intersubjective realities" (1985: 61) and language is a major mechanism of socio-ideological construction. He further argues that there are two types of linguistic practices by which social control is exercised by the powerful: directives and constitutives. Directive practices in the context of the courtroom include manipulative and coercive speech acts such as commands, requests, interrogatives and interpersonal devices like address and reference terms. Consitutive practices, on the other hand, are more subtle as they refer to the way in which language encodes ideology in the text by foregrounding systems of beliefs that legitimate particular ideological world-views to the detriment of others. Lexical choices, syntactic structures, forms of speech-representation are the main forms through which language articulates ideology and power relationships.

In my analysis I shall draw on the directive and consitutive practices outlined by Fowler and I will seek to determine to what extent discourse dynamics within the courtroom and at the author-readership discourse level reflect and construe aspects of the institutional context as well as features of the larger socio-cultural environment. I will also seek to determine to what extent the concept of reified power is subject to contestation and resistance on the part of the less powerful participants and to what extent this resistance has to be assessed on the basis of their social status and ideological values. This will require:

1. investigating the complex relational work operating between defendants and professionals and defendants and witnesses.
2. identifying the main defence strategies adopted by prisoners and analysing their distribution across the century.
3. examining the trial text as a communicative act between the author and the future reader with special attention to the way in which political ideology is rooted in court recording.

To address these issues I shall draw on a number of linguistic approaches including speech act theory, (im)politeness, and (critical) discourse analysis maintaining the necessary caution with respect to the applicability of modern day principles to old language materials (Kryk-Kastovsky 2006). Different types of trial cases will be taken into account: from high treason to religious subversion, from murder to felony and misdemeanour.

1.5 A description of my dataset

This study is based on a corpus of 33 trials dating from 1616 to 1693. The data have been selected from three primary sources: the *Corpus of English Dialogues*, the *State Trials* and the *Old Bailey Proceedings Online*[3]. Each of the three sources presents advantages

3 18 trials are taken from the CED (Trial of Lady Frances 1616, Trial of Robert Carr 1616, Censure of Dr Bastwicke, Mr Burton and Mr Prynne 1637, Trial of Lord Macguire 1644, Trial of John Lilburne, Trial of Mr Love 1651, Severall Tryals of Sir Henry Slingsby, Dr Hewett and John Mordant 1658, Trial of Colonel Turner 1663, Trial of Edward Coleman 1678, Trial of Robert

as well as drawbacks. The *Corpus of English Dialogues*, for example, is particularly suitable for a quantitative investigation but it is not always useful for an analysis of the arraignment section or the evidence phase in trials where only one of the two sections has been transcribed and not fully (e.g. Trial of Sidney 1683, Trial of J. Lilburne 1649). In these cases I have therefore also referred to the full version contained in the *State Trials*. Where possible, however, preference is given to the *Corpus of English Dialogues* for its higher level of accuracy. Besides, both the *Corpus of English Dialogues* and the *State Trials* are not representative of ordinary criminal trials such as felony, housebreaking and larceny, which is why I have also included samples from the *Old Bailey Proceedings*.

1.5.1 The Corpus of English Dialogues (1560–1760)

The *Corpus of English Dialogues 1560–1760* (henceforth CED) was compiled by Merja Kytö from Uppsala University and Jonathan Culpeper from Lancaster University. It covers a two hundred year time span and contains 1.2 million words of authentic and fictional speech taken from five text types (prose fiction, comedy drama, courtroom proceedings, witness depositions and handbooks in dialogue forms). The trial section consists of 302,027 words dating from 1571 to 1759. Although there is some overlap with the *State Trials* with regard to the trials included, the CED has some major advantages over this. First of all the corpus is in elec-

---

Green etc. 1678/79, Trial of John Giles 1680, Trial of Stephen Colledge 1681, Trial of Nathaniel Thompson 1682, Trial of Thomas Pilkington, etc. 1682, Trial of Algernon Sidney 1682, Trial of Charles Lord Mohun 1692). 9 trials are selected from the ST (Trial of John Lilburne 1649, Trial of Pordage 1654, Trial of Crooks 1662, Trial of William Penn and William Mead 1670, Trial of Benjamin Keach 1662, Trial of Algernon Sidney 1682, Trial of Strafford 1641, Trial of William Laud 1643, Trial of Hamilton 1648). 6 trial accounts are taken from OBP (29th April 1674, 17th January 1676, 5th April 1676, 6th April 1678, 23rd February 1682, 15th January 1690).

tronic format, thus allowing for a more systematic computational analysis with the aid of computer programs. Secondly only trials with publication dates within 40 years of the speech event they represent are used to guarantee the preservation of contemporary language usage. Thirdly trial texts resemble modern stenographic trial transcripts in that they report only minimum scribal interference. Last but not least, each trial has been rigorously checked against related data to ensure its authenticity (Archer 2005: 14).

Along with these points of strength, the corpus also has some minor weaknesses. One of these is the fact that only c. 10,000 word portions of larger trials have been transcribed, so that we lack a complete transcription of all the phases of the trial proceeding. Secondly the reduction of the scribal interference hinders what could be an equally valuable analysis of the dialogic interaction existing between the recorder's stance and the direct speech of the participants (especially in famous political trials e.g. the trial of Strafford, the trial of Hamilton). Finally the 17th-century trial section is not fully representative of 'ordinary crimes' (e.g. robbery, larceny, felony). In fact it mainly accounts for cases of high politics and homicides, with only one case of bigamy (Trial of Mary Moders, 1663) and housebreaking (Trial of Colonel Turner 1663).

1.5.2 The State Trials (1163–1858)

The *State Trials* (henceforth ST) represent the best example of historical texts in quantitative terms (Archer 2005: 12). First published in 1719, revised and expanded three times in the 18th century and definitively published between 1809–1826 by T.B. Howell and his son, they cover the period from Norman down through Stuart and Georgian times. The edition that I have consulted for the present analysis is the third edition of 1742 in six volumes (1388–1741) which is available on-line. Despite the influence of the ST on the history of criminal trials, Langbein (1978) outlines three major drawbacks. Firstly, they were retrospectively compiled by authors who patched together their accounts of trials in former centuries from a variety of sources, many of which are now suspect. Secondly, compilers of 17th-century trials seem to have privileged sources of Puritan and Whig orientation (see Clark 1967: 92–114, Plucknett 1983), though the reliability of the records increases towards the end of the century as a result of the larger use of professional scribes and the speed at which their work was printed. As Langbein claims:

> Major trials were transcribed in short hand by professional scribes, promptly published in pamphlet editions represented to be accurate and complete, and scrutinized by contemporary audiences that included many of the official participants.
>
> (1978: 265)

Thirdly, the ST mainly contains trials involving high politics, with no representation of other types of trial. Only after the mid-17th century is it possible to find non-political cases, however still with the exclusion of minor crimes such as shop-theft, housebreaking, sheep stealing and larceny.

Even so this corpus may still be considered a valuable source of analysis in several respects:

1. it provides a full account of each trial, from the reading of the charges to the arraignment section and the evidence phase up to the final verdict
2. it maintains authorial interventions and comments thus allowing for an analysis of trial presentation strategies (especially in political trials)
3. it includes both trials reported by professional writers and trials recorded by defendants themselves in a first person *a posteriori* transcription, thus documenting two 17th-century practices of trial rendition

1.5.3 *Old Bailey Proceedings On-line (1674–1913)*

The *Old Bailey Proceedings On-line* (henceforth OBP) makes available a fully searchable, digitised collection of all surviving editions of the Old Bailey Proceedings from 1674 to 1913, and of the Ordinary of Newgate's Accounts between 1676 and 1772. It allows access (free of charge for non-commercial use) to over 197,000 trials and biographical details of approximately 2,500 men and women executed at Tyburn. The trial texts are accessible through both keyword and structured searching.

As Langbein claims, the Proceedings are "probably the best accounts we shall ever have of what transpired in ordinary English criminal courts before the later eighteenth century" (1978: 271; 2003: 190). Although initially aimed at a popular rather than a legal readership, the material reported was neither invented nor significantly distorted. The Old Bailey Courthouse was a public place, with a big audience, and the reputation of the source would have rapidly suffered if the reporters had indulged in fabricating. The authenticity of the Proceedings was one of their strongest marketing points, and a comparison of these texts with other manuscript and published accounts of the same trials confirms that what they reported was for the most part reported accurately.

One major problem with these trial texts is that they do not report *verbatim* what was said in court. This is especially the case with trials dated from the 1670s to the 1710s. In this period the accounts are short summaries where details of the evidence and points of law have been compressed and omitted to the point that it is impossible to reconstruct the dynamics of courtroom discourse (Langbein 1978, 2003). Nonetheless these anonymous squibs written by nonlawyers enable us to cast some light on the practice of ordinary crimes in 17th-century England as well as on the defendants' general behaviour in confrontational situations.

By drawing together samples from the three sources my dataset is intended to provide a more comprehensive account of 17th-century courtroom discourse/practice:

- as reported in verbatim transcriptions with minimum or no scribal interference
- as presented by professional(?) scribes with strategic interlacements of reported speech and authorial comments
- as occurring both in political/religious and non-political cases.

1.6 Features of the 17th-century courtroom

17th-century trials strike us for the many respects in which they differ from their modern equivalent. Scholars from the late 1970s onwards have investigated the discrepancies which exists between EmodE courtroom and the adversarial system of today's courts, singling out the presumption of innocence and the presence of lawyers as the major achievements of modern times.

The dogma that everyperson is to be regarded as innocent until proven guilty is at the base of modern Anglo-American law but it was still unknown to the EmodE Court where defendants had to struggle against a statutory presumption of guilt. The same was true for the accompanying principles that "the onus of the proof of guilt lies on the accuser" and that "no man is bound, required or expected to prove his own innocence" (Beattie 1986: 341). The 17th-century common assumption was that if the accused was innocent s/he ought to be able to demonstrate it to the jury by the quality and character of his/her reply to the prosecutor's evidence (Beattie 1986: 341; Langbein 1999: 315; Archer 2005: 85). This ascribed a very active role to defendants in the trial, all the more so since for most of the century defendants could not rely on the assistance of a lawyer answering on their behalf to the charges put to them. Things changed by the end of the century when defence counsels were first introduced in treason cases (1696) and later on, around the 1730s, in ordinary criminal trials along with the introduction of prosecution counsels.

According to Beattie (1986) EmodE jury trial was an altercation between the prosecutor and the defendant. It generally began with the prosecutor telling his/her story to the jury, where the term 'prosecutor' refers to the citizen, i.e. the victim of the offence, and as such must be distinguished from the professional prosecutor. There followed the witness for the Crown, often including a constable who might testify about the circumstances of the prisoner's apprehension. These witnesses gave their evidence under an oath and they risked a prosecution for perjury if they were found to have lied (witnesses for the defence and the defendants on the other hand did not testify on oath until 1702 and 1878 respectively (Langbein 1999: 311)). Although trial records reveal that some prosecutors and witnesses simply made a statement about the matters at issue, the common practice envisaged that the judge guided them through their testimony, acting as both examiner and cross-examiner until he was confident that all the particulars of a case had emerged. Judges had therefore a very active role in that, rather than simply presiding over the Court while lawyers unfolded the case before them, they considerably contributed to the trial's framing and production. The courtroom process consisted of five specific phases: the reading of the charge, the prosecutor's presentation of the case, the witness testimony given during (cross) examination, the prisoner's defence, the summary of the judge and finally the jury's verdict. The next sections will be devoted to an analysis of the role and functions of some of the main participants in the trial: judge, jury, defendants and lawyers.

1.6.1 The role of judges

The judge was seldom alone in the trial, at least officially. As Langbein points out, it was customary for two Royal court justices and the recorder (a kind of judge) to be commissioned to sit, though it may be hypothesised that for routine dockets the judges spelled each other, so that most of the time only one judge was actually present (1978: 292 n 84). This was not the case in treason trials where the full commission did sit and the trial bench was collegial.

Even if more than one judge was sitting at the bench, the trial transcripts reveal that the leading judge was very much in charge of the examination process. The fact that the ordinary criminal trial was generally conducted without the involvement of the prosecution and defence lawyers enhanced the primary role of the judge in making first the prosecutor and then the witnesses tell their stories (Beattie 1986: 342). It is worth pointing out, however, that in ST the Crown was invariably represented by prosecution lawyers as early as the 16th century (usually the Attorney General and the solicitor). The right to defence lawyers, on the other hand, was officially granted in treason cases only from 1696 while it was recognised in "misdemeanour" cases throughout the entire century. By misdemeanour cases we mean a variety of matters that would be considered today as civil – for example the liability of property owners and parishioners for the upkeep of the roads (Langbein 1978: 308). Even so the judge maintained his dominant role of examiner in chief and was fully engaged in shaping the trial and moving it through its necessary sequence.

The leading role of the judge was also manifest in his relationship with the jury. Indeed, when instructing the jury the judge had almost unrestricted power to comment on the merits of the case, thus biasing their evaluations of the events and of the prisoner. The records of the OBP suggest that the judge did not regard the jury as autonomous fact-finders, and although it was the jury's task to give the final verdict, he had no hesitation about schooling it as to how to vote (Langbein 1978: 285). By and large the jury was eager to follow the judge's guidance, though there are trials in which the judge's will was strongly confronted and resisted (Langbein 1978: 289, 295). One case in point was the trial of William Penn and William Mead (1670), which constituted the legal precedent for the jury nullification act. The jury nullification act represents one of the greatest libertarian achievements in modern courtroom practice, as it represents the process whereby the jury has the right to nullify a law or disregard the judge's instructions by acquitting the defendant (Watts 1978; Stern 2002). Penn and Mead had been arrested in 1670 for illegally preaching a Quaker sermon and disturbing the peace, but four jurors, led by Edward Bushell, refused to find them guilty. Instead of dismissing the jury, the judge sent them back for further deliberations but in the end they unanimously found Penn guilty of 'speaking in Gracechurch street' but not of speaking to an unlawful assembly and acquitted Mead of all charges. As punishment, the jury was first kept for three days without food or drink and then imprisoned until they paid a fine to the Court. The four jurors who had originally objected to the judge's will refused to pay and remained imprisoned until Chief Justice Vaughan, sitting on the Court of Common Pleas, discharged the writ, released them and forbade judges from punishing jurors for returning a verdict with which they disagreed (Stern 2002: 1822–1823). He claimed that:

> [I]f the judge having heard the evidence ... shall tell the jury ... the law is for the plaintiff or for the defendant, and you are under the pain of fine and imprisonment to find accordingly, ... every man sees that the jury is but a troublesome delay ... and therefore the tryals by them may be better abolish'd than continued; which were a strange new found conclusion, after a tryal so celebrated for many hundreds of years.
>
> (Bushell's Case, 124 Eng. Rep. at 1010)

Among the judge's duties was also that of being counsel for prisoners and ensuring that they were given every opportunity to prove their innocence (Beattie 1986: 345). This aspect of criminal procedure led contemporaries to praise the English Law and the English Courts as exceptionally humane and tender with regard to the prisoner's rights. Sir Thomas de Veil, for example, claimed that English judges acted with tenderness and humanity towards those that "however bad they may be, are still our fellow creatures" (1748: 81). This view was echoed in the press and among law writers, thus contributing to the idea of judicial benevolence as a primary feature of English Law Courts. Such commendable morality, unfortunately, often remained purely at the intellectual level. Indeed, when prisoners entered the courtroom, they rarely found judges who helped them formulate their defence or acted as their advocates (Archer 2005: 87). A case in point is the trial of the leveller leader, John Lilburne. Even before having heard his defence the presiding judge – who was supposed to be counsel for him – told the jury: "I hope the Jury hath seen the Evidence so plain and so fully, that it doth confirm them to do their duty, and to find the Prisoner guilty of what is charged upon him". He concluded, after Lilburne's defence, that "never was the like Treason hatched in England" (in Hostettler 2006: 27).

1.6.2 *The jury*

The modern idea of a silent jury engaged in mere listening and observing often clashes with the reality of the 17th-century courtroom where jurors appear to have been more talkative than we expect. Several 17th-century trials often feature a juror asking questions of the witnesses or the accused, or asking for certain witnesses to be called, or making observations about the fact or about a particular testimony or about the character of a witness accused (Langbein 1978: 288). Consider the following extract taken from John Hampden's trial for high-misdemeanour in 1683:

> [Jury-Man] My Lord, We desire that my Lord Howard would name those Scotch-men that were to come.

> [L.Howard] There was my Lord Melvin, Sir John Cockram, and one Cambel, one that was of my Lord Argyles Name and Family; and there was another Name, but I can't remember what that Name was.

In this quite chaotic atmosphere, it was not unlikely to see judge and jurors talking about the matter at issue during the trial. While the modern jury is taciturn also in the sense that it does not give reasons for its verdict, the EmodE jury can either volounteer the explanation for its decision or provide it under judge's questioning.

1.6.3 *The role of the defendant*

Although the power of the judge could be exercised either in favour or against the defendant, some trials were particularly hazardous for prisoners (Archer 2005). In treason trials or trials against dissenters there are cases in which prisoners were victim of the judges' rudeness and the number of acquittals was low in comparison with ordinary criminal prosecutions. It is hard to establish to what extent different treatments of the defendant depended on the character and attitudes of single judges. What is more certain is that with the Act of Settlement of 1701 judges were freed from direct ties to the Crown and as a result they slowly developed a less hostile and more impartial stance towards prisoners (Beattie 1986: 348; Archer 2005: 88).

The 17th-century defendant appears particularly disadvantaged to modern eyes for a number of reasons: a) the prosecution was organised by the State (i.e. witnesses against the defendant were bound in recognisance to ensure their presence in the courtroom); b) the burden of proof actually lay with the prisoner in practice; c) most prisoners were without counsel for most of the century so that they had to cross-examine witnesses and speak in their own defence. To make things harder, prisoners were expected to make their main defence only after the prosecution case was completed and the jury had already formed its impression of the facts. Besides, prisoners had no right to remain silent on the grounds that they would otherwise be liable to incriminate themselves. Should a defendant refuse to speak, the Court interpreted this silence as a sign of his/her impossibility to deny the truth of the prosecution evidence.

As early as the 16th century and throughout the 17th century defendants in political trials complained about the disparity existing between the prosecution represented by counsel and the defence which was a do-it-yourself activity. The reply was always that the judge was to serve as defence counsel for the accused and that the accused was more expert about the facts laid to him than any lawyer. Discussing the refusal of counsel to Stephen College, Roger North claimed: "Criminals of that Sort should not have any Assistance in Matters of Fact, but defend upon plain Truth, which they know best, without any Dilatories, Arts and Evasions" (in Langbein 1978: 308). Hawkins expressed the same view when he argued that the prisoners' best defence was their own natural and spontaneous response to the charges:

> [I]t requires no manner of Skill to make a plain and honest Defence, which in Cases of this Kind is always the best; the Simplicity and Innocence, artless and ingenuous Behaviour of one whose Conscience acquits him, having something in it more moving and convincing than the highest Eloquence of Person speaking in a Cause not their own. [On the other hand] the very Speech, Gesture and Countenance, and Manner of Defence of those who are Guilty, when they speak for themselves, may often help to disclose the Truth, which probably would not so well be discovered from the artificial Defence of others speaking for them.
>
> (Hawkins 1721: 400)

Hawkin's belief that an innocent risking his/her life at the bar was well suited to display his/her innocence was met with criticism and distancing irony in the following centuries (Langbein 1978: 311).

At the time therefore defendants acted as counsel for themselves. The extent to which they actually managed to mount a defence, however, depended on a number of factors: a) if they had objections of substance to offer; b) if they had been able to prepare for the trial; c) if they were able to talk effectively in the public setting; d) their actual physical and emotional state, as most were brought to the trial from their prison cells in a dishevelled and hungry state. Even if some of them were 'old offenders' and could rely on their own experience from previous trials, most miserably failed according to Beattie (1986: 350). Court records report numerous instances in which guilt was only nominally contested – where the accused is expressly said to make no reply or defence; or where no defence is mentioned in the face of strong evidence; or where the accused makes only hopeless denials as his/her total defence; or where the accused brings only character witnesses and does not attempt to contradict or explain the prosecution evidence (Langbein 1978: 279). In other cases defendants ventured into some ineffective comments that hampered rather than benefitted their cause. Difficulties increased if prisoners had confessed at their examination and the confession was introduced during the trial and certified as authentic by the magistrate or his clerk. One case in point was the trial of Lord Macguire.

> Then the Lord Macguire proceeded to make his defence, wherein he first of all denied his Examination (although testified as before by so many credible witnesses) and said that he knew no such Examination [...]
> [Serjeant Whitfield] My Lord Macguire does forget himself what he acknowledges under his own hand.
> [Then the Examination being shewed him he said] Theres my name but not my hand.
> [Judge] I am sorry to hear it, I did rather expect, that you should have acknowledged it; Here are two able witnesses that can testifie it against you, your denying your own hand, which is so manifestly proved, will be a great discredit to what you say; you acknowledged it at two severall times.
>
> (Trial of Lord Macguire 1644)

There were also cases in which a witness's testimony that the prisoner had acknowledged their guilt to them was enough to incriminate the defendant. In the contemporary courtroom the hearsay rule ensures that reports of what has been said out of court are excluded from the jury but in the 17th century hearsay evidence was generally accepted with the exception of some judges who disapproved of it.

Even when defendants – who could rely on friends outside – were able to arrange counter-evidence and organise witnesses for their defence, their efforts were useless as they did not know the precise evidence that would be given against them. All things considered, the successful prisoner who asked probing questions and spoke effectively to the jury appeared to have been more the exception than the norm. What is more, as Archer points out, skills did not always equate acquittals (2005: 89). This may be shown by comparing the trial of John Lilburne (1649) with that of Edward Coleman (1678) (both accused of high treason). In the first case the defendant's expertise in trial procedure and his pragmatic skills helped him to counter the judges' resistance and obtain acquittal, whereas in Coleman's trial, the prisoner's oratory could do nothing against the hostility of the judge:

> [Prisoner] I hope (my Lord) if there be any Point of Law, that I am not skill'd in, that your Lordship will be pleased not to take the advantage over me. Another thing seems most dreadful, that is, the violent prejudices that seem to be against every man in England, that is confess'd to be a Roman Catholick [...]
> [L. C. Justice] You need not make any preparations for us in this matter, you shall have a fair, just, and legal Trial; if Condemned, it will be apparent you ought to be so; and without a fair Proof, there shall be no Condemnation. Therefore you shall find, we will not do to you, as you do to us, blow up at adventure, kill people because they are not of your perswasion; our Religion teacheth us another Doctrine...
>
> (Trial of Edward Coleman 1678)

The extract represents one of the several cases in which 17th-century English Courts directly manifest their power over the interrogated through forms of verbal defamation, which are no longer accepted in modern courtroom (Kryk-Kastovsky 2010: 157). As long as the criminal trial was a mere altercation between citizen accuser and citizen accused, the disparity between the parties was not perceived (Langbein 1999: 315). With the introduction of prosecution lawyers, however, the sense of balance in the courtroom disappeared to the point that only the introduction of defence lawyers could restore a semblance of equity and justice.

1.6.4 *Introduction of lawyers*

In important State Trials the case for the Crown was commonly put by the Attorney General assisted by other counsels from as early as the 16th century. Ordinary criminal cases, on the other hand, were generally lawyer-free records documenting only few prosecuting counsels engaged before 1714. Beattie (1986: 355) dates a more conspicuous presence of prosecutors from the 1720s–1730s, which coincides with Langbein's findings (1978).

The presence of prosecution lawyers was in all probability encouraged by the government which had to face a variety of disturbances and Jacobite plots, as a result of the popular discontent of the time. Several presumed enemies were brought before the secretaries and privy council for examination and were prosecuted in the Courts. The Walpole administration also contributed to the appointment of prosecution lawyers as it widely and assiduously prosecuted men and women overheard uttering treasonable words as well as printers and sellers of ballads and pamphlets (Beattie 1986: 353). The impact of prosecuting counsels, however, did not affect trial procedure dramatically as lawyers simply replaced the judge's examining role, only acting more effectively. It was the introduction of their defence colleagues that led to fundamental changes in the conduct of trials. The latter, in fact, were employed to do things that had not been done before (Beattie 1986: 356).

1.6.5 *Defence counsels*

In the late 1670s and 1680s complaints about the injustice inherent in the rule prohibiting defence counsel dramatically increased. These decades represented a turbulent period in the history of England, characterised by "the highly political use of charges of treason (the Popish Plot, the Bloody Assizes, and the seven Bishops), some serious miscarriages of justice and the consequential decline in the reputation of the judges and the courts" (Archer 2005: 91). In the

Popish plot cases innocent men were unjustly executed and this strongly affected public opinion. State trial defendants denounced the hostility of the Court and their complaints were echoed in the press. A contemporary Sir John Hawles in his famous *Remarks* on the trial of Stephen College for high treason attacked as "vain" the argument that the judge acts as counsel for the accused. He claimed that in College's trial and elsewhere the judges inevitably supported the interests of their "better client, the King", thus betraying their poor client. He also argued that since the truth is not always self-evident and requires demonstration, "keeping a man in prison and then denying him the help of a lawyer in court was downright tying a man's hands behind him, and baiting him to death" (Hawles 1689: 22–23). Archer interestingly notices that although these commentaries post-date the Treason Act of 1696 which allowed defence counsel in treason cases, they reflect the kinds of sentiment that led to its introduction (2005: 92).

Several factors in treason trials in the 1680s had caused discontent: a) the accused had to defend himself/herself against charges of which s/he had had no clear prior knowledge; b) s/he was expected to respond immediately to an accusation which had required hours of oral testimony to be constructed; c) the prisoner was deprived of any help or assistance in preparing for trial or in conducting his/her defence in the courtroom. In this last respect, 17th-century State Trials document several cases in which the prisoner's requests to consult with a counsel before trial were systematically rejected. According to Langbein as late as the 1680s the Courts exhibited hostility towards the pre-trial contacts of accused and counsel and interfered with the accused's use of notes based upon the counsel's advice (1978: 309).

The 1696 Treason Act marked a turning point in the history of English trial procedure. The first defence counsel operating under the Act – Sir Bartholomew Shower – still showed difficulties in dissociation himself from the prosecutor's accusation of his client, though he constructed a very good defence (Hostettler 2006: 22). Although the defendant was found guilty, the trial set a precedent by vigorously defending an alleged traitor. Forty years later the right to defence counsel was extended to criminal trials too as it was eventually acknowledged that the disparity existing between the prosecution represented by a lawyer and a do-it-yourself defence was no longer justifiable. Even if the 1730s are officially recognised as the period of the employment of defence counsels in felony trials, in my data I have found ordinary criminal cases dated from 1680 to 1683 which document the presence of a defence counsel (i.e. the trial of John Giles 1680, Nathaniel Thompson 1682, Thomas Pilkington 1682 and John Hambden 1683) (see Archer 2005: 170). While in the 1680 trial, the defendant cooperates with the counsel in the construction of his defence, in the 1683 trial the defence is almost entirely managed by the lawyer. The difference in the examination practice may be due to the judge's stronger or weaker interference in the defence counsel's role and functions. Indeed, as one barrister noticed in 1741, judges rarely stuck to the same rule and the defence counsel's freedom of action varied significantly from trial to trial.

> Some have gone so far, as to give leave for counsel to examine and cross-examine witnesses; others have bid the counsel propose their questions to the Court; and others again have directed that the prisoner should put his own questions: the method of practice in this point is very variable and uncertain.
>
> (Langbein 1978: 313)

Despite possible restrictions, defence counsels could still do much for their clients. They were able to spot errors, or appeal to technical grounds to optimise the defence or dismiss some charges (Archer 2005: 93). The area in which the defence counsel exerted his greater influence was in cross-examination of prosecution witnesses. Indeed as trial procedure progressively assumed an adversarial character, a new questioning strategy emerged, which would later be defined as the "art of interrogation" (Wigmore 1904).

1.7 Previous literature in the field of EmodE courtroom discourse

In the last decade there has been an increase in the number of studies on EmodE courtroom discourse. Some of the reasons for this flourishing research drive may be found in:

1) the emerging interest in historical trial texts as valuable sources for investigating discourse functions of the past and relating them to the present
2) a shift of emphasis from the structural analysis of legal language in terms of lexico-syntactic features towards a functional approach to the text as reflective of the complex dynamics characterising language use in Court (i.e. the participants' social roles, the power relations between them).

Both factors are deeply related to the rise of historical pragmatics with its large variety of methodological approaches ranging from address term theory to (im)politeness framework, from speech-act analysis to Grice's conversational maxims. In recent years all these methods of inquiry have been productively applied to the investigation of the pragmatic and discourse analytic intricacies of the EmodE courtroom. Below I shall review some of the basic studies which have contributed to the full development of this research area.

1.7.1 Studies related to English trials

The studies on English trials comprise three main research fields:

1) pragmatics, including speech acts (question/answer), address terms, turn-taking, other features of orality
2) facework dynamics ((im)politeness and power)
3) discourse analysis of narrative structure.

The first research trend has been the most popular since the development of historical pragmatics. Some of the most interesting contributions began to appear in 2000 with Culpeper and Kytö's studies on aspects of spoken interaction in 17th-century trials (in "Data in historical pragmatics: spoken interaction recast as writing") and their analysis of gender implications in the dynamics characterising the judge-witness exchange in the 17th-century courtroom (in "Gender voices in the spoken interaction of the past"). The former study documents the closeness of trial proceedings to 'real' spoken interaction and represents one of the first legitimations of this speech-based text-type as reliable source for the analysis of the spoken discourse of the past. The latter shows the different distribution of question-types in relation to the different gender of the witness in four 17th-century trials (from the *Corpus of English Dialogues*). Despite the acknowledged limited size of the corpus, the authors notice a tendency for judges to construct female witnesses as crime-narrative givers (as a result of their frequent use of prompters when addressing them), while male witnesses appear to be particularly involved in intense cross-examination through challenging or rhetorical questions.

The interest in orality also characterises Kryk-Kastovsky's study "Representations of orality in Early Modern English trial records", which appeared in the same year. In her article, Kryk-Kastowsky combines the pragmatic investigation of speech acts (in terms of in/direct question strategies) and address terms with considerations on facework dynamics and deviations from the expected formality of the courtroom. A case in point is provided by the following example where the judge repeatedly addresses the witness using insulting address forms:

> [Lord Chief Justice Jeffreys] *Sirrah*, I charge you in the presence of God, tell me true. What other Persons did you see that Night?
> [L.C.J. Jeffreys]: But you *Blockhead*, I ask you whether you did see any body else?
> [L.C.J. Jeffreys]: Why, *thou vile Wretch* didst not thou tell me just now that thou pluck'd up the Latch?
>
> (from the Trial of Lady Alice Lisle, 1685)

Address term usage in historical courtroom discourse has always attracted historical linguists. In his 2005 article "'Sir, I am not an ordinary prisoner': terms of address and self-presentation in the trial of Charles I", Brownlees examines the ideological implications inherent in the choice of address terms in the king's trial. In particular he analyses how the king's deviation from the expected norms of address in the courtroom, as well as the prosecution's denial of Charles I's Royal status reflect the political and ideological tension existing between the two opposing forces. Results show that although both the king and the Lord President skilfully rely on address term usage to sanction their own political and juridical position as regards the other, it is the king who mostly flouts the socio-political norms of address in the attempt to highlight the Parliament's outrage.

The year 2005 also saw the appearance of the first monographic study on EmodE courtroom written by Dawn Archer and entitled *Questions and Answers in the English Courtroom (1640–1760): A Socio-pragmatic Analysis.* The author's analytic approach is innovative in the sense that she combines a socio-pragmatic analysis of questions and answers with an annotated corpus-based methodology so as to make possible the quantitative investigation of functional aspects of discourse. Archer elaborates an annotation scheme for questions and answers classified on the basis of their interactional intent (i.e. the position an utterance occupies in the discourse as well as what the speaker intends to achieve by it), force and where possible form. The annotated scheme is then applied to the trial section from the *Corpus of English Dialogues*, which is rebaptised *Sociopragmatic Corpus* (SPC). Since a particular question type can be used in different ways for different purposes, the annotation scheme also includes information about the role of the speaker, of their addressee and the context of interaction. One of the most relevant findings of Archer's research is that both powerful and powerless participants alike utilise the four eliciting devices of 'question', 'request', 'require' and 'counsel'. From an in-depth analysis of the questioning strategies Archer comes to the conclusion that the question-answer sequence is not the only structuring device utilised in the trial. Indeed judges and defendants are also responsible for commands and requests/requires which make the panorama of courtroom discourse dynamics far more variegated. The topic is further elaborated in her 2006 article on "(Re)initiating strategies: Judges and defendants in the Early Modern English courtroom", whose findings confirm that the judges' interaction with defendants did not strictly follow the question-answer format we expect. In fact the judges' utterances often had the force of 'informs' or 'requires' whereas defendants relied on 'requests' and, to a lesser extent, 'requires' in order to manage their defence. Archer's study highlights the need to study more than questions and answers if we want to achieve a fuller understanding of the dynamics of EmodE courtroom discourse.

As far as the second trend of research is concerned, i.e. facework dynamics, Kryk-Kastovsky applies the concept of impoliteness to two EmodE trial records. In her 2006 article "Impoliteness in Early Modern Courtroom Discourse", she attempts to demonstrate how a model originally worked for synchronic data can equally be suitable for diachronic pragmatics, provided that some adjustments are made. After drawing a distinction between structural (syntactic) and semantic/pragmatic impoliteness, she examines whether an utterance can be judged as impolite on the basis of its representation (i.e. overt impoliteness), or whether the impoliteness of an expression emerges as a result of an inferential process and as such works as an implicature (i.e. covert impoliteness). Kryk-Kastovsky's model has the merit of capturing the complexity of an utterance-meaning by combining linguistic and extra-linguistic variables. Her claims are further elaborated in her 2010 article on "Power in Early Modern English Courtoom" where she concludes that in 17th-century English Courts "power was a more salient phenomenon than it is today, since in modern courtrooms power is manifested in a more covert way" (2010: 169).

The impoliteness approach to the study of historical trial talk also characterises Archer's 2008 article on "Verbal aggression and impoliteness. Related or synonymous?". The author assesses to what extent it is possible to talk about impoliteness in historical courtroom discourse. To do so she distinguishes between 'verbal aggression' , i.e. the linguistic behaviour that although not motivated by some personal sense of spite can result in an offence being taken, and prototypical impoliteness, i.e. the linguistic behaviour motivated by some personal sense of spite. By drawing on Penman's distinction between the speaker's primary and secondary goals in interaction (1990), she advocates the elaboration of an intentionality scale which can help differentiate between the speaker's stronger and weaker intent to harm the addressee. After applying this scale model to a group of EmodE trials taken from CED (1647–1722), Archer comes to the conclusion that prototypical impoliteness was rare in the context of the courtroom. Her scale model is particularly praiseworthy as it allows to account for subtle nuances in facework dynamics, which fall oustide the traditional politeness and impoliteness labels. I will provide a detailed account of Archer's model later on in my analysis in order to investigate the relational work between professionals and defendants in the arraignment section of 17th-century trials.

The topic of facework dynamics in forensic linguistics is continuing to attract scholars'attention as documented by the special issue that the Journal of Politeness Research has dedicated to Im/politeness across legal contexts edited by Luchenbrojers and Archer (2011). The volume gathers together studies on politeness and impoliteness as it pertains to legal contexts, raising issues which help our understanding of facework in the field of language and the law. By and large the papers suggest a need to go beyond the politeness/impoliteness labels in order to analyse *linguistic* facework dynamics in their own right.

The third trend of research regards studies on the narrative structure of witness testimonies. Wright was among the first to shift the focus of attention to EmodE courtroom narratives provided by witness during examination. In her 2000 article "On the construction of some Early Modern English courtroom narratives", she shows how some of the basic components of Labov's model of narrative framework (1967) disappear as a result of the question-answer format of the trial and the witness succession at the bar to reconstruct the macrostory. In this sense, the witness narrative, rather than a spontaneous monologue autonomously constructed to attract the listener's attention, becomes part of a wider discussion which is dialogically structured and involves many speakers.

A similar approach has been taken in the present writer's "Witness narratives in 17th-century trial proceedings: a case study of historical courtroom public discourse" (2010). This study aims to capture the specificity of 17th-century witness testimonies by identifying their primary functions and by examining the discourse strategies through which these functions are actualised in the narrative. The results of the analysis show the hybrid nature of witness testimonies where features of communicative immediacy (resulting from the dialogic interaction with professionals and from the re-enactment of spontaneous conversations occurring outside the courtroom) merge with aspects of formality and publicness dictated by the institutional character of the setting and by the persuasive and approval-seeking purposes of the witness.

1.7.2 *Studies related to American trials (the Salem Witchcraft trials)*

The Salem Witchcraft Trials contained in Bayer and Nissenbaum's *Salem Witchcraft Papers* (1977) constitute another very productive source for the analysis of 17th-century courtroom discourse in colonial America. Linguists have approached the data from three main different angles: 1) a sociopragmatic investigation of the interactional pattern between defendants and judges (Archer 2002; Kahlas-Tarkka and Rissanen 2007); 2) an analysis of the narrative patterns characterising the defendants' confession (Doty and Hiltunen 2002); 3) the role of the scribe in reporting and constructing discourse (Doty 2007; Hiltunen and Peikola 2007).

Archer (2002) analyses the magistrates' questions and their controlling force on the responses of the accused. In particular, she focuses on the way in which judges adopt a 'guilty but unwilling to confess' reality paradigm when confronting defendants, which transforms their questions into accusations. Her study reveals interesting similarities between the incriminating strategies of the Salem magistrates and those used by lawyers today.

In "The Sullen and the Talkative" Kahlas-Tarkka and Rissanen (2007) continue the analysis of the discourse strategies adopted by defendants in terms of politeness theory and Grice's cooperative principle. The authors draw a broad distinction between successful and unsuccessful discourse strategies. The former entail cooperativeness both in the form of detailed report of the events and conflict-avoidance with the examiners. The latter are characterised by lack of cooperativeness, including denial of any involvement in witchcraft, questioning of the validity of the accusation and doubting of the wisdom of the Court. The authors conclude that although tools of synchronic pragmatics such as Grice's cooperative principle and the notion of politeness cannot be uncritically applied to historical data, in this case they can cast light on some of the main features of 17th-century courtroom discourse.

Doty and Hiltunen (2002) take into account discourse features and narrative structure of confessions provided in the Salem trials (1692). The pragmatic analysis concerns records in direct discourse and focuses on the strategies of the examiner and the accused. The results confirm that magistrates rely on presumptions and assumptions in order to elicit confessions during examination. Records in reported discourse, on the other hand, are investigated by applying Labov's model of narrative structure. The analysis shows that narratives, though not chronologically organised, give vivid representations of the sociohistorical context, the accused and the devil.

Another crucial issue for historical courtroom discourse is the role of scribes in providing a reliable written rendition of the original spoken production. The studies of Doty (2007) and Hiltunen and Peikola (2007) are particularly relevant in this regard. Doty (2007) analyses the role of scribes as discourse "creators". She draws on 68 trials from the *Salem Witchcraft Papers* to show how the reconstruction of the events described in the trial is carried out in two main speech modes: direct and indirect discourse. Hiltunen and Peikola's research (2007), on the other hand, is part of a longer international project aimed at publishing a chronologically structured edition of the Salem material. Like Doty, the authors take as their focus individual scribes and their role in the editing of the documents. In the attempt to provide a more exhaustive picture of the pragmahistorical context, they examine aspects of dialectical variation, orthography and the writing skills of the scribes. Their study shows how sensitivity to both scribal variation and the manuscript context sheds new lights on the complex textual process behind the elaboration of the Salem papers.

More recently the researchers' attention has moved to the attitudes of the defendant during examination. In his 2009 article Chaemsaithong analyses the prisoners' response strategies in terms of "what they thought others thought of them", which he equates with their "face" (2009: 56). In this way he defines self-politeness as "strategies or expressions that a person develops to mitigate self-face threats, in accordance with his/her calculation of what others may think of him/her" (2009: 63). A similar interest in the defendants' responses characterises Kahlas-Tarkka and Rissanen's article "Attitudes of the accused in the Salem Witchcraft trials" (2011). By adopting a more intuitive approach the authors consider each defendant in relation to his/her socio-cultural background and identify types of replies "from the point of view of various ways of convincing the Court that the accused is not a witch" (2011: 242).

Part one

The interactional role of defendants in 17th-century trial texts

Chapter 2

Defendants and professionals: verbal duelling in the arraignment section[4]

2.1 Object and aims of the analysis

Trial proceedings begin with the reading of the charge to the defendant who is then called and ordered to plead. This introductory phase of the trial is known as the arraignment section and consists of a protocol of adjacency pairs where the judge requires prisoners first to answer to their charge and second to state by which authority they will be tried. The preferred seconds expected from the defendants are institutionally fixed: either "guilty" or "not guilty" (to the former require) and "By God and the Country", meaning the jury (to the latter).

This apparently simple and linear procedure was not immune from objections and disputes in the 17th century. Coke CJ, writing in 1628, observed that "more jangling and questions grow upon the manner of pleading, and exceptions to form, than upon the matter itself, and infinite causes [are] lost or delayed for want of good pleading" (Baker 1990: 102). There were cases in fact in which prisoners deliberately deviated from normative behaviour and ventured into a set of dispreferred seconds in the form of requests and – to a lesser extent – requires. The pragmatic distinction between requests and requires was first drawn by Archer (2005, 2006). In

4 This chapter is a revised and extended version of an article of mine entitled "Power confrontation and verbal duelling in the arraignment section of 17th century trials" published in *Impoliteness and facework across legal contexts – Special Edition of the Journal of Politeness Research*, vol. 7, 101–121 (2011).

her analysis of (re)initiating strategies in the EmodE courtroom, she notices that speakers use a request when they want something to happen and hope to do it/get the addressee to do it, e.g. "I do humbly move that I may have time allowed to me by the Court to send for my witnesses". Requires, on the other hand, are used when the speaker wants (and expects) the addressee to do something in spite of his/her reluctance to do it, e.g. "My Lord, I demand this, to have the Commission read" (2006: 189). These eliciting devices are very common in the pleading phase as the absence of defence counsel made defendants remarkably talkative and bold in comparison to what happens in the modern courtroom. Furthermore, prisoners often arrived at the bar without having received any advice in matter of pleading and this prompted their requests to the judges about the consequences of their pleading or the reasons and justification of their charges. The refusal to plead had very self-face damaging consequences for defendants. In cases of high treason and misdemeanour, for example, the non-plea corresponded to an acknowledgement of guilt, and after sufficient warning, the prisoner was punished as if s/he had pleaded guilty.

The aim of this chapter is to examine instances of deviation from normative behaviour and classify the discourse strategies by which the reified power of the Court is challenged and resisted by less powerful participants in specific contexts. In particular I will be seeking to determine whether and to what extent:

> 1) Archer's (2008) suggestion that impoliteness is rare in historical courtroom discourse is corroborated by my findings.
> 2) "resistance" to the Court's power and control is a practice involving defendants of lower as well as upper classes.
> 3) differences in terms of crime committed and social status can determine a different relational work between judges and defendants[5].
>
> (Cecconi 2011: 104)

5 The term "relational work" has been taken from Locher (2004: 51) and covers the entire continuum from polite and appropriate behaviour to impolite and inappropriate behaviour during interaction between at least two participants.

The examples will be analysed in terms of offensive and counter-offensive pairs. Following Archer (2008) I shall refer to the notion of the speaker's multiple goals and to a scale of intentionality in order to distinguish (prototypical) impoliteness (as intended in Culpeper 2005 and Bousfield 2008a) from mere verbal aggression. In this respect special attention will be given to the hearer's cognitive construction of the face threat. Since professionals and defendants often appeal to different norms of behaviour in order to evaluate the (in)appropriateness of their interlocutor's conduct, Culpeper's four types of 'behavioural norm' will be adopted to examine cases of relational mismanagement between participants (2008).

The trials selected for analysis are organised into three groups: 1) treason cases transcribed by professional scribes, 2) trials against dissenters recorded by the defendants themselves *a posteriori* (with one exception: the trial of Keach), 3) trials for ordinary crimes (e.g. theft, housebreaking, burglary).

Treason trials (from CED znd ST)	Trials against dissenters (from ST)	Criminal trials (from OBP)
Trial of J. Lilburne (1649) (CED)	Trial of B. Keach (1664)	29th April 1674
Trial of Dr Hewett (1658) (CED)	Trial of J. Pordage (1654)	17th January 1676
Trial of John Mordant (1658) (CED)	Trial of John Crooks (1662)	5th April 1676
Trial of R. Lilburne (1660) (CED)	Trial of William Penn (1670)	6th April 1678
Trial of Colonel Sidney (1683) (ST)	Trial of William Mead (1670)	23rd February 1682
		15th January 1690

The chapter is organised as follows. First, I will provide an overview of modern research in the field of power and impoliteness, with special reference to the situation of the courtroom. In this respect, Locher's checklist (2004) for the identification of an exercise of power will be analysed systematically so as to capture all the socio-linguistic components related to the notion of power in context. Impoliteness will then be considered in relation to an exercise of power. After having reviewed some of the basic models of impoliteness (Austin, Lachenicht, Culpeper, Bousfield), I will focus on Archer's theoretical framework (2011a, 2011c) specifically elaborated for the analysis of facework dynamics in the courtroom. Next, I will undertake a linguistic analysis of my data which includes: 1) an inquiry into the way in which defendants frame their off-script requests to the judges 2) an analysis of facework dynamics between professionals and defendants in larger stretches of discourse. This second section will be subdivided into three main sub-sections corresponding to the different trials analysed: treason trials, trials for religious subversion and ordinary criminal trials. In the conclusion I will argue that an exercise of power is not necessarily related to the status of the speaker and that instances of prototypical impoliteness (Bousfield 2008) – though apparently common in trials against dissenters – appear exceptional in the other cases.

2.2 Theoretical considerations: power and impoliteness

In the arraignment section of treason and state trials defendants commonly adopt a "willing to plead if the Court proves its legitimacy" paradigm. This line of argument challenges the judges' and prosecutors' positive and negative face in two ways: 1) by questioning their institutional authority, 2) by urging them to prove it with clear evidence. As the defendant ventures into an escalation of face threatening requests and requires, the powerful party counters the face attack through a set of defensive and – if these are not enough to solve the conflict – offensive turns. In order to investigate the relational work in the asymmetrical context of the courtroom, I shall refer to the interrelated notions of power and impoliteness.

2.2.1 *Power*

Power is a complex notion which has been generally discussed in relation to politeness. Brown and Levinson ([1978] 1987) were among the first to assimilate power to the concept of face, defining it as an "asymmetrical social dimension of relative power, roughly in Weber's sense. That is ... the degree to which H can impose his own plans and self-evaluation (face) at the expense of S's plans and self-evaluation" (1987: 77). It is worth pointing out that power is here defined as "relative" as opposed to "absolute" and strictly connected to the face negotiation operating between S and H (Culpeper 2008: 34). Since Brown and Levinson's pioneering work there has been a proliferation of studies on power and politeness (e.g. Watts 2003; Mills 2003; Holmes and Stubbe 2003; Locher 2004), which have recently extended to include considerations on impoliteness (e.g. Locher and Bousfield 2008). In order to provide an overview of some of the basic findings in the field, I shall refer to Locher's checklist, derived from her review of the literature on power. Each proposition will be explained and related to the next.

- Power is (often) expressed through language
- Power cannot be explained without contextualization
- Power is relational, dynamic and contestable
- The interconnectedness of language and society can also be seen in the display of power
- Freedom of action is needed to exercise power
- The restriction of an interactant's action-environment often leads to the exercise of power
- The exercise of power involves a latent conflict and clash of interests, which can be obscured because of a society's ideologies.

(Locher 2004: 39–40)

Language is one of the major mechanisms for the exercise of power. Brown and Gilman's notions of power and solidarity semantics (1960, 1989) explain how people use language in order to maintain power differentials in a society which has been traditionally built on inequality. In order to interpret how power is actualised in social interaction, contextualization is crucial. People assume different roles in different contexts and even within the same exchange roles may fluctuate so that one person can exercise power at one moment and have power exercised upon them in the next. Waternberg (1990: 7, 161) adopts the term "situated power" in order to express the close relationship which exists between power and situation. Next, power is defined as relational, dynamic and contestable. It is relational in the sense that it does not exist as a fixed propriety of an agent but only as a result of the relational work at play between participants in interaction. To become fully effective, power aspires to achieve reification and be seen as something "solid, real and material", something which is institutionally recognised as being an established commodity of an agent (Clegg 1989: 207). Even reified power, however, can be met with resistance as is the case with historical courtroom discourse, where the judge's authority may occasionally be challenged by the private and public interests of defendants. Power is therefore a dynamic concept which is contextually negotiable and contestable and which cannot be taken for granted in any relationship. To take this further, since language and society are interconnected (Fairclough 1989), power also reflects aspects of society. In some cases, society's ideologies can obscure the exercise of power to the point that it comes to be accepted as natural and unchangeable. This is what happens in the legal setting, where professionals exercise a power which is institutionally recognised and socially maintained through linguistic practice.

Moving to a more concrete level, a person can exercise power if s/he has freedom of action. This term has been used by Watts and is crucial to the analysis of the defendant's interactional behaviour:

> An individual *A* possesses power if s/he has the freedom of action to achieve the goals s/he has set her/himself, regardless of whether or not this involves the potential to impose *A*'s will on others to carry out actions that are in *A*'s interests
>
> (Watts 1991: 60)

Freedom of action can be considered as a prerequisite for the exercise of power over someone and corresponds to Watts's notion of power-to as distinct from power-over. While power-to refers to the socio-institutional pre-conditions to exercise power, power-over defines the actual exercise of power:

> *A* exercises power over *B* when *A* affects *B* in a manner contrary to *B*'s initially perceived interests, regardless of whether *B* later comes to accept the desirability of *A*'s actions.
>
> (Watts 1991: 62)

In the arraignment section, for example, defendants self-attribute a freedom of action as English freemen (i.e. power-to) which – in their view – authorises them to exercise power over the Court.

Another factor related to the identification of an exercise of power is the restriction of the interlocutor's action-environment. The notion is consistent with Warternberg's acknowledgement of a social space within which each social agent can act. This space can be altered and thus restricted by the actions or even the mere presence of a more powerful participant:

> A social agent *A* has power over another social agent *B* if and only if *A* strategically constrains *B's* action-environment.
>
> (Wartenberg 1990: 85).

Whether a restriction is recognised as such by the interlocutor depends on his/her evaluation of the situation.

Both Watts's and Wartenberg's definitions of power include the notion of latent conflict and clash of interests. Courtroom discourse is generally described as a setting where conflict is obscured by the participants' mutual agreement with respect to status differences and the exercise of power (Locher 2004: 38). As previously anticipated, however, even the courtroom may become an arena of conflictual discourse where powerless participants (defendants) challenge a power which – though presented as institutionally sanctioned – is not recognised as legitimate. By perceiving the professionals' stance as openly hostile and abusive, prisoners attempt to defend their rights at the cost of incurring overt disagreement with the Court. In these cases, the relational work between the parties brings to the surface their mutual perception of a clash of interests which is at the origin of the verbal duelling. In this sense, I agree with Locher's conclusion that "it is the combination of restrictions placed on an interactant's action-environment and the perception of a real conflict and clash of interests, which most reliably identifies the exercise of power in linguistic data" (2004: 39).

I wish to conclude this overview on power by reporting Wartenberg's classification of types of power as this will be useful when discussing my dataset. Wartenberg (1990) identifies three types of power, whose use is determined by the different status, role and character of participants. They are force, coercion and influence:

> FORCE: an exercise of power by an agent *A* over an agent *B* is an exercise of force if and only if *A physically* keeps *B* from pursuing the action-alternative that *B* wishes to pursue or causes a certain behaviour to apply to *B* that *B* would avoid if possible.
>
> (1990: 93, emphasis added)

> COERCION: A social agent *A* exercises *coercive power* over a social agent *B* if and only if 1) A has the ability to affect *B* in a significant way; 2) *A threatens* to do so unless *B* acts in a certain way; and 3) *B* accedes to *A*'s threat and alters the course of action.
>
> (1990: 96, emphasis added)

> INFLUENCE: an agent *A influences* another agent *B* if and only if *A communicatively* interacts with *B* in such a way that, as a result, *B* alters his assessment of his action-environment in a fundamental manner.
>
> (1990: 105, emphasis added)

When influence comes to be exercised in a hidden manner, this use of it is called manipulation. Wartenberg distinguishes between emotional and cognitive manipulation:

> In the case of *cognitive manipulation* an agent *A* manipulates *B* by influencing *B* for her own purposes or ends while keeping this fact concealed. [...]

> *Emotional manipulation*, on the other hand, succeeds by appealing to an agent's emotions. An agent *A* emotionally manipulates *B* by influencing *B* by means of an appeal to *B*'s emotions that keeps *B* from being able to make a fully rational decision.
>
> (1990: 111, emphasis added)

Given the asymmetrical character of courtroom discourse, judges can appeal to the entire range of power forms, whereas defendants mostly attempt to exercise power through influence, especially in the form of manipulation. In the following extract, for example, the defendant strategically appeals to the reasonableness of the Court in order to solicit the desired behaviour:

> [Hewett]: "My Lord, I hope it is not the *Sense* of the whole Court, that they should proceed against me, either to Sentence, or any other way, till first they clear themselves to me".
>
> (The trial of Dr Hewett, 1658)

His manipulation, however, is not effective as professionals recognise the outrageous challenge inherent in the overturning of roles: [Mr Att.Gen.]: "Pray, who is the Judge? You must clear yourself to him".

In many cases, however, the exercise of power with its aggravating potential extends beyond the level of the single dispreferred second to "escalate" across the exchange (see Culpeper 1996 and Mills 2003). By means of illustration, the systematic reiteration of the request over a sustained period of time reveals the defendant's intent to *dominate* the Court. Wartenberg describes *domination* as a specific behaviour in which power is used "repeatedly, systematically, and to the detriment of the dominated agent" (1990: 117). The extract below shows to what extent face aggravation may lie not so much on the level of the single utterance, but rather on its reiteration accompanied by an aggravating shift from requests (I desire) to requires (I demand, I claim):

> [Mr Mordant]: My Lord I desire I may hear the Commission read by which you sit.
> [L. Pres.] You are impeached of High Treason: We require your Answer.

> [Mr. Mordant]: I desire the Commission may be read, and the Commissioners names.
> [L. Pres.]: You are to be tryed by the Laws of England, Act of Parliament, and Commission under the Great Seal of England, in pursuance of that Act.
> [Mr. Mordant]: I claim it as my right, I am ignorant in Law, I desire it may be read.
> [L. Pres.]: It is not granted to any.
> [Mr. Mordant]: My Lord, Will you take away that liberty that we shall not know by what Commission we are tryed, and who are our Judges? I desire I may not be made the first president.
> [L. Pres.]: It is visible who are your Judges, they are named by Act of Parliament: We are your Judges.
> [Mr. Mordant]: My Lord, if the Act specifie any such thing that it may not be read, I have done: I desire it may be read, that I may have a legal and just proceeding.
> [L. Pres.]: The Act of Parliament doth not require it.
> [Mr. Mordant]: The Act doth not deny it.
> [L. Pres.]: You shall have all the privileges that may be; but you must first plead.
> [Mr. Mordant]: My Lord, I demand this, to hear the Commission read.
> [Mr. Att. G.]: My Lord, Pray let him know what is done, to warn him, lest he fall into the same condemnation. There was one but a little before you that demanded the same thing, and the Court hath ruled it otherwise, and he hath received his Sentence. I tell you of it that you may beware, and know how to carry your self. If Mr.Mordant will be pleased to answer whether or no guilty of those Crimes, then he shall have a fair Trial, and full Examination: If otherwise, the
> same Sentence must be required as before; that is, upon refusall, the Judgement pronounced for High Treason.
>
> (The trial of Mordant, 1658)

The examples show how the exercise of power entails a restriction of the interlocutor's action-environment which tends to be perceived as face aggravating. In order to assess the degree of face damage related to conflictual exchanges in historical courtroom discourse (HCD), I shall adopt an impoliteness framework with special reference to Archer's distinction between verbal aggression and its sub-category impoliteness (2008). Before providing a detailed description of Archer's facework model, I will briefly outline the development of impoliteness research.

2.2.2 *Outline of impoliteness research*

Traditional politeness theories (Brown and Levinson 1978, 1987; Leech 1983; Lakoff 1989) focus on the communicative strategies adopted by participants in order to promote or maintain social harmony in conversation. Brown and Levinson claim that all competent members of a society have face, i.e. that public self-image that is emotionally invested and that can be lost, maintained or enhanced in interaction. They conclude that "in the context of mutual vulnerability of face, any rational agent will seek to avoid face threatening acts (FTAs) or will employ certain strategies to minimize the threat." (1987: 68). There are however circumstances in which vulnerability of face is unequally distributed and motivation to cooperate is no longer a priority. In his pioneering study of 1996 Culpeper notices that situations characterised by an imbalance of power between participants are very likely to host forms of impolite behaviour, where the powerful speaker uses linguistic strategies with the clear aim of attacking the interlocutor's face. Courtroom discourse is a case in point. Research conducted by Lakoff (1989) and Penman (1990) on the barrister-defendant and barrister-witness interaction reveals to what extent the former's "almost unlimited capacity to threaten and aggravate" the powerless speaker's face clashes with the "latter's limited capacity to negotiate positive and negative face wants" (Penman 1990: 34).

Despite the central role played by impoliteness in various contexts and activity-types, the concept has only recently received the deserved attention. Traditional approaches to politeness have in fact relegated impoliteness to a subservient position, usually defining it as the violation of politeness norms of behaviour. Eelen (2001) notices how leading theories of politeness – despite their claims to account for the politeness-impoliteness distinction in a neutral way – have generally centred on the polite side, with the result that their description of impolite behaviour has been often inadequate and conceptually biased (i.e. concepts used to explain politeness phenomena are considered as straightforwardly applicable to impoliteness as well). In the last decade the interest in impoliteness has noticeably increased and face-aggravation has become a notion in its own right. One of the most recent definitions of impoliteness is provided by Bousfield (2008) who considers it:

> as the broad opposite of politeness in that rather than seeking to mitigate face threatening acts (FTAs), [it] consitutes the communication of intentionally gratuitous and conflictive verbal FTAs which are "purposefully delivered": i.) Unmitigated in contexts where mitigation is required and /or ii) with deliberate *aggression,* that is with the face threat exacerbated, 'boosted' or maximised in some way to heighten the face damage inflicted.
>
> (Bousfield 2008: 72)

In reviewing existing models of impoliteness Bousfield singles out three main approaches: Austin's (1990), Lachenicht's (1980) and Culpeper's (1996). The models have a lot in common in the sense that they take Brown and Levinson's framework as the point of departure and both Austin and Culpeper use the notion of face attack. A crucial difference however is that while Austin concentrates on the reader's role in interpreting utterances as offensive, Culpeper and Lachenicht emphasise the role of the speaker and the concept of 'intentionality'. Lachenicht, for example, defines 'aggravating language' as a deliberate attempt to hurt the addressee's positive and negative face (1980: 607) and elaborates four aggravating strategies to actualise the threat: off record, bald on record, positive aggravation and negative aggravation. Bousfield (2008: 89) acknowledges the merit of Lachenicht's work in having provided a large repertoire of linguistic strategies to aggravate face and in contemplating the possibility that these strategies can be mixed. At the same time, however, he also points out two major weaknesses in the model. First is Lachenicht's straightforward application of politeness variables to aggravation strategies, which leads him to the perhaps over-simplistic conclusion that off record strategies are typically used against powerful interlocutors, positive aggravation against intimates, and negative aggravation against those who are socially distant. Second is the fact that his model is not based on real life data and as a result his claims require testing in order to establish their validity.

Culpeper's approach shows similarities with Lachenicht's as he also defines impoliteness as that linguistic and non-lingusitic behaviour which attacks the addressee's positive and negative face wants, causing social disruption. Unlike Lachenicht, however, Culpeper develops a parallel structure to Brown and Levinson's politeness strategies, which consists of five impoliteness super-strategies: i) bald on record impoliteness strategies, deliberately used to damage the interlocutor's face, ii) positive impoliteness deployed to damage the addressee's positive face needs, iii) negative impoliteness meant to aggravate the interlocutor's negative face wants, iv) sarcasm referring to polite behaviour which is clearly insincere in a given context and thus remains a surface realisation and v) withholding of politeness in contexts where politeness is expected. In his 2005 revised model Culpeper draws upon Spencer-Oatey's approach (2002) to face as a more contextually and culturally sensitive notion. In a more recent contribution Spencer-Oatey (2007) takes her distance from Brown and Levinson's notion of face as restricted to individual sensitivities and advocates a more multi-faceted approach which also accounts for face in its collective and social dimension. Such a perspective will be particularly suitable to the analysis of my data as in many cases it is not so much the individual face of the judge or Attorney General to be challenged, but rather the face of the legal institution they represent (cf. Levorato 2009: 165).

Culpeper's work (1996, Culpeper et al. 2003) has the merit of being based on real-lfe data, nonetheless Bousfield remains critical in regard to the distinction between positive and negative impoliteness superstrategies. Indeed, he claims that such a clear-cut distinction does not exist in real life as one utterance can simultaneously attack the positive and negative face of the addressee. In his simplified version of Culpeper's model, Bousfield (2008) merely distinguishes between on-record and off-record impoliteness. The former includes all those strategies which are used to attack the addressee's positive and negative face wants in an unambiguous manner; the latter comprises all those face threatening strategies which work indirectly, i.e. the damage to the interactant's face is constructed by means of an implicature (cf Grice [1975] 1989) and can be cancelled, though "...one attributable intention clearly outweighs any others" (Culpeper 2005: 44) given the context in which the FTA occurs. *Sarcasm* and *Withhold impoliteness* are included in the off-record category (Bousfield 2008: 87). Culpeper's impoliteness strategies are still applicable within Bousfield's model and in the course of my analysis I will often refer to them in order to investigate how face aggravation is actualised in discourse. Another criticism of Culpeper's impoliteness application comes from Dawn Archer (2008) who questions his association of impoliteness "as a type of aggression" with courtroom discourse as the "legitimate form of [that] verbal aggression" (Culpeper 1998: 86). Archer wonders to what extent it is possible to talk in terms of impoliteness (as intended by Culpeper, 1996 and Bousfield 2008) in the context of the courtroom where "some participants are legally licensed to aggravate the face of other participants because of their role in the interaction and in which there is likely to be a high expectation of conflictive talk amongst participants" (2008: 182). This consideration leads her to the elaboration of a facework model which accounts for the complex facework dynamics characterising (historical) courtroom discourse (2008, 2011).

2.2.3 *Archer's model of verbal aggression/impoliteness in HCD*

In this section I will provide a detailed account of Archer's model of verbal aggression and impoliteness as it constitutes the theoretical basis of my present analysis. Archer's work (2008) places itself within the debate around the notion of systematic impoliteness in certain activity types like the courtroom. As far back as 1996 Culpeper acknowledged that impoliteness is not always "a haphazard product of say a heated argument" as in some activity types it can be used by participants "in a systematic way as part of what they perceive to be their job" (1996: 359). Some linguists such as Watts (1992, 2003) and Locher and Watts (2008) are critical of the concept of systematic impoliteness, as they maintain that impolite behaviour which is systematic should be considered as the norm in certain contexts and, therefore as politic/unmarked as opposed to salient/marked. They are also dubious as to whether participants perceive utterances as impolite in activity types where conflictive talk is the norm (Mills 2005: 270). Archer agrees with Watts's and Mills's claim that systematic impoliteness should be considered as normative and therefore politic. At the same time, however, she argues that facework models can still be useful in order to explain the complex relational dynamics in institutionally sanctioned, conflictive contexts such as the courtroom (2008: 182). Hence her elaboration of a facework model takes into account the relationship between the rights of various participants and the acceptability of their face attacks in courtroom discourse. The notion of acceptability recalls Watts's definition of politic behaviour as that "linguistic behaviour which is perceived to be appropriate to the social constraints of the ongoing interaction" (2003: 19) and which guarantees the maintenance of balance in social relationships. After suggesting that prototypical impoliteness is relatively uncommon in the Early modern English courtroom, Archer (2008) advocates a distinction between impoliteness and face-aggression and proposes a way of making this distinction by using Goffman's three categories of face attack: intentional, incidental, accidental (1967: 14). Intentional face attack occurs when "the offending person may appear to have acted maliciously and spitefully, with the intention of causing open insult". The incidental face threat, on the other hand, "arises as an unplanned but sometimes anticipated by-product of action". In other words it refers to an action the offender performs in spite of its offensive consequences, though not out of spite. Finally, the accidental face threat covers those cases in which the offending person "may appear to have acted innocently; his offence seems to be unintended and unwitting". While Culpeper et al. (2003) used their impoliteness strategies to account only for those cases of intentional face attack (i.e. where the intention is to cause face damage), Archer understands impoliteness as a sub-category of verbal aggression and proposes the use the Culpeper (1996, 2005) and the Culpeper et al. (2003) strategies to investigate all of Goffman's distinctions. She therefore re-labels the impoliteness strategies as face aggravating strategies and applies them both to cases of "verbal aggression", defined as "that linguistic behaviour which, although not motivated by some personal sense of spite, can result in an offence being taken" (corresponding to Goffman's incidental category) and to cases of impoliteness intended as "that linguistic behaviour motivated by some personal sense of spite and maliciousness" (corresponding to Goffman's intentional face threat) (2008: 191).

In order to classify the speaker's speech-acts as forms of impoliteness or verbal aggression, Archer draws on Penman's distinction between primary and subsidiary goals in trial talk (1990) and suggests the elaboration of an intentionality scale which can differentiate between strong and weak intent to harm/insult on the part of the speaker. By borrowing from Penman the idea that powerful participants may occasionally manipulate their multiple goals in interaction for some strategic purpose, Archer's model attempts to capture the dynamic relationship between verbal aggression, impoliteness and the fuzzy area that exists between the two. In this regard, she has recently elaborated a new *ambiguous-to-speaker-intent* zone (2011a, 2011c), corresponding to that indeterminate area located between Goffman's incidental (i.e. verbal aggression) and intentional face threat (i.e. impoliteness). The notion is particularly useful for an analysis of facework strategies in the cross-examination phase of modern, adversarial trials (Archer 2011c), though it may also be profitable to account for facework dynamics in the arraignment section of 17th-century trials. Indeed this new zone enables us to account for:

> a level of verbal aggression which does not demonstrate a primary intent to harm/personal sense of spite (cf. Goffman's 1967: 14, intentional level) and yet is more planned and more systematic than Goffman seemed to assume when initially constructing his *incidental* level (which, for him, captured actions that constituted an *unplanned* 'by-product' of an interaction).
>
> (Archer 2011a: 5)

The lawyer's questioning strategies in the cross-examination phase testify to the frequent usage of this intermediate facework level. Indeed it is common practice for professionals to embed covert evaluative comments within their utterances in the attempt to discredit the defendant, while all the time preserving the illusion that they are acting within their insitutionally sanctioned role. Below is an example that Archer (2011a: 6) re-adapts from Matoesian (1993: 163–164):

Lawyer	Did you ever say that three people got into your car?
Witness	Yes, I did.
Lawyer	How often did you say that?
Witness	A few times.
Lawyer	Before you talked to the prosecutor in this case?
Witness	Yes.
Lawyer	Was that because you thought that made your story sound better?

Additionally, Archer's model takes into consideration those cases in which witnesses and defendants perceive offence for the lawyers' questions and construe their utterances as impolite, even when no harm/maliciousness was originally intended. As Penman (1990: 25) notices, lawyers' questions sometimes have a mere seeking-information purpose as opposed to attempting to frame the witness's behaviour negatively. These instances of relational mismanagement between professionals and lay people fall within an accidental facework zone (as intended by Goffman 1967: 14) which interacts with Archer's intentionality scale. Both the intentionality scale and the accidental zone can overlap with a movable politic zone, as shown in the following diagram:

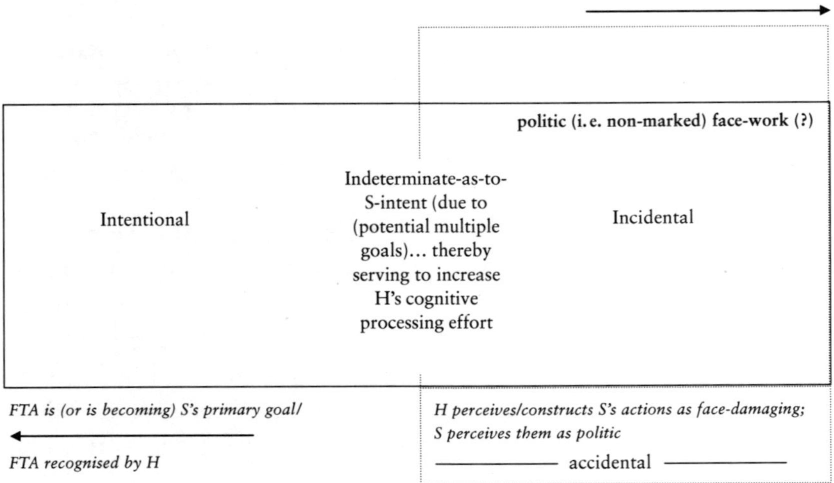

Figure 1. The relationship between politic facework and (non)intentionality (Archer 2011a: 7).

Insofar as professional activities overlap with the politic zone they have to be considered as legally sanctioned and therefore apparently incidental – though they would undoubtedly be perceived as impolite outside the courtroom. The politic zone also overlaps with the accidental zone in the courtroom – thus accounting for those cases in which lay people perceive utterances differently from professionals – and with the *indeterminate-as-to-speaker* intent zone (described above) to capture the ambiguity inherent in the lawyers' use of undermining and challenging strategies, whilst nevertheless being seen to act within their sanctioned role (Archer 2011a). The problem of how participants assess their interaction is particularly felt in (historical) courtroom discourse where professionals on the one hand and lay people on the other often appeal to different norms of behaviour in order to evaluate the (in)appropriateness of their interlocutor's conduct. Below I will set out Culpeper's classification of behavioural norms which will be useful for investigating instances of relational mismanagement in my dataset.

2.2.4 *Culpeper's classification of behavioural norms (2008)*

Culpeper (2008) distinguishes four types of norms relevant to an individual engaged in an activity type:

- personal norms based on the totality of X's social experiences
- cultural norms based on the totality of X's experiences in a particular culture
- situational norms based on the totality of X's experiences in a particular situation in a particular culture
- co-textual norms based on the totality of X's experiences of a particular interaction in a particular situation in a particular culture.

(Culpeper 2008: 30)

These norms are hierarchical in the sense that the cultural norms are embedded in the personal norms, the situational are contained in the cultural and the co-textual in the situational. Generally speaking, in courtoom discourse (CD), the first two categories contribute to shaping the experience of defendants and witnesses and are those against which they evaluate the professionals' behaviour. The last two categories, on the other hand, are the ones primed by professionals to assess the defendants' and witnesses' demeanour. This explains why CD is the arena of several relational mismanagements (falling within the accidental zone) where professionals and lay people take offence by applying different experiential norms of behaviour. As Culpeper notices "the salience of face-attacking linguistic and non-linguistic behaviours against personal and cultural norms can engulf local norms which might otherwise "neutralise" a judgement that is impolite" (2008: 31). In my data, however, not all defendants are ignorant of the Law. In the trial of Doctor Hewett (1658), the prisoner mentions legal precedents in order to enhance the legitimacy of his claims. Offering an account to justify one's requests is a mitigating strategy which is often used by defendants to reduce the face damage of the dispreferred second (Bousfield 2008). The example, however, shows that, despite the good intentions of the speaker, reporting evidence from other cases may be perceived as a face aggravating tool deliberately used to restrict the freedom of action of the Court. By means of illustration, in the following passage, Hewett's combination of request and account is met with the humorous comment of the Attorney General.

> [Dr Hewet]: My Lord, if you sit by the Act, sit according to the Act, and then I shall submit. It was resolved by all the Judges of the King Bench in the 13. of Eliz. In the Earl of Leicester's Case, see Plowden fol. &C.
> [Mr Attorney General]: The Doctor did profess his ignorance in the Laws, yet pretends more knowledge than the Court...

The Attorney General's reply represents an interesting combination of defensive/offensive relational work. In fact, if on the one hand he underrates face damage through humour, on the other hand, he seems to be aiming at aggravating the prisoner's face for his improper attempt to enter a field which is beyond his competences. Though in this example the Attorney General still frames his utterance as ambiguous in terms of his primary goal (instruct the prisoner, or intentionally cause face damage), in the next extract the judge manifests his resentment far more overtly. The defendant John Lilburne, the leader of the levellers movement, attempts to prove the legitimacy of his request by mentioning his trial at the king's Commission at Oxford as a legitimate legal precedent. The extract is taken from the ST:

> [Lieut. Col. Lilburne]: There was arraigned with me at *Oxford* Colonel *Vivers* of *Banbury* now alive, and Captain *Catesby* who is dead: I will bring Colonel Vivers to depose here upon his Oath, that my Lord *Heath*, and the rest of the Commission...proffered me Counsel, and allowed me and him Counsel before ever so much as any Witnesses were produced, to prove the lease Matter of Fact. And if you will not be so just towards me as the Caveliers were, and allow me Counsel as they did, I have no more to say, but resolve upon this score to stand, and here to die upon the principles of an *Englishman*...
> [Judge Nichols]: If you will not be led by the proceedings of Law, it will be worse for you; and you are to know this is not *Oxford*.
>
> (v. II, 32)

The judge counters the perceived offence to his freedom of action by exercising coercive power over the prisoner. Though most of the face damage remains hinted at ("you are to know this is not Oxford"), the threat is such that Lilburne's reiteration of his requests at this point may only be highly self-face damaging.

2.3 Request-types in the arraignment section

The analysis of my dataset begins with an account of the kinds of requests made by defendants and interpreted as impolite/improper by judges and Attorney Generals. Defendants self-attribute a freedom of action as *English Freemen* and deviate from the pleading-script by:

a) asking to have their Commission read
b) challenging the validity of the Indictment
c) asking to have counsel assigned
d) asking for a copy of the Indictment
e) asking for advice during the trial
f) asking for speaking rights

The fulfilment of their requests is advocated as being the *sine qua non* of their future pleading. Although defendants will learn the intransigence of the Court at their own expense, their linguistic behaviour reveals an unprecedented awareness of people's rights as *English Freemen,* especially among members of the higher classes and professionals (colonels, captains, ministers). An analysis of the defendants' requests shows the variety of forms adopted to negotiate power. In order to account for the request-types used in the arraignment section and in the evidence phase (cf chapter 3), I have drawn upon Blum-Kulka's classification between direct and conventionally indirect requests (1982, 1985, 1987, 1989). Her model has been reproposed in Culpeper and Archer's analysis of requests and directness in Early Modern English trial proceedings and play texts (2008).

On a scale of directness Blum-Kulka et al. (1989: 278–281) distinguish between:

a) direct requests (impositives) which are actualised by means of
   - mood (mood derivable imperative)
   - performatives (e.g. I demand, I request, I ask)
   - hedged performatives (e.g. I beseech, I beg)
   - obligation statements (e.g. I must speak to you)
   - want statements (e.g. I desire, I would like, I wish)
b) conventionally indirect requests
   - suggestory formulae
   - query preparatory (e.g. let-clause, will you…, if you please…)
c) non-conventionally indirect (hints)
   - strong hints
   - mild hints

In their investigation of EmodE courtroom and drama dialogues Culpeper and Archer (2008) notice that the borders between the categories are not always clear-cut, especially when discourse is examined from a diachronic perspective. In particular, they identify want statements as a problematic area. While, according to the present day interpretation provided by Aijmer, these express a "speaker's wishes directly" and are considered "as direct and assertive as a request" (1996: 154–156), Kohnen – in his diachronic study of English directives – claims that some verbs like *would*, *desire* and *wish* are not "straight commands but are more or less polite requests" (2002: 169). Culpeper and Archer follow this line of argument and favour an interpretation of the desire and wish forms of want statements as closer to conventionally indirect requests. At the same time, however, they insist on the necessity of examining individual linguistic strategies in context in order to make sense of the complexity of the category (2008: 64). In my analysis I shall adopt Culpeper and Archer's understanding of want statements as closer to conventionally indirect requests.

Request types in the arraignment section[6]	No.
Want statements	71
Imperatives	30
Let-clauses	23
Hope (you will/won't)	15
Hedged performatives	12
Performatives	9
Will you	9
Obligation	3

2.3.1 *Want statements*

The majority of requests are verbalised in the form of want statements *(desire, crave)*. This seems to be due to the fact that "the institutional context does not necessarily accommodate the 'wants' of all participants, notably those with less power, such as the defendant" (Culpeper and Archer 2008: 72). The strategy is often used to negotiate speaking rights, which are denied to the prisoner before the pleading. Here are some examples:

1) I am not to own every person that will sit to judge me, therefore I desire to know by what Commission you sit. (Trial of Dr. Hewett, 1658)
2) My Lord I desire that the Act may be read to know whether I am to be excluded of Jury and Councel. (Trial of John Mordant, 1658)
3) I humbly desire Councel. (Trial of Mordant, 1658)
4) Under favour I desire Counsell, for matter of Law, and not for Matter of Facts: My Indictment I believe in Law is all matter of Law, and I have something to say it in Law. (Trial of J. Lilburne, 1649)
5) I desire I may have a copy of it before I plead to put in my Exceptions. (Trial of Benjamin Keach, 1664)

6 For the present quantitative investigation I have considered those trials which are reported in the direct format as it is easier to identify and categorise the encoding of the request. The trial of Pordage which is recorded in indirect format and the narrative accounts in the OBP have not been included in the counting.

6) The Indictment is so very long, that I cannot remember half of it, nor have I been accustomed to plead to indictment therefore I desire a Copy of it and liberty to confer with Counsel about it in order to put in my Exceptions and then I shall plead to it. (Trial of Keach 1664)
7) Sweet Sir, I crave but one word more, I am upon my Life... (Trial of J. Lilburne 1649)

In some cases requests receive internal or external modification which is intended to mitigate the potential challenge of the speech act. Indeed, as Locher points out, "the exercise of power is often accompanied by displays of unmarked or positively marked relational work in order to maintain the social equilibrium and negotiate identities" (2004: 100). The most frequent marker of internal modification is the adverb "humbly". External markers include alerters (such as "My Lord" and "Sweet Sir"), expressions of deference (such as "By/Under your Favour") and grounders, i.e. support moves which have the function to provide the reason for the request, thus mitigating or aggravating (depending on the hearer's cognitive construction of the utterance) its pragmatic force (Blum-Kulka et al. 1989). In the examples above grounders occur in initial (nos. 1 and 6) and, far more frequently, in final position (nos. 2-4-5-6-7) as a result of the end-focus principle (e.g. "to know whether I am to be excluded of Jury and Councel", " to put in my Exceptions", "I am upon my Life...").

2.3.2 *Imperatives*

The second category of requests is represented by mood derivable impositives. Given the status differential between participants the frequency of imperatives confirms the findings of Culpeper and Archer (2008) who notice that in 17th-century courtroom discourse the lack of distance associated with imperative forms has neutral or even positive value. Their view is consistent with Kopytko's (1995) conclusions that EmodE society seems to be more willing to abide by positive than negative politeness strategies. Even so, it is worth noticing that 26 out of the 30 occurrences of imperatives in my dataset are accompanied by support moves such as vocatives, the internal modifer *pray,* and the external modifiers *I pray you/ I beseech you* and grounders. This suggests that in the arraignment section defendants are conscious of the deviating character of their requests and as a result they feel the need to legitimate them by using negative politeness strategies. Below are some instances of impositives with modifiers and grounders:

1) And *pray* be pleased to do that Justice to yourself as to vindicate the legality of your Judicature and then Ile proceed. (Trial of Hewett)
2) *My Lord, if you sit by the Act,* sit according to the Act, and then I shall submit. (Hewett)
3) *Pray My Lord* give me a day to consider of it. (Trial of Sidney 1683)
4) *Truely, Sir, I am upon my Life, and shall my Ignorance of the Formalities of the Law in the practick part thereof destroy me? God forbid!* Therefore give me but leave to speak for my Life. (J. Lilburne 1649).
5) *I pray Sir,* do not now go about to tire the jury with tedious repetitions. (J. Lilburne 1649)
6) *Sir, I beseech you,* produce your Act of Parliament in Queen Maries time, *to prove, in cases of Treason, there ought to be but one single Witness.* (J. Lilburne 1649)
7) *My Lord* convince me by this Act that I am to lose the right of the Jury. (Mordant 1658)
8) *My Case is not their, yet they have their Accusers; and may I not call for mine?* And therefore call for them, for you ought to do so. (Trial of Crook 1662)

(my emphasis)

Along with vocatives (nos. 2-3-4-5-6-7), the support moves “pray” “I pray” and “I beseech you” are the most common modifiers in imperatives (nos. 1-3-5-6). They generally occur in initial position and they are semantically similar to present-day “please”. Being acts of supplication, they are used to acknowledge and stress the superior power of the interlocutor, thus counterbalancing the face threatening potential of the impositive. Grounders, on the other hand, occur both in initial and final position (nos. 4-6-8). In some cases the support moves can be mixed up, as happens in example 6 where the initial vocative and the *I beseech you* form combine with the final grounder. The very few instances of imperatives without modification (4 out of 29) testify to the defendants' need to rely on negative politeness strategies when performing off-script requests.

2.3.3 *Let-clauses*

Let-clauses are conventional indirect requests which were generally spoken by powerful participants in the courtroom, for example judges and Attorney Generals. Culpeper and Archer (2008) noticed that the only relevant case in which let-clauses were used by a defendant is the trial of Charles I, where the 'special'prisoner still acts according to his double role of king and ruler in the legal setting (2008: 66). In my dataset let-clauses come third in the frequency list. Interestingly, however, 20 out of the 23 occurrences are found in the trial of John Lilburne (10 times) and in the autobiographical trial of the Quaker John Crook (10 times). This suggests that individual variables – i.e. the prisoner's social and ideological identity outside the courtroom – can appreciably alter the results. Caution is nonetheless in order especially in the Quaker's case where the autobiographical character of the record may have prompted some kind of ***a posteriori*** manipulation of the original encoding of the requests. Below are some examples of let-clauses from John Lilburne's trial:

- Here's the Statute Book, let the Jury hear it read *(no support move)*
- *I beseech you* then, let there be no more added to the testimony, than right and truth
- *By your favour, Sir,* then let me have a little time to consult with counsell.
- *I beseech you Sir,* let me hear but the grand Jury speak, *for I understand from some of themselves, they never found me guilty of Treason, but doe conceive themselves wronged by some words yesterday, that passed from some of the Judges*
- *I pray* let me hear them speak.
- *I pray you* let me do it in the Court

(my emphasis)

It is significant that in eight cases out of ten Lilburne feels the need to mitigate his let-request with external support moves like "I beseech you" (three times), "I pray you" (two times), grounders (two times) and with the mitigator "By your favour" (one time). A different attitude emerges in Crook's trial:

- Let me seen my Accuser, *that I may know for what Cause I have been six weeks imprisoned*
- Let me be cleared of my Imprisonment, and then I shall answer to what is charged against me
- *I stand at your Bar as a Delinquent, and am brought hither by Force, contrary to the Law*; therefore let me see my Accuser
- *How can I help myself when you have Out-lawed me?* Therefore let Proclamation be made in the Court that I was brought by Force hither, and let me stand cleared by Proclamation, as you ought to.

(my emphasis)

As we can see, the prisoner never softens his let-requests with vocatives (Sir, My Lord), mitigators (by your favour) and moves like "I beseech you" or "pray/I pray you". The only support move adopted are grounders, though at times they seem to be used more as a means of aggravating the injustice of the Court than as a legitimation of the request. Again, it is problematic to establish to what extent the directness of Crook's speech-acts corresponds to his real behaviour in the courtroom and to what extent it may have been fabricated *a posteriori* so as to highlight his boldness against the illegitimacy of the Court procedure.

2.3.4 Hope (you will/won't) structure

The "hope you will" structure is a relatively frequent form of indirect request with a strong persuasive function. The mental verb indicates the axiologic-evaluative orientation of the speaker as to the desirability of a certain action on the part of the interlocutor. The main verb is followed by the volitional "will" referring to the addressee's willingness to do something. As Culpeper and Archer hypothesise the interlocutor's volition is the *sine qua non* for the accomplishment of the speaker's requests (2008). The defendant exercises influence over judges so as to convince them that what s/he wants somehow coincides with their own interest in proving the justice of the Court. In this sense the *hope you will* structure can be included in Archer's macro-category of "counsel", according to which "S wants to convey something to A which will help prevent/result in Y [= an event not in A's best interests]" (Archer 2005: 127). This is especially the case in example number one taken from Hewet's trial:

1) And withal I hope they will remember what befell the Judges in the case of Shipmoney in the time of the late King, and therefore I hope they will be cautious themselves in doing anything that is contrary to Law. (Trial of Hewett 1658)
2) I hope you will not goe about to ensnare me and take away my life for punctilios. (Trial of John Lilburne 1649)
3) Therefore I hope the Court will not deny me the right and benefit of the Law, as being an *Englishman.* (Trial of Crook 1662)

2.3.5 Hedged performatives

The next category is hedged performatives (e.g. I beseech/pray/beg/entreat). A quantitative analysis features 35 occurrences though in 23 cases they function as support moves premodifying imperatives or let-clauses, as we have seen in the previous examples. Only in 12 cases are hedged performatives used as encoders of the actual request. They all entail an overt act of supplication which reflects the defendant's acknowledgement of the superior position of the interlocutor:

1) *My Lord*, everybody will acknowledge , that there have been … vitious Indictments. Now if I plead to an erroneous Indictment and am acquitted, I may be indicted again. Bills of Attainder have been upon Errors in original Indictments, as that of the Duke of *Somerset.* Now, if there be here several Things distinct in Nature, distinguished by Law that are put

together, 'tis impossible to make a positive Answer to any one [...] here I don't find anything specified, or can tell upon what Statute I am indicted [– GROUNDER]. I pray I may feel the record. (Trial of Sidney 1683)

2) There are a great many snares, and a great many niceties in the practick, that are formall proceedings of the Law, and seeing I know not certainly, whether if I proceed to matter of proofe, before in Law I make my exceptions against your Indictment, as to matter, time and place, I be not in Law deprived of that benefit, which I principally aime at the preservation of my Life, [= GROUNDER] therefore I beseech you and *most earnestly* entreat you, to assign me Counsell to consult with. (Trial of John Lilburne 1649)
3) Sir, By the Petition of Right, I am not to answer to any Questions concerning my selfe; therefore I humbly entreat you to afford me the Priviledges of the Laws of England (Trial of J. Lilburne)
4) *My Lord* you sit there as Judge I beseech you to let me know by what Commission you sit there (Trial of Dr Hewett, 1658)
5) I beg *my Lord* that my ignorance of the Laws may not prejudice me (Trial of Mordant, 1658)

(my emphasis)

The examples show that, despite their overt deferential character, hedged performatives are usually combined with vocatives and grounders in order to boost the legitimacy of the request.

2.3.6 *Performatives and* will you+ *verb*

Though performatives belong to the direct request type and *will you* verb to the conventionally indirect request, they share the same low frequency in my dataset. This may be partly due to the fact that in Middle English *will* could be taken as a performative of some kind (Kohnen 2002) and, as a result, its usage in Emod English data may represent a legacy of its role in more direct requests. In this regard, Culpeper and Archer (2008) notice that both performative and *will you*+verb are generally used by people of relatively high power/status, mainly professionals. This would explain the small number of occurrences in the defendants' speech-contributions. As far as performatives are concerned, five out of the nine instances are found in the trial of John Mordant, a gentleman who presumably shared the same status of the judge (Archer 2005: 279):

1) My Lord your Indictment is matter of Law and upon that I may safely demand Counsell
2) I ask a President for this
3) I claim it as my right
4) I urge My Lord Cooke for Authority for a Copy of the Indictment
5) My Lord I demand this to have the Commission read

In three cases (nos. 1-4-5) the illocutionary force of the performative is softened with modifiers: the modal *may* (suggesting that the defendant is in the legitimate position to have the permission granted) and vocatives. The *will you*+verb structure, on the other hand, is mostly used by John Lilburne (six out of nine occurrences) who, in line with his libertarian principles, feels he is authorised to 1) ask for the professionals' willingness to do something or 2) question the professionals' willingness to act against him:

1) Pray, will you give me but 8 dayes time then
2) Will you let me have some friend by me?
3) Sir, will you put a man to more then a horse is put to, or is able to go through with, the righteous man is merciful even to a very beast.
4) Good Sir, would you have me to answer to impossibilities, will you not give me breath?

The *will you*+verb structure is modifed by the support move *pray* (no. 1) and vocatives (nos. 3-4).

2.3.7 Obligation statement

This category is marked. Institutionally speaking, in fact, defendants are not in the position to demand, require or express the addressee's obligation to do something. This explains why the few occurrences of obligation statements used by defendants are speaker-oriented in the sense that the obligation is placed on the speaker (I must) and not on the hearer (you must). This type of locution represents a more indirect/implicit way "of conveying the illocutionary point which involves action on the part of the target" (Culpeper and Archer 2008). In this sense, it differs from Blum-Kulka et al.'s hearer-oriented obligation statements, which are included in the direct requests category. Consider the following examples.

1) Truly Sir I must then make my Protest against your unjust and bloody proceedings with me (Lilburne 1649)
2) My Lord, I must first know whether the Court be a lawful judicature before I give my defence. (Hewett 1658)
3) My Lord, I must know the persons, whether they be all here. (Hewett 1658)

As we can see, defendants adopt alerters to soften the threat of the utterance and verbalise the deontic "must" as foregrounding the speaker's obligation to perform the request, only implicitly conveying the addressee's obligation to do something[7].

---

7 In the autobiographical trial of the Quaker John Crook there are 20 occurrences of the modal verb *ought to* to frame requests. The modal is mostly used in the form *you ought to* (14 times) overtly conveying the judges' obligation to do something. In the rest of my dataset, there are only three cases of *ought to* and the obligation is always conveyed indirectly either in the form *I ought to* (as in Robert Lilburne's trial: *I ought to have counsell*) or in the form *it ought to* (as in Dr Hewett's trial: *it* [Counsell] *ought to be allowed as in my Lord Cook and Dyer*). The modal *should* is also found in my database (about 20 occurrences) but it is mostly used indirectly either in the form of *I/we should* or *it/they should*: "Are these according to the rights and privileges of an Englishman that we should not be heard…?" (Trial of Penn and Mead, 1670); "My Jury who are my judges, ought not to be thus menaced, their verdict should be free and not compelled" (Trial of Penn and Mead 1670). In the few cases of the more direct *you should* the appeal to the required normative behaviour of the Court is inserted within the *why*-interrogative construction: "Why should you run upon the hazard of my life?" (Trial of John Lilburne 1658); "If it contains that law you say I have broken, why should you decline to produce that law?" (Trial of Penn and Mead 1670).

2.4 The dynamics of requests in the arraignment section

I now intend to investigate how the defendants' request-types are used in extended stretches of discourse and how they contribute to the engendering of impoliteness/verbal aggression in context. In normal circumstances, verbal aggression is not given in a vacuum but is always the result of contextual and discourse dynamics which need to be taken into careful consideration in order to account for its delivery and resolution. As Bousfield notices, an offending event prompts an impolite response which could be itself seen as

> further triggering offending situation, which could, in turn, lead to feeling of frustration or anger in the interlocutor which could, in turn, lead to the expression of an impolite utterance and so on and so forth [...] To put it in another way, when impoliteness is triggered, the impoliteness expressed and communicated could trigger the expression and communication of impoliteness in response, and so on.
>
> (2008: 187).

Once an initial offending event has been perceived (be it construed as intentional, incidental or accidental), the interlocutor can choose either to respond or not to respond to the offence. If s/he chooses to respond, s/he can either accept the face attack, for example, by acknowledging responsibility for it and agreeing with the interlocutor's impolite assessment contained in the FTA, or s/he can choose to counter the threat. This latter option can be actualised in the form of offensive and defensive counterstrategies, which constitute the basic discourse dynamics in the defendant-professionals exchange. While the offensive strategy counters face attack with face attack, the defensive strategies primarily defend one's own personal and institutional face.

The analysis is divided into three sub-sections. The first investigates facework dynamics in treason trials. The examples will be classified in terms of offensive-defensive pairing (an impolite offence met with an impolite defence as a counter), offensive-offensive pairing (impolite offence met with an impolite offence as a counter) and offensive-defensive/offensive pairing where the interlocutor's response is twisted in such a way that the former part appears in the form of an "account" while the latter is charged with off-record aggravation. The second section illustrates the relational work between defendants and professionals in trials of dissenters accused of religious subversion and heresy. Finally, the third section takes into account the defendants' refusal to plead in cases of larceny, theft and housebreaking reported in the Old Bailey Proceedings. In the course of the analysis attention will be drawn to how confrontation ends. Vuchinich (1990), in his study on conflict termination, identifies five types of possible resolutions: 1) submission to opponents, 2) dominant third party intervention, 3) compromise, 4) stand off, 5) withdrawal. In courtroom discourse the defendant-judge exchange appears to contemplate only two of the options above, either defendants submit to the authority or they are compelled to withdraw. One last consideration concerns the three party interaction pattern which often occurs in the trial and which is responsible for more complex dynamics of face aggression. There are in fact cases in which the defendant addresses the supreme authority of the judge even if he is questioned by the Attorney General. This behaviour is dictated by the hierarchical structure of the Court where the judge is considered as the supreme authority capable of decision-making.

2.4.1 Treason trials

I start my analysis with offensive-defensive pairs in treason trials: the offending event is initiated by the defendant who deviates from normative behaviour by making requests before pleading. Judges/prosecutors initially opt for defensive moves either in the form of "account" or "abrogation" (Bousfield 2008). The first example is taken from the trial of Dr Hewett. John Hewett was chaplain to King Charles I and a faithful servant of the Royalist cause. His loyalty to Charles II during his exile was manifest in the collections he made in his church to help a "distressed friend". In 1657 he was actively engaged in a correspondence with Royalist rebels and in April 1658 he was accused of plotting the return of the king. When brought to the bar, he refused to plead claiming the right to a trial by jury. In the end the judge forced him to withdraw from the Court and found him guilty by default.

The example below occurs almost at the beginning of the trial. It represents the first attack on the power of the Court as, by means of the request, Hewett challenges its legitimacy and casts doubts on its legality.

1) [Dr Hewett]: I am not to own every person that will sit to judge me, therefore I desire to know by what Commission you sit and who are the judges and then I shall say more.
[President]: Those that are to judge you are very well known, you consented yourself to the judges, we are all chosen by the Act of Parliament, the Parliament hath consented to it; we are chosen judges and are your judges by the Act of Parliament.

The challenge articulates itself through an initial grounder that aggravates, rather than mitigates, the threatening force of the utterance: "I am not to own every person that sits to judge me". Hewett indirectly accuses the Court of lacking the institutional power to try him. His face attack appears incidental insofar as it is dictated by the need to have an impartial and lawful proceeding but, given the prisoner's political orientation, it may equally express a subsidiary intention to insult an Institution which is not recognised as legitimate. Initially the judge replies to the challenge by opting for a peaceful resolution based on consent rather than mutual face aggravation. To this purpose he offers an account by means of which he attempts to explain and legitimise the power of the Commission: "Those that are to judge you are very well known, you consented yourself to the judges, we are all chosen by the Act of Parliament, the Parliament hath consented to it; we are chosen judges and are your judges by the Act of Parliament". *Offer an account – explain* is identified by Bousfield as a defensive move that reduces "the face damage of the verbal aggression received by, for example, having it retracted, or showing it to be erroneously issued in the first place" (2008: 198). It is in other words a way to convince the interlocutor of the reified power of the Court thus urging him to opt for a safer path and submit to the Authority. *Offering an account* is a common practice among judges and Attorney Generals in the initial phase of the conflict.

The second example is taken from the trial of Colonel Sidney. Algernon Sidney was a republican and a fervent opponent of Charles II. When the king ordered the dismissal of the Parliament in 1681 he plotted against the Royal tyranny of a "face without authority". He was later accused of a scheme to assassinate the king and was imprisoned though only one witness gave evidence of the plotting. Sidney appealed to the Law – according to which conviction has to be rested on the testimony of two witnesses – and demanded a second witness. At the crucial point, his own writings were offered as evidence against him. Despite his strong argumentation, Sidney was found guilty and sentenced to death.

2) [Sidney]: My Lord, will you oblige me that am an ignorant Man and confess my self so, upon hearing my Indictment for things I know not of, a long Thing, presently to raise a point of Law?
[L. President]: 'Tis not we oblige you, Mr Sidney, 'tis the Law obliges you. We are the Ministers of the Law…Therefore you don't go away and say we as Men sitting here impose upon you, we sit here only to administer the justice of the Nation.

By means of a response-seeking challenge, the defendant indirectly accuses the Court of abusing his rights, putting him in the position of defending himself without counsel. In terms of relational work the *will you* question: "My Lord will you oblige me… presently to raise a point of Law?" acts as a verbal trap which restricts the interlocutor's action-environment, forcing him to provide an answer which is ultimately self-damaging. The judge perceives the challenge to his power and ethics and replies by means of a dispreferred second where he explains the reason for his apparently unjust behaviour. To do this he adopts a common defensive strategy among powerful participants, i.e. *abrogation or role-switching*. Abrogation is a counterstrategy by which "the utterer attempts to deny responsibility for the offending situation which has caused him/her to become the focus of an impolite face attack" (Bousfield 2008: 195). In the example the judge appeals to a switch in social and discourse roles in order to justify his conduct. By distinguishing between private individuals and ministers of the law, i.e. between individual and collective face, the judge intends to make it clear that the Court is acting in a representative role, as a "mouthpiece", "an administrator" and not as an author: "'tis the Law obliges you. We are the Ministers of the Law… Therefore don't go away and say we as Men sitting here impose upon you, we sit here only to administer the justice of the Nation".

The examples from Hewett's and Sidney's trials are representative of a common attitude among EmodE defendants in the pleading phase. Given their inferiority position and politeness requirements, prisoners do not openly or performatively refuse to answer the charge but they rather allege lack of knowledge, need for further information or time to consider it (Martinez-Insua 2010: 186). As prisoners insist on their requests, professionals shift into more offensive moves. The first instance of an offensive-offensive pair is taken from Hewett's trial:

> [Dr Hewett]: I hope you will have patience to heare me for vindication of my selfe, and satisfaction of my own conscience and all persons whatever; and withall, for the clearing of your selves that you doe not bring blood upon your selves by taking that power that is not justifiable –
> [Att. General]: Truly my Lord this is insufferable; Mr.Doctor hath had as much respect as ever any had. I have attended many, I never saw the like in my time; you have had the patience to heare him oppose your selves, your Authority, your persons, and to strike at the root of all. Mr. Doctor I would have you to carry your selfe with more respect. This shews that much of what is charged against him is true: If you will scorn the Court say it positively.
> [Dr Hewett]: My Lord, I humbly submit my selfe to the Laws of the Land; I shall not dispute Acts of Parliament, but I conceive (if you will please to give me a little patience) an house of Commons is not of Authority enough –

Lukes claims that the supreme exercise of power is to make others have the desires you want them to have – "that is to secure their compliance by controlling their thoughts and desires" (1974: 23). Dr Hewett attempts to construe the Court's wants as coinciding with his own through the following strategies:

> a) the use of "I hope you will" structure: by means of the mitigating verb "I hope" the defendant assumes – and attempts to establish – that it is in the Court's interests, for the preservation of its face, to accommodate his requests (in six cases out of seven *hope* is used to articulate positive/negative aggravation).
> b) Speaking for others in order to enhance the pragmatic force of his requests: "and satisfaction… of all persons whatever"
> c) Indirect reference (in end-focus position) to the Court's face loss should it refuse to grant him permission to make his points: "and withal, for the clearing of your selves, that you do not bring Blood upon your selves by taking that Power that is not justifiable".
>
> (Cecconi 2011: 107)

Hewett's indirectness is not sufficient to mitigate the face threat. Indeed, the Attorney General's response makes it clear that serious offence has been taken from his verbal behaviour. The question, however, is to what extent Hewett has been intentionally impolite towards the Court. Given the fact that his life is at stake, it is reasonable to argue that his primary goal is not to insult the Court but rather to ensure that his rights as *English Freeman* are recognised. In order to do so, however, he inevitably aggravates the institutional and individual face of the authorities: "I conceive an House of Commons is not Authority enough". I will therefore interpret his behaviour as an example of Goffman's incidental face attack (corresponding to Archer's notion of verbal aggression as distinct from impoliteness) where the speaker's primary goal is not to wilfully cause face damage but face damage nonetheless occurs as an unplanned by-product of the interaction (i.e. it occurs in spite of its potentially offensive consequencies) (Archer 2008: 197).

The Attorney General's reply is equally interesting in terms of facework. First he constructs the defendant's conduct as impolite/

improper and then frames it as reflective of his guilt. To establish now whether the prosecutor is acting within his institutionally sanctioned role (i.e. politic/normative behaviour) or out of a personal sense of spite and maliciousness is rather problematic. Lawyers in fact often take advantage of the ambiguity existing between personal and institutional goals in order to disorient the prisoner and exercise power over him through cognitive manipulation. Especially in cross-examination, Archer (2011a, 2011c) notices there are several cases in which defendants and witnesses construe the professionals' utterances as intentionally face-damaging, while professionals systematically justify their conduct as "doing their job", i.e. as consistent with their sanctioned role and therefore acceptable/politic (Weizman 1989: 125). The extract taken from Dr Hetwett's trial shows that this kind of "systematic verbal aggression" on the part of professionals is also used in the arraignment section whenever the defendant deviates from the pleading script and creates a conflict of power. In this sense, Archer's theorisation of an *ambiguous-to-speaker-intent zone* is also applicable to the pleading phase where the professionals' manipulation of their multiple goals (e.g. administer the Law, give advice but also convince the jury of the defendant's guilt, vent their prejudices against the defendant) make their utterances ambiguous as to their real intentions. Oscillating between the incidental and the intentional face threat cline, the Attorney General's behaviour increases the cognitive efforts of the defendant, with the result that any reply runs the risk of becoming highly self-damaging. Even if contemporaries celebrated the magnanimity of English Courts towards prisoners, the analysis of linguistic evidence shows that professionals maintained a strong power imbalance in Court, which cast the defendant in a no-win situation from the onset of the trial.

The defendant's face attack shifts from weaker to stronger aggravating goals in the next example taken from the trial of John Mordant. A Royalist nobleman and a Catholic, Mordant conspired against Cromwell's Protectorate. In 1658 he collaborated with the Marquis of Ormond on a visit to London to coordinate Royalist conspirators in England. Cromwell's agents discovered the connivance and Mordant was arrested. Charged with treason he was tried together with Dr John Hewett and Henry Slingsby. While Hewett and Slingsby were both condemned to death, Mordant was acquitted by the casting vote of the Lord President. Like Hewett, he refused to plead unless the Court proved its legitimacy and recognised his rights. The passage selected for analysis occurs at the end of the arraignment section after the defendant has shown his domineering attitude through the systematic reiteration of his requests.

> [Mr Mordant] I am not convinced at all, but forced upon it and it is a hard Thing; it is reason that my Reason should be convinced. If this Act doth say in any place that I must lose these Privileges, or if the Judges will declare it to be so, I will submit to it. If the Judges will declare that I must be tried thus, God's Will be done; I desire to stand and fall by the Laws.
> [...]
> [Mr Att, Gen] The Parliament hath thought fit to go this way, and it is not to be disputed. They that live in this Nation are not to dispute it. If that Gentleman will please to recollect himself, and not, my Lord, thus expostulate and dispute with the Court of Justice, if he please to put himself upon a Tryal, if he thinks himself innocent, I think it is best; and if he refuse it, his Sentence is from himself.
> [Mr Mordant]: I do not, my Lord, dispute the Power of the Court, but I desire my Reason may be convinced, and that I may have Counsel
> [Ld President]: We are clearly of Opinion, we have not Power in this case to appoint any other Jury, not to summon a Jury, we our selves have taken an Oath. You would do well to plead.
> [...]
> [Mr Mordant]: Seeing I am here overuled, tho' not convinced in my Reason, I shall demur to the Court, and plead Not Guilty. I desire a copy of my Indictment, and Time to plead.

The exchange documents instances of accidental face-threats between the parties where the hearer perceives face damage even when this does not seem to be primarily intended by the speaker. Accidental facework dynamics are quite common in courtroom discourse as they originate from a clash of behavioural norms between lay people (defendants and witnesses) and professionals. In this sense Culpeper's classification of norms of behaviour turns out useful to explain cases of relational mismanagement in the pleading section. Mordant, for example, appeals to his experiential and socio-cultural norms of behaviour in order to assess the acceptability of the Court's procedure. He maintains that legitimate behaviour must be based on human reasonableness and insofar as his reason is not satisfied, he denounces the professionals' behaviour as a manifestation of their personal rather than institutionally motivated hostility against him. In the first part of the exchange Mordant's face attack appears incidental: "I am not convinced at all but forced upon it...". As was the case with Hewett, his primary goal is to have his rights recognised and the consequential face damage is weak and performed in spite of its offensive resonances on the Court. Even so, caution is in order, as the indirect framing of the face threat through conditionals ("If this Act doth say in any place that I must lose these Privileges, or if the Judges will declare it to be so, I will submit to it"), passivisation with agent-omission ("I am not convinced but forced upon it"; "I am here overruled"), honorification ("My Lord") and reasons for the request ("it is reason that my Reason should be convinced") is not to be necessarily underrated as something accidental or ingenuous. As Archer notices, in fact, the indirectness of more controversial goals is often occasioned by "a perceived need to be able to deny any implicature that was deemed to be potentially [self-face damaging]" (2008: 197). In this sense the pragmatic relevance of weaker, hostile intentions is by no means to be dismissed or discounted in the utterance.

Although the defendant takes care to move within a *politic zone*, i.e. he attempts to frame his criticism in line with what he considers normative/acceptable behaviour, the Attorney General construes his utterances as impolite/non-politic. The mismatch derives from the professional's appeal to co-textual and situational norms of behaviour according to which Law is above all and insofar as the decisions of the Court are institutionally sanctioned, any attempt to question them is outrageous and more face-damaging to the initiator of the offence than to its receiver. The relational mismanagement between the parties urges the defendant to appeal to plausible deniability (Weizman 1989) in order to invalidate the negative interpretation of his behaviour and to protect his own face: "I do not, my Lord, dispute the Power of the Court, but I desire my reason may be convinced, and that I may have Counsel". The same tactic was used by Hewett, when he attempted to foreground the politic character of his behaviour: "My Lord, I humbly submit my selfe to the Laws of the Land; I shall not dispute Acts of Parliament, but I conceive (if you will please to give me a little patience) an house of Commons is not of Authority enough". In both cases the defendants manipulate their utterances in such a way that the first part denies any intent to challenge the Court while the second does exactly the opposite, reactivating power confrontation.

If up to this point, the defendant's requests have been mitigated through indirectness and vocatives, his last move triggers a stronger intent to aggrieve the Court's positive face. Indeed, Mordant ventures into a more direct criticism in order to denounce the Court's abuse of power before submitting to injustice: "seeing I am here overuled though not convinced in my reason, I shall demur to the Court and plead Not Guilty". In the example the shift from weaker to stronger aggravating goals coincides with the defendant's progressive loss of power over the Authorities.

A similar face-attack on the Court is enacted by Robert Lilburne in his trial (1660). Colonel Robert Lilburne was the brother of John Lilburne. During the interregnum he supported Oliver Cromwell and after his death he was in favour of the Rump Parliament. When Charles II was restored to the throne, he was arrested and found guilty of High Treason (1660). In the arraignment section, he asks for counsel before pleading and when the Court denies it, he replies as follows:

> [Robert Lilburne]: My Lord, if you over rule me, I cannot help it
> [Judge]: Sir, Pray let not such words fall from your mouth
> [Lilburne] My Lord, I must say in matter and form as I stand indicted, I am not guilty.

His utterance is construed as face-aggravating to the point that Lilburne avoids more dangerous and potentially self-damaging acts by immediately submitting to the legal procedure. It is interesting that the same criticism towards the Court's abuse of power is treated differently in the two trials. While in Lilburne's case the judge takes offence and reproaches him for his inappropriate conduct, in Mordant's trial the judge decides to ignore the FTA so as to avoid exacerbating the conflict. The fact that Mordant's words are nonetheless offensive is documented by the Attorney General who requests the judge to warn the defendant not to use such inappropriate expressions in the Court: "...but my Lord I beseech you he may forbear to say he is overborn." The difference in the judges' response to the same criticism may be due to several reasons: 1) the different social status of the defendants, Lilburne being a lieutenant and Mordant a nobleman, 2) aspects of their character or 3) the fact that Mordant's improper conduct was considered as instigated by the ill advice of John Hewett and as a result it was more easily tolerated (Archer 2005).

Despite the stronger aggravating goals of Mordant's and Lilburne's utterances, I would still be reluctant to consider their behaviour as prototypically impolite (according to Bousfield's definition). In both cases, in fact, the defendants encode their criticism in a subordinate clause (an *ing*-clause in Mordant's case and an *if*-clause in Lilborn's), which frames it as subsidiary to their resolution to submit to the Court's will, which is verbalised or anticipated in the main clause. By and large the defendants' acknowledgement of their subordinate position in the trial prevents them from going bald on-record, with the result that their face-threatening goals are generally encoded as subservient to their primary aim to be treated fairly.

I wish to conclude the analysis of OFF-OFF pairs by examining an exchange between the leveller John Lilburne and the judge where face aggravation is enhanced by aspects of supra-segmental phonology. John Lilburne was a political agitator in the years before and after the English Civil War. He spent his life fighting for the basic rights of every Englishman as a freeborn human being. He was tried and arrested several times for pamphleteering and this explains his familiarity with courtroom discourse in the trial of 1649 where he was charged of high treason[8]. In the extract below verbal aggression is manifested in turn-taking management and voice tone.

> [Lilburne]: One word more, and I shall have done; and that is by the Law of England_______[*but being interrupted he cried*]. With your favour Sir, I will come to the main thing; I hope you do not goe about to circumvent me, therefore, hear me, I beseech you.

Lilburne claims his right to talk by virtue of the Law of England but the judge denies it by blocking his turn. Although turn-interruption on the part of professionals is institutionally sanctioned and therefore politic, the defendant constructs it as intentionally face-damaging and as such non-politic. Again, the clash between norms of behaviour leads the defendant to perceive offence where it was not presumably intended and to reciprocate it by "crying". The verb may refer to various feelings such as anger, desperation but also self-confidence. What is certain is that the voice tone is louder than required by the setting. This generates a flouting of the maxim of manner which conveys the speaker's hostility/resentment towards the interlocutors (2008: 137). Lilburne's shouting is combined with an implied criticism of the Court's illegitimate use of power. By means of the "I hope you do not…therefore hear me" request, the defendant attempts to exercise influence over the Court by implying that it is in their interest – for their face preservation – not to exhibit so blatant an abuse of a man's right. Lilburne mitigates his utterance with the external modifier "with your favour Sir" – uttered in a loud tone in order to re-gain the floor – and the additional formula "I beseech you" at the end

8 In one of his trials, in 1637 he claimed his right against self-incrimination. Before the star chamber he refused to take an oath which required that he answered truthfully any questions. He accused the Court of trying to ensnare him and he claimed that the Law of God and the law of the land did not authorize professionals to lead the prisoner to self-accusation. His trial was quoted by jurists and scholars in the USA as being one of the historical foundations of the Fifth Amendment to the United States Constitution.

of the imperative with a downplaying purpose. In both cases there is an obvious disjunction between the protocol of formal politeness adopted by the defendant and the verbal aggression inherent in the pragmatic force of his turn. The clash between the conventional meaning of honorifics and the challenging character of the utterance reveals to what extent the institutional power imbalance between participants – though formally preserved – is consistently undermined in the attempt to negotiate and protect one's own discourse and social role (Cecconi 2008). As happened in the previous cases, the defendant's primary goal is to be heard and the consequential face aggravation can be neutralised as incidental. Even so, his combination of turn-interruption and shouting reveals a stronger consciousness of a prisoner's rights, which constitutes a serious threat to the institutional power of the Court.

The final example illustrates those cases in which the offensive act performed by the defendant is reciprocated by a sequence of defensive-offensive counterstrategies, which may destabilise the prisoner as to how to construe the judge's utterance, either as a face maintaining or face aggravating act. The extract is taken from the trial of Coleman

> [Mr Coleman, *gentleman, for High Treason*] I hope (my Lord) if there be any Point of Law, that I am not skill'd in, that your Lordship will be pleased not to take the advantage over me. Another thing seems most dreadful, that is, the violent prejudices that seem to be against every man in England, that is confess'd to be a Roman Catholick. It is possible that a Roman Catholick may be very innocent of these crimes...
> [Lord President] You need not make any preparations for us in this matter, you shall have a fair, just, and legal Trial; if Condemned, it will be apparent you ought to be so; and without a fair Proof, there shall be no Condemnation. Therefore you shall find, we will not do to you, as you do to us, blow up at adventure, kill people because they are not of your perswasion; our Religion teacheth us another Doctrine, and you shall find it clearly to your advantage. We seek no mans blood, but our own safety.
>
> (from CED, 1678)

The defendant's request indirectly casts some doubts as to the impartiality of the Court. The implication inherent in the *I hope you will* structure is that the Court is generally willing to take advantage of people of a different creed, despite their innocence. Although the defendant's request appears to be dictated by the primary goal to play safe and ensure that his positive and negative face is respected, it indirectly conveys a criticism of the legal system, which cannot pass unnoticed by the judge. The latter's outburst of resentment is articulated into two parts: a formal defence of the Court's reliability and justice in terms of an *account* and a quite direct face attack through *dissociation from the other* in the form of we Protestants vs you Catholics pronouns (Bousfield 2008: 95). If the first part of the judge's turn sounds reassuring to the defendant, the next assumes an unexpected tone shifting into a more direct confrontation. The we/Protestants vs you/Catholics opposition re-enacts the religious and political framework which sees Catholics as traitors of the king and as the main enemies of England. By means of dissociating from the interlocutor, the judge reaffirms his moral and ethical superiority and criticises the Catholics' partiality as opposed to the Protestants' sense of equality and justice. The strong power of religious prejudices over legal judgment is such that the fate of the prisoner is sealed from the start.

2.4.2 Trials of dissenters

This group of trials differs from the others in the more exacerbated tone of the judge-defendant interaction and better exemplifies Bousfield's notion of prototypical impoliteness. The trials – with one exception – are all related by defendants themselves *a posteriori*. This autobiographical aspect gives us an interesting insight into how prisoners – as reporters – construe and assess the interaction of which they are part in order to denounce the Court's abuse of power and prejudices. Although the partial stance of the writers – in their double role of prisoners and recorders – may contaminate the authenticity of the records, the data may still represent a valuable testimony of when 17th-century speakers deem impoliteness to have taken place and how impoliteness is strategically (re)enacted to bias negatively the readers' impression-formation of the Court's behaviour. The analysis shows that while in the trials previously examined verbal aggression was generally mitigated by modifiers (grounders, conditionals, 'hope you will...' structure, support moves) and honorifics ("with submission", "under favour", "my Lord", "Sir", "Gentleman") intended to preserve a certain degree of formal deference, in this group mitigators are almost non-existent or are exploited for sarcastic purposes[9].

All the proceedings belonging to this group are against dissenters, a social category which was treated with contempt and open hostility in the 17th century. Dissenters were English Christians who separated from the Anglican Church since they refused its doctrine and worship as reported in the Act of Uniformity (1662). They proliferated in the period of the Interregnum thanks to the more tolerant attitude of the Puritans. Most of them supported Cromwell during the Civil War and put their hope in him for the reformation of the Church but when the reforms fell short of their expectations, each sect brought forward its own model of the Church and the State independently. Because of their Cromwellian past, dissenters were suspect in the eyes of the government during the Restoration. Their radical views in religious matters were soon associated with radical politics and they were accused of subversion and disloyalty to the king. In particular in the reign of Charles II, they were widely persecuted and legally excluded from full participation in the country's civil and political life until the 19th century. In the period of the Interregnum many sects existed among which, Baptists, Quakers, Levellers, Diggers, Fifth Monarchists, Behmenists, and Independents. In the trials

9 Irvine distinguishes between honorification, a convention of linguistic form which belongs to sentence-meaning, from (im)politeness, a communicative effect determined by a person's behaviour in interaction, which belongs to utterance-meaning. She notices that it is only by means of this distinction that it is possible to account for those sarcastic uses of honorifics, whose purpose is quite the opposite of politeness and deference (1995: 2).

selected for analysis the defendants are Baptists (1), Quakers (3) and Behmenists (1) (see Watts 1978).

Quakerism was a political, social and religious movement which developed in England in the early 1650s. Its founder, George Fox, was a key figure in the history of the English Radical Reformation. Quakers rejected the hierarchical structure of society and advocated a new structure based on their own religious views. They considered all godly men as equals in that they possessed the same inner light of Christ and they were against clerical ordinations and forms of Church interference in the State. As supporters of a very plain life style, they rejected sacramental and ceremonial traditions of worship as well as religious sumptuousity in manner, custom and appareil, which, in their view, documented the corruption of the Church. In addition to their radical religious views, they refused to recognise the power of civil and legal authorities and their laws. Their non-conformist stance brought them into direct conflict with the Church and the State as is evident from the confrontational character of their linguistic behaviour in the courtroom. Quakers were also known for their deliberate violation of formal etiquette in language and manners. Their rejection of the polite form *you* in favour of the regular use of *thou/thee* to refer to all members of society developed as a clear sign of separation. Even the protocol of not doffing their hats or removing them as a sign of respect and deference to superiors was well established as a distinctive marker of their refusal to recognise status differences (see Dandelion 2008). Quakers were associated with other radical sectarian groups including the Behmenists – a Christian movement based on the teaching of the German mystic Jakob Böhme and the Baptists who rejected baptism of infants and instituted baptism only of believing adults[10].

10 For specific reading on the Baptists see Underwood, A. C. (1947) *A History of the English Baptists*. London: Kingsgate Press and for a reading on Behmenists, see Thune, Nils (1948) *The Behmenists and Philadelphians: A contribution to the study of English mysticism in the 17th and 18th centuries*. Uppsala: Almquist and Wiksell.

Under Charles II, they were regarded with suspicion and by 1670 most of the early leaders were dead while others had emigrated to America to found their model of society in a more tolerant environment. Below I shall analyse some of their trials in detail.

The first extract is taken from the ordinary trial of Benjamin Keach contained in the State Trials (1662). This is the only example in my dataset of a trial against dissenters reported by an external author and therefore non-autobiographical. Keach was a Baptist leader when Baptism was seriously persecuted as religious heresy. He was accused of writing and publishing a seditious book entitled *The Child's Instructor* where he diffused a Christian catechism which did not conform to the Liturgy of the Anglican Church. Chief Justice Robert Hyde sentenced him to the stocks in the public square while copies of his book were burnt before his eyes. Although Hyde was not always opposed to non-conformists, in Keach's trial he adopted a very hostile tone and arbitrary manner. His conduct is interesting from a socio-pragmatic point of view as it seems to fall beyond his institutional role of arbiter and be prompted by an intense, personal dislike of the defendant. Before the reading of the indictment the judge alternates institutionally sanctioned face-aggravation (i.e. politic behaviour) with gratuitous impoliteness (i.e. non-politic facework).

> [Keach]: My Lord, as to those Things...
> [Judge]: You shall not preach here, nor give any reasons of your Damnable Doctrine, to seduce and infect his Majesty's Subjects. These are not things for such as you are to meddle with, and to pretend to write Books of Divinity: But I will try you for it before I sleep...
> [Indictment read]

The exchange features the judge blocking the defendant's floor and venting his hostility against him. Turn-interruption can be justified by the situational constraints of the courtroom, which do not acknowledge the right of the defendant to make his point before pleading and can thus be neutralised as politic behaviour. What appears as deviant, on the other hand, is the judge's unmitigated attack on the defendant's positive and negative face ("these are not things for such as *you* are to meddle with") and the final face threat "But I will try you for it before I sleep" which though consistent with the judge's "job/duty" reflects a strong personal malevolence. After the reading of the indictment, conflict continues:

> [Keach]: The Indictment is so very long, that I cannot remember half of it, nor have I been accustomed to plead to Indictments: therefore I desire a Copy of it, and liberty to confer with Counsel about it, in order to put in my Exceptions, and then I shall plead to it.
> [Judge]: 'Tis your Intention, I perceive, to delay your Trial to the next Assize.
> [Keach]: No, My Lord, I have no design by this to delay my Trial.
>
> (from State Trials, 1662)

Before pleading, Keach makes a set of requests which, though interpreted as improper by the judge, do not seem to express any malicious intent. In this regard, the good faith of the defendant is corroborated by his prompt submission to the Court and his resolution not to take advantage of his right to be tried at the next Assize. Nonetheless the judge strategically assumes evil intentions on his part and negatively biases the jury's impression formation of him. His utterance: "Tis your Intention, I perceive, to delay your Trial to the next Assize" is construed in a way which assumes confirmation on the part of the prisoner and engineers self-face damage. Face-aggravation however is performed indirectly: since the judge (even more than lawyers) is not permitted to state overtly that the defendant is trying to gain time to fabricate aspects of his defence, he embeds within his reply a covert evaluative comment relating to the prisoner's malicious intentions. Although it is part of the judge's goal to frame his utterance as ambiguous/indirect, the implied accusation is such that Keach's self-defence can only reduce but never eradicate its negative effects on the mind of the jurors. This is the last example in my dataset in which professionals generally perform FTAs indirectly, moving within Archer's *ambigious-to-speaker-intent* zone. From now on, the trials examined are all autobiographical and feature professionals engaged in overt manifestations of impoliteness against the defendant.

The first trial is that of John Pordage, an Anglican priest and the founder of the English Behmenist group. He was charged with heresies comprised in nine articles which accused him of a mystical pantheism. He was acquitted of all charges in 1651 but in 1654 he was summoned again. New articles were brought against him along with the already existing ones. Despite his eloquent rebuttal this time the Commissioner found him "ignorant and very insufficient for the work of ministry" and ordered him to leave his rectory in Bradfield. Below is an extract taken from the arraignment section of the 1654 trial.

> I further replied I hoped they would give me the liberty of a Felon who, after Trial and Acquitment, cannot be questioned for the same thing again. To which Mr Dunch replied, with much seeming Fierceness, you are worse than a Felon, for ought I know, which language coming from a judge to the Defendant before Trial, let all sober Persons judge of, who are acquainted with the Rules of Civility, Morality or Christianity.

The defendant's off script request is countered with bald on record impoliteness on the part of the judge, who uses the derogatory expression "you are worse than a felon" in order to attack the integrity and honesty of the man. Pordage assesses the judge's behaviour as improper/non-politic on the basis of his consciousness of what is socio-pragmatically acceptable in the situational context of a judge-defendant encounter in the courtroom: "which language coming from a judge to the Defendant before Trial, let all sober Persons judge of…". His comment reveals the pragmatic competence of a 17th-century man who refers to participants' roles and activity type in order to evaluate and construe the opponent's behaviour as "not sober". The judge's utterance: "You are worse than a Felon for ought I know" constitutes an open insult to the individual and collective face of the defendant and is indicative of the judge's personal hostility against him and the religious category he represents. Unlike what happens in other trials where the judges' FTAs appear to be neutralised/justified by their institutionally sanctioned role, here the judge's behaviour exceeds the scope of his office and is remarkable for its intentionally unmitigated rudeness. It is interesting to notice that Pordage gives voice to his resentment only in his *a posteriori* comment and not at the time of the interaction. This suggests that the strong power imbalance between judge and defendant was such that the less powerful speaker found himself at a great disadvantage, having only very little space to retaliate with impoliteness. In the on-line encounter Pordage preferred to suffer face loss rather than venture into a self-face damaging escalation of face threats.

Immediately afterwards, the defendant directs a similar criticism to the judge's assistant, Mr Hewes:

> Here Mr Hewes the Minister interposed, affirming that a Felon might be acquitted at one Assize, and gang for the same thing at the next [...] To which I replied only this, that it could not be for the same thing he was acquitted before. But I seeing that he had gone *ultra crepidam,* beyond his Office, and beyond Reason, said no more to he; though he was very bitter and pragmatical, speaking often as judge, although he was but an Assistant, and that only in reference to Ignorance and Insufficiency.

It is interesting that since Hewes's rudeness might be justified by Pordage's overt contradiction of his argumentation, the defendant/recorder mitigates his dispreferred second through the downtoner *only* in "I replied only this". The hedge is intended to bias the readers' opinion, showing that his remark did not deserve such a violent slapping back on the part of the Court. Although the defendant does not report the exact words spoken by the assistant, his diegetic comments reveal the excesses of the professional's conduct, all the more so given that he lacked the supreme sanctioned authority of a judge. By and large in Pordage's records judge and assistant are portrayed as insensitive not only to the socio-cultural norms of the time (in terms of reasonableness and civility), but also to the situational and co-textual norms of behaviour expected in a neutral courtroom (as they are represented as going beyond their Office).

A more direct criticism against the impoliteness of the Court is found in the trial of the Quaker, John Crook. Crook was an early convert of George Fox. Before joining the Quaker movement, he was a justice and his legal competence is evident in the trial. He was accused of not taking the Oath of Allegiance, which was a very common offence among Quakers as they refused to take any oath in accordance with what Matthew said in the Holy Scriptures: "swear not at all". He was tried by Justice Forster, who was an ardent Royalist and showed great zeal in the trials of the regicides as well as strong prejudices against dissenters accused of plotting the king's death.

> [Crook]: […]I desire the benefit and observance of them [Laws of England]: And you that are Judges upon the Bench ought to be my Counsel, and not my Accusers, but to inform me of the benefit of those Laws; and wherein I am ignorant you ought to inform me, that I may not suffer through my own ignorance of those advantages which the Law of England afford me as an *Englishmen.*
> [Chief Justice]: We sit here to do Justice, and are upon our Oaths, and we are to tell you what is Law, and not you to us: Therefore, Sirrah, you are too bold.
> [Crook]: *Sirrah* is not a Word becoming a Judge; for I am no Felon; neither ought you to menace the Prisoner at the Bar…Therefore you ought to hear me to the full what I can say in my own Defence, according to Law, and that in its season, as it is given to me to speak: Therefore I hope the Court will bear with me, if I am bold to assert my Liberty as an Englishman and as a Christian: and if I speak loud, it is my Zeal for the Truth, and for the Name of the Lord; and mine Innocency makes me bold______
> [Judge]: It is an evil Zeal [interrupting John Crook]
> [Crook]: No, I am bold in the Name of the Lord God Almighty, the everlasting Jehovah, to assert the Truth, and stand as a Witness for it; Let my Accuser be brought forth, and I am ready to answer any Court of Justice_______
> Then the Judge interrupted me, saying *Sirrah*, with some other Words I do not remember: But I answered, *You are not to threaten me, neither are those Menaces fit for the Mouth of a Judge: for the Safety of a Prisoner stands in the Indifferency of the Court; And you ought not behave yourselves as Parties; seeking all advantages against the Prisoner, but not heeding anything that may make for his clearing or advantage*________
> The Judge again interrupted me, saying
> [Judge]: Sirrah you are to take the Oath, and here we tender it to you [*bidding me to read*]

The defendant's request and his criticism of the judges' partiality is retaliated with impoliteness. The judge perceives the implied coercive force of the speaker's utterance and reciprocates the threat by re-establishing the status and power differential between them. The *we-you* opposition is here instrumental in re-affirming the reified power of the Court against any form of resistance or interference on the part of the less powerful participant: "we are to tell you what is Law and not you to us". If the judge's remark may be said to be consistent with his sanctioned role of arbiter initially, the final part of his utterance represents a clear instance of socio-institutional abuse of power. Indeed the judge goes bald on-record and deliberately attacks the defendant's positive face through the insulting address term "Sirrah". This is the only instance in my dataset of a judge using the derogatory term "sirrah" to address the defendant[11]. If we take Crook's report at face-value it may be hypothesised that judges reserved derogatory address forms and epithets for addressing dissenters only, though it may also be the case that the use of taboo expressions and harsh language depended upon the personal character of the judge and was not recognised as part of their judicial common practice. Crook reproaches the judge for his impolite conduct and restates his rights using a loud voice-tone which he justifies as reflective of his good faith. In line with the Quakers' customs, he transforms his testimony into an

11 In the trial of Lady Alice Lisle (1685), which is not part of my data, Jucker and Taavitsainen (2000) and Kryk-Kastovsky (2006) have found several instances of name-calling and derogatory epithets addressed by the judges to the witness. The vocative "Sirrah" was one of them: "[Lord Chief Justice]: Sirrah I charge you in the presence of God, tell me true, What other Persons did you see that Night?" During the testimony Mr Dunne kept contradicting himself and gave very confused accounts of the events. This may be the reason why the judge lost his temper though the low social status of the witness (a baker) may have considerably contributed to his face-vulnerability. It is also worth bearing in mind that the judge in question was George Jeffreys, the so-called "hanging judge", who was famous for his harsh manners and coarse language in trials.

occasion for preaching so much so that the judge repeatedly blocks communication. The judge's turn interruption is marked off as abusive and impolite to the prisoner's positive and negative face. In order to maximise the challenge the judge opts for the repetition of the insulting vocative "Sirrah", which acquires a double conflictual force at this point in the interaction. In fact after the defendant has taken offence at it, its reiteration functions as a means for snubbing his face wants and triggers an escalation of FTAs which ultimately shows where power stands. Quakers are famous for their strong resistance to being subdued and Crook – unlike Pordage – represents himself as never withdrawing into silence when confronted with abuses of power. In one of his exacerbated replies to the judge "You are not to threaten me, neither are those Menaces fit for the Mouth of a Judge..." he gives voice to that criticism which Pordage verbalises only as relator in the *a posteriori* narration. However both Pordage and Crook were found guilty and sent to prison.

Only a few years later, two famous Quakers William Penn and William Mead were called to the bar. Their 1670 trial has been the most quoted in the literature of the Quaker movement as it represents the legal precedent for what is known as *jury nullification* (Watts 1978, Stern 2002). Penn was the son of an Admiral. He became a close friend of George Fox and the leader of the Quakers in London. He wrote a comprehensive explanation of Quakerism thus becoming the first theorist and legal defender of the movement. Because of his fervent pamphleteering he was arrested several times, though the 1670 trial was the most famous. Despite the jury's opposition Penn and Mead were sent to prison and only later released on an agreement to leave for America in a mass migration. After being freed Penn published a succesful book about his trial, which resulted in legal reforms and in the punishment of the judges who had tried him. Penn and Mead's eloquence convinced the jury though it has to be borne in mind that their trial was very atypical. At the time, in fact, Quakers were swiftly convicted with juries made up of Quaker haters. Even so, their proceedings have the merit of illustrating the depravity that existed among the Protestant officials.

The first extract selected for analysis takes as its focus the way in which the defendant's boldness is reciprocated with judges' impoliteness.

> [Penn]: [...] I say again, unless you shew me, and the People, the Law you ground your Indictment upon, I shall take it for granted your Proceedings are merely Arbitrary.
> [Recorder]: The Question is whether you are Guilty of this Indictment?
> [Penn]: The Question is not whether I am Guilty of this Indictment, but whether this Indictment be legal. It is too general and imperfect an Answer, to say it is the Common-Law, unless we knew both where, and what it is: For where there is no Law, there is no Transgression; and that Law which is not in being, is so far from being Common, that it is no Law at all.
> [Recorder]: You are an Impertinent Fellow, will you teach the Court what Law is? It's *Lex non Scripta,* that which many have studied thirty or forty years to know, and would you have me to tell you in a Moment?
> [Penn]: Certainly, if the Common Law be so hard to be understood, it's far from being very Common...
> [Recorder]: Sir you are a troublesome Fellow, and it is not for the Honour of the Court to suffer you to go on.
> [Penn]: I have asked but one Question and you have not answer'd me; tho' the Rights and Privileges of every *Englishman* be concerned in it.
> [Recorder]: If I should suffer you to ask Questions till to Morrow Morning, you would be never the wiser.
> [Penn]: That is according as the Answers are.
> [Recorder]: Sir we must not stand to hear you talk all Night
> [Penn] I design no Affront to the Court, but to be heard in my just Plea: And I must plainly tell you, that if you will deny me *Oyer* of that Law, which you suggest I have broken, you do at once deny me an acknowledged Right, and evidence to the whole World your Resolution to sacrifice the Privileges of *Englishmen* to your sinister and Arbitrary Designs.
> [Recorder]: Take him away. My Lord, if you take not some Course with this pestilent Fellow, to stop his Mouth, we shall not be able to do anything to Night.
> [Major]: Take him away, take him away, turn him into the Bale-dock.
>
> (Trial of W. Penn, 1670)

Penn challenges the legality of the Indictment through an escalation of unmitigated off-script requests, which reveal his domineering attitude. Convinced of his rights as an English Freeman, he attempts to exercise coercive power over the Court by threatening to denounce the illegality of their procedure, unless they prove the legitimacy of their charges. The recorder snubs the requests and peremptorily restates the Court's power by requiring him to plead. Penn refuses to comply and overtly contradicts the recorder, criticising the evasiveness of his answers. There follows an increasing verbal tension between the parties. The recorder causes positive and negative face attack on the defendant by means of: 1) insulting epithets (e.g. "impertinent Fellow", "troublesome Fellow", "pestilent Fellow") 2) rhetorical challenging questions (e.g. will you teach the Court what Law is? It's *Lex non Scripta,* that which many have studied thirty of forty years to know, and would you have me to tell you in a Moment?). The defendant counters the Court's attacks through: 1) conflictual dispreferred seconds: ("Certainly..."); 2) enforced role shift, whereby Penn forces the Court out of its discoursal role of asking questions into that of answering questions and giving explanations for its conduct: "I have asked but one Question and you have not answer'd me"; 3) reciprocation of off record insult which falls within Culpeper's strategy of "condescend, scorn or ridicule – emphasise your negative power; be contemptuous" (1996: 358):

> [Recorder]: "If I should suffer you to ask Questions till to Morrow Morning, you would never be the wiser".
> [Penn]: "That is according as the Answers are"

The conflictual spiral of the exchange reaches its crisis when the recorder threatens to force the defendant out of the courtroom: "Sir, we must not stand to hear you talk all Night". At this point Penn takes a step back and claims that it is not part of his intentions to insult the Court, suggesting that his facework has to be read as incidental, i.e. as dictated by the necessity to have his rights recognised rather than by a personal dislike of the Institution. The concession, however, does not last long as immediately afterwards Penn inflicts the final blow on the authorities through a skilful combination of coercion and manipulation: "And I must plainly tell you, that if you will deny me *Oyer* of that Law, which you suggest I have broken, you do at once deny me an acknowledged Right, and evidence to the whole World your Resolution to sacrifice the Privileges of *Englishmen* to your sinister and Arbitrary Designs". By means of the conditional clause and his reference to the world as witness to the legal procedure, Penn attempts to convince the Court to comply with his requests, unless it wants to lose its public face. As other defendants have done before him (e.g. Lilburne, Hewett, Mordant), Penn strategically intends to show that it is in the Court's interests not to act unjustly and improperly against him. His coercion, however, is not sustainable according to the norms of 17th-century courtroom and the judge resolves to force the defendant out of the room. Penn is taken away and cast into the Bale-dock. The same treatment was accorded to John Hewett for having attempted to influence and manipulate the Court. What distinguishes this trial from Hewett's case, however, is the degree of directness characterising Penn's utterances, where mitigators are replaced with overtly insulting expressions (i.e. "your sinister and Arbitrary Designs"). The professionals' behaviour is also striking for its deliberate face-aggravation. If in Hewett's trial the prosecutor's behaviour still moved from an incidental to an *ambigious-a-to-speaker* intent level, in Penn's trial (as well as in the trials of other dissenters) the recorder's utterances are closer to impoliteness than institutionally sanctioned verbal aggression.

The final extract is taken from the trial of William Mead. The relational work between the parties is represented in such a way that the defendant's dispreferred seconds are countered with bald-on record impoliteness in the form of scornful gestures and with off record impoliteness through Culpeper's sarcasm strategy.

> Mead, turning his Face to the Jury, saith, You Men of the Jury, who are my Judges, if the Recorder will not tell you what makes a Riot, a Rout, or an unlawful Assembly, *Coke,* he that once they called the Lord Coke, tells us what makes a Riot, a Rout, and an unlawful Assembly ___A Riot is when three, or more, are met together to beat a Man, or to enter forcibly into

> another Man's land, to cut down his Grass, his Wood, or break down his Pales.
> [Observer]: *Here the Recorder interrupted him and said,* I thank you Sir, that you will tell me what the Law is; *scornfully pulling off his Hat.*
> [Mead]: Thou may'st put on thy Hat, I have never a Fee for thee now.
> [Brown]: He talks at random, one while an Independent, another while some other Religion, and now a Quaker, and next a Papist.
> [Mead]: *Turpe est doctori cum culpa redarguit ipsum*
> [Major]: You deserve to have your Tongue cut out.

After usurping the professional's role and explaining to the Jury the legal difference between a lawful and an unlawful assembly, Mead is interrupted by the Recorder. This is another instance of hindering communication strategy, which is represented by the defendant/reporter as socially abusive and as a clear marker of the Court's negative impoliteness. There follows the Recorder's activation of the sarcasm strategy intended to ridicule Mead's pretentiousness to show off his expertise in matters of Law. Culpeper defines sarcasm as FTA that is performed with the use of politeness strategies that are obviously insincere and thus remain surface realisations (1996: 356). In the utterance "I thank you Sir that you will tell me what Law is" the thanking is clearly ironic and the polite address term "Sir" enhances deference when the opposite is intended. The sarcasm of the utterance may have been further stressed by prosodic aspects of communication, for example a tonal emphasis on the *you-me* opposition. To maximise mock-deference and therefore face aggravation, the recorder accompanies his utterance with the gesture of pulling off his own hat. Mead's reply is rude in insulting the recorder by intentionally misinterpreting his gesture. The expression "Thou may'st put on thy Hat, I have never a Fee for thee now" is in fact intended to hint at the lawyers' general inclination to corruption. The conflictual relational work between the parties continues in the next exchange where Justice Brown attacks the positive and negative face of the defendant by associating his linguistic behaviour with that of surreptitious religious sects (including Papists), implying that his beliefs can be as dangerous. Mead intentionally exacerbates the conflict by returning his offence in Latin. The double face threat perceived in the choice of language and content triggers Lord Major's full resentment as is evident from his bald-on record counterattack: "You deserve to have your tongue cut out".

2.4.3 *Trials for theft and housebreaking*

In the trials which I have examined so far the defendants who refuse to plead belong to the middle and upper social classes. They are army professionals, gentlemen, ministers, dissenters with an education. This seems to suggest a correspondence between power and socio-cultural status. Nonetheless, an analysis of the narrative accounts of the Old Bailey Proceedings from 1674 to 1700 reveals that the non-plea practice was also present in trials for ordinary crimes with defendants of lower status. Unlike John Mordant, John Hewett or John Crook, who justified their refusal on the basis of a certain legal expertise and libertarian principles, in the accounts below lower-status defendants refuse to comply with the legal procedure for the most diverse reasons.

In one case the defendant accused of housebreaking and theft refused to plead unless the constable returned him the money that he had taken from him at the moment of the arrest:

> There was two others for breaking the House of the Duke of Buckingham, and stealing a great deal of Plate to the value of 400 pounds who being brought to the Bar; their Indictments being Read; one of them Pleaded not Guilty, and the other would not Plead, upon pretence that the Constable had taken from him eight pieces of Gold that was his own money, and so stood for the first two days; whereupon the Court was pleased to read the Statute to him, declaring the punishment which ought to be inflicted upon all such persons that would not plead to their Indictments by Pressing; and he hearing such grievous pu- [sic] there prescribed the next day pleaded to his Indictment not Guilty: but the Evidence proving it so clearly against them the Jury brought them in both Guilty: and Sentence was past upon them. (April 1674)

In the next three trials the defendants refused to plead until their wives and friends, accused with them of the robbery were released:

> There was another arraigned for Fellony and Burglary, but would not Plead till his Wife, who was accused with him might be released; The Court urg'd him in vain, and told him the Press was ready: he confidently replyed, that he was as ready for the Press: but the Court having enough to do that day, did let him alone till another, and ere that time was expired, possibly he would alter his Resolution. (17th January 1676)

> William Stevens being Indicted, together with Agnes his Wife, for stealing one pair of Curtains and Vallins, one Counterpain, one Rug, two Mantles, one pair of Sheets one Pillowbare, and one silver Cup , from Mathew Howlet, of the Parish of St. Clement Danes , one the 26th. of February last; Upon his Arraignment refused to plead, unless his Wife, (who did not appear in Court) might be first acquitted, but the Court granting him the Favour to consider for some time, of the danger he was like to incurr by such a Refusal; he upon a second time being brought to the Bar, pleaded guilty. (1678)

> Joseph Taylor and Samuel Eades of St. Andrew's Holbourn , were Indicted, Taylor as principal, Eades as Accessary, for stealing one Silver Tankard value 6 l. on the 25th of December last, the Goods of John Stanton: Taylor would not plead at first, until Eades was cleared, and being ask'd several times to plead, they both refused it; but having a little respite, and the Court telling them the danger of standing mute, viz. That they should be immediately Pressed, &c. at last they both pleaded Not Guilty (1690)

There was even the peculiar case of a wife accused of theft along with her husband who refused to plead because she had to keep her husband's secrets:

> There was a Youngman and his supposed Wife that were Arraigned for stealing of Thirty pair of Cloath-coloured Stockins: He (understanding there were many other Indictments against him) pleaded guilty to all Felonies within the benefit of Clergy: But she refused to plead, saying, That she was his Wife, and therefore bound to keep his secrets but at last she pleaded, she was acquitted, and he found guilty. (April 1676)

And here is the trial of John Price who refused to plead unless he was allowed to see his accusers.

> John Price being Indicted for a Fellony and Burglary for stealing a Brass Frying pan and other things to the value of 5 s. from one James Bennet, he refused to plead, and not with standing all endeavours were used by the Court, in which there were at least two hours spent, to perswade him to plead Guilty or not Guilty, he obstinately refused it unless he might see his Accusers: so that Sentence was passed upon him to be pressed by ten of the clock on Saturday, unless he conform to the Law, and recant his former stubborn obstinacy.
>
> (OBP 23rd Feburary 1682)

In all the summaries the reporter accounts for the enduring resistance of defendants to plead, despite the escalation of coercive strategies adopted by professionals: from the reading of the Statute – threatening them that serious punishment would follow if they did not submit to the law – to the passing of the sentence for physical torture. Although the squibs do not allow for an in-depth analysis of the discourse behaviour of the two parties, time and manner adverbs (confidently, in vain, at last, upon a second time, obstinately, several times) testify to the long power negotiation going on between judges and defendants as well as the boldness and stubborness of the latter. In the first account, for example, one unknown thief is said to have stood for two days confronting the authority of the judge before pleading; in the second squib the reporter highlights the vain efforts of the Court to convince the defendant to plead and the way in which he "confidently" resisted their threats; in the last account the Court is said to have spent at least two hours persuading the defendant to give up resistance, while he "obstinately" refused to plead unless his request was satisfied. The "stubborn obstinacy" of the defendants shows that prisoners attempted to dominate the Court through the systematic reiteration of dispreferred seconds in the same way as defendants of higher status and education did for more serious crimes. Unfortunately, however, the narrative style of the court record does not allow for a pragmatic analysis of speech-acts in terms of directness/indirectness, politeness/impoliteness. Even the judges' behaviour recalls the strategies adopted by the Commission for high treason and religious subversion as they also negotiated their power for long periods before exercising *force* in the form of physical torture or removal.

2.5 Conclusion

My analysis of the 17th-century arraignment section documents cases in which the reified power of the Court is met with resistance on the part of defendants. The resistance is exemplified in the form of off-script requests (dispreferred seconds) where prisoners ask for justification of the Court's procedure and counsel before pleading. Conscious of their off-script behaviour, defendants soften their utterances through hedges, vocatives and grounders, in the attempt to preserve social equilibrium and negotiate important rights before pleading. Professionals, in their turn, systematically construe their requests as improper/impolite thus revealing the rigid relational protocol of 17th-century Courts. Their behaviour testifies to the high deference expectation in the 17th-century courtroom especially when compared with the greater sense of rights on each side that characterises today's Court. At the same time, however, it may also be argued that the professionals' face-work responds to their aim to frame the prisoner as a disrespectful individual, whose off-script attitude is indicative of his guilt.

In order to investigate the relational dynamics at the basis of the professional-defendant interaction, I have selected three groups of trials which differ from one another in terms of defendants' status and crime committed. The first group of high treason trials involves defendants of higher status, i.e. army professionals, gentlemen and ministers. The second group consists of cases of religious subversion through refusal to take oaths, illegal assembly and incompetent ministry. The defendants are all dissenters and belong to the middle and high social class. Finally the third group shows defendants of lower status accused of burglary, housebreaking and theft. The different contextual aspects of each subcorpus account for differences in the relational work going on between judges and defendants.

In the first group for example occurrences of prototypical impoliteness are rare. Although professionals construe the defendants' dispreferred seconds as intentionally aggravating (i.e. impolite), an analysis of their utterances shows that their criticism of the Court's conduct is generally incidental and subservient to their primary goal to be treated justly. In this sense, the prisoners' behaviour may be said to equate to verbal aggression as opposed to impoliteness. Similar considerations may be drawn in relation to the professionals' facework. As a result of the activation of different norms of behaviour, defendants interpret their utterances as 'falling outside their institutionally sanctioned office' and thefore as intentionally face aggravating. Nonetheless, judges and prosecutors consistently justify their criticism/accusation of the defendant's attitude as 'doing their job' and therefore as politic/normative. Given their multiple goals in interaction, it is hard to establish when certain malicious intentions (i.e. discredit the defendant, frame him in a negative way) have the better of their institutionally sanctioned task (i.e. instruct the defendant as to how to behave, administer the Law). In this sense, Archer's notion of an *ambigious-to-speaker-intent* zone located between the incidental and intentional face threat cline proves useful in order to account for those cases in which the professionals' facework remains indeterminate as to its real intention.

By and large, if in this group of trials professionals and defendants still tend to preserve an aura of formal distance when addressing each other – no matter how hostile their pragmatic intentions may be – in the next group of autobiographical records, formal etiquette disappears in favour of open insult. The ruder character of the interaction seems to be primarily ascribed to the status of defendants as dissenters. Even so, it is significant that while in the non-autobiographical trial of Benjamin Keach the judge's replies still moved within an *ambiguous-to-speaker-intent* zone, with only one case of more overtly malicious face aggravation, in all the autobiographical trials both defendants and professionals ventured into instances of prototypical impoliteness. In many cases the judges' FTAs along with the prisoner's boldness are maximised to the point that it is hard to establish to what extent impoliteness has actually been engineered by the original speaker and to what extent it has been purposefully enacted by the recorders/defendants in the *a posteriori* transcription in order to denounce the Court's abuses in the eyes of public opinion. Even admitting the potentially fictitious character of the exchange, the data testify as to when 17th-century non-professional participants deem impoliteness to have taken place and when it is perceived as such by the contemporary readers.

The last group of trials taken from the OBP reminds us that the challenging behaviour of defendants is not necessarily to be associated with their status and education as bearers of power. In fact, even defendants of lower status may occasionally venture into a strong refusal to comply with the legal procedure, thus instigating an escalation of counter-threats on the part of professionals. Unfortunately, being mere summaries, this particular dataset does not allow for a detailed analysis of the participants' linguistic behaviour. As a result it is not possible to comment on the weaker or stronger goals of the speaker and on the receiver's cognitive construction of the utterance.

By and large the analysis of verbal duelling in the arraignment section has ultimately highlighted the need to go beyond the 'politeness' and 'impoliteness' labels in order to catch more subtle nuances in discourse and to account for facework dynamics in their own right.

Chapter 3

Defence construction in the evidence phase

3.1 Forms of defence

In the evidence phase of 17th-century trials defendants articulate their defence through two main discourse practices: a) their reply to the prosecution evidence b) their right to examine witnesses. The former is realised by means of representatives with an informative and expressive purpose; it includes answers to questions, accounts, denials, confessions and – in a few cases – evaluative comments. The latter encompasses all those cases in which the defendant intends to obtain information from witnesses. It is actualised in the form of a) direct questions addressed to witnesses, b) requests addressed to the judge to elicit answers from the witness.

Defendants' question types do not basically differ from those utilised by professionals. This seems to be due to their tendency to borrow examining forms from experts in the attempt to shape the interlocutor's evidence in a way favourable to their cause. Archer (2005: 24–71) provides an exhaustive account of the interrogative forms and functions adopted by defendants in EmodE trials (1640–1760). In this chapter first I shall outline the question and request-types used by defendants during the examination phase. Next I shall provide a quantitative and qualitative analysis of the distribution of directives (questions and requests) and representatives (accounts, denials, answers) in my dataset. Finally I shall focus on the defence strategies adopted by defendants and actualised in the form of directives and representatives. My dataset consists of 16 trials dating from 1616 to 1692 and amounts to about

114,000 words[12]. I shall start with an analysis of the question categories which are most commonly directed to witnesses: wh-questions, polar and negative polar questions, tag-questions.

3.1.1 Question-types

Wh-questions in the 17th century do not markedly differ from their Present Day English counterpart, the only peculiarities being the use of ***what*** for referring to people and things and the non-periphrastic inversion (i.e. How know you him?) which continues to coexist along with the use of *did/do/doth*. They are defined as "questions that ask for information about the referent of the interrogative adverb or pronoun that initiates them" (Walker 1987; Rigney 1999). They may be broad (those asking about why? what? how?) in the sense that they accept/expect longer answers, usually narratives:

> [Colledge, the defendant]: What do you know of Haynes?

or narrow, insofar as they elicit only information about specific details of the story version represented (who, where, when, how long):

> [Giles, the defendant]: How long ago was this?
> [Bridges]: This was, my Lord, about a Twelve Month ago.

12 The Trial of Lady Frances (1616), the Trial of Robert Carr (1616), Censure of Dr Bastwicke, Mr Burton and Mr Prynne (1637), the Trial of Lord Macguire (1644), the Trial of Lilburne (1649), the Trial of Mr Love (1651), Severall Tryals of Sir Henry Slingsby (1658), the Trial of Colonel Turner (1663) the Trial of Edward Coleman (1678), the Trial of Robert Green etc (1678/79), the Trial of John Giles (1680), the Trial of Stephen Colledge (1681) the Trial of Nathaniel Thompson (1682), the Trial of Thomas Pilkington, etc. (1682), the Trial of Algernon Sidney (1682), The Trial of Charles Lord Mohun (1692). All the trials have been taken from the CED with the exception of the Trial of Lilburne, whose evidence phase has been taken from the State Trials, as it has not been transcribed in the CED.

They are generally considered low control questions as they allow the witness a certain freedom of action in the elaboration of the answer, though narrow wh-questions can take on a coercive function in contexts (Archer 2005: 81):

> [Sir H Slingsby, the defendant]: Mr Overton, what date did that Commission which I then delivered bear?
> [Mr Overton]: This is the same Commission and I here see it is dated 12 March 1657.
> [Sir H Slingsby]: I deny that that Commission I then delivered did bear that date.

Along with wh-questions there are also imperative forms which are used to elicit longer narratives from witnesses:

> [Colledge]: Pray tell the Court how these papers that are called the "Raree-shew" came to be in my House.

Polar, negative polar and tag-questions on the other hand are classified as coercive questions for the high degree of restriction that they try to impose on the answer. EmodE polar questions are similar to Present Day English ones. They are called polar as they must be answered with either "yes" or "no". This means that the witness is only called to confirm or deny the content of the question as it has been worded and conceptualised by the examiner. In this way defendants (as well as lawyers) can "speak to the jury directly without the witness-intermediary" (Woodbury 1984: 215), which is crucial to make their points especially in cross-examination:

> [Sir H Slingsby]: Was that Commission which you read dated 12 March?

Negative polar questions are negative grammatical yes/no questions which incorporate the speaker's expected/desired answer. As Woodbury claims, they signal the speaker's surprise with regard to the information he has just received. When the examiner asks: "Didn't you enter the house at that time?" The covert message is "I thought you did and now you appear to contradict this belief"

(1984: 202). In this sense they represent a valuable strategy in the examination of hostile witnesses in order to cast doubts as to the consistency and reliability of their testimony.

> [Giles]: ...Do you hear Sir, Were not these the words that I said when you charged me to be a Papist, That I knew of no Popish Plot, and they that said I was a Papist, or knew any of the Plot, were Rogues, or Whores, or worse.

Tag questions are also defined as coercive questions. They consist of declarative sentences followed by a tag. In particular, the category of checking tags – either negative or positive – functions as a demand to affirm or deny the prepositional content of the declarative. The following example is taken from the direct examination of a friendly witness where the defendant attempts to make his point by leading the witness to confirm his story version.

> [Turner, the defendant]: I drank not with him, did I
> [Dawes]: Not that I saw.

Although the amount of control inherent in a question type cannot be assessed on the basis of its grammatical form alone (Archer 2005: 78), Woodbury (1984: 205) claims that question types can be organised hierarchically according to a "continuum of control", as shown below

Amount of control	Type of question
Least	Broad wh-
↑	Narrow wh-
	Alternative
	Grammatical yes/no
	Negative yes/no questions
	Prosodic (i.e. declarative questions)
↓	Tag
Most	

Figure 2. Woodbury's (1984: 205) 'continuum of control'.

Woodbury's contuuum has been subsequently revised by Archer (2005: 79) who notices that, although the scale helps us understand the amount of control an examiner "may be attempting to exercise over the discouse", it does not consider the kinds of responses that these question types typically require. In her adapted continuum shown in figure 3, we can see how the higher amount of control exerted by certain question types ((negative) polars, declartatives, tag questions) displays a greater expectation of an answer.

Type of questions	Amount of control	Conducivity	Type of response question types typically expect
1. Broad wh-	Least	Low	– Open range
2. Narrow wh-	↑		– Naming of specific variable
3. Alternative		↑	– Choice of answer restricted to 1 of 2 provided by questioner
4. Grammatical yes/no			– Yes/no
5. Negative gram yes/no			– Anticipated response whether affirmative or negative
6. Declarative		↓	– Confirmation of proposition
7. Tagged declarative	↓ Most	High	

Figure 3. Archer's revised continuum of control (2005: 79).

Figure 3 will be particularly useful when analysing instances in which the defendant's use of certain highly conducive questions (e.g. Giles's use of polar and negative polar questions in cross-examination in 3.3.3) is not accompanied by the corresponding expected answer. This in a way confirms Archer's claim that "the various questions are less likely to exhibit the same amount of control when asked by less powerful participants" (Archer 2005: 79).

In my data defendants generally opt for wh-questions and (negative) polar questions whereas prosodic and tag questions remain the exclusive province of professionals. In the 17th-century courtroom the formal protocol requires that defendants frame their questions in the form of requests to the judges, as a result most of their questions are indirect. With the exception of one trial where the defendant asks a considerable number of direct questions in direct examination (Trial of Stephen Colledge, 1681), requests are the most frequently distributed category in my dataset used to elicit information.

3.1.2 Request-types in the evidence phase

There are two main ways in which prisoners word their requests to ask questions of witnesses: a) asking judges to pose the question for them, b) asking permission to pose the question themselves. The reason for such a ritual is that questions coming from defendants have to be approved by judges before being answered by witnesses. In those cases in which questions are directly addressed to the witness, the judge has previously authorised the defendant to do so (see the trial of Colledge, 1681 and Mohun, 1692) or the defendant has previously asked for permission (see trials of Pilkington 1682, Giles 1680, Sidney 1683). In order to examine request strategies I shall adopt Blum-Kulka's classification as reported in chapter 2. Since my data are mostly taken from the CED, my findings conform to those of Culpeper and Archer (2008). Their frequency scale features a major presence of impositive strategies – imperatives being the most common – followed by want statements – which I consider as indirect requests – and other conventional indirect requests, especially let-construction and *will-you* structure. A similar distribution occurs in my specialised dataset of defendants' requests to judges in the evidence phase. I distinguish between (a) requests in which defendants ask judges to pose the question for them and (b) requests in which defendants ask for the judges' permission to pose the question.

– *Requests (a): impositives*

In the evidence phase of the trial, defendants who ask judges to pose the question for them do so mostly through the use of imperatives:

1) [J. Lilburne]: Ask him the Question thus, whether was I the Corrector of the Thing printed, or the Looker on upon the printed Copy? And whether or no, he can swear that printed Sheet, that he says I had, was corrected and revised, and was a true and perfect Sheet, according to the Original? (Trial of John Lilburne 1649)
2) [Mr Love]: My Lord, I pray ask him, whether any of these pretended or supposed letters, were ever received by me, any one of them, or that I writ one of them, or mended one of them. (Trial of Love, 1651)
3) [Mr Love]: Ask him whether I gave my consent to the sending away of this he calls a Commission… (Trial of Love, 1651)
4) [Mr Turner]: Pray ask Sir Thomas whether I did not promise him to do all I could. (Trial of Iames Turner 1663)
5) [Mr Coleman]: Pray ask Mr Oates whether he was not as near to me as this Gentleman is, because he speaks of his eyes being bad? (Trial of Coleman, 1678).

In the evidence phase, several impositives used by defendants have no support at all (nos. 1, 3) or are premodified only by vocatives and external markers like *pray/I pray* occurring in initial position before the head act (nos. 2,4,5). The vocative functions as an alerter. "It calls the hearer's attention to the ensuing speech-act" (Blum-Kulka et al. 1989: 277) and offers the possibility of "marking a particular social relationship between participants" (Culpeper and Archer 2008: 73). In my corpus the vocative *My Lord* is used by defendants as a politeness marker to signal the power differential between speaker and judge. Also the support move *pray/I pray* enhances the relative power of the interlocutor by casting the speaker in the role of a supplicant. Grounders, on the other hand, are scarcely used (no. 5) and are less frequent than in the arraignment section. This seems to suggest that in the context of the examination phase the defendant's requests to judges as examiners are officially sanctioned and as such there is no need to legitimate them through much negative politeness facework (e.g. Culpeper and Archer 2008). In this sense, less power does not necessarily correlate with the use of indirect/polite formulae since it is the institutional recognition of the defendant's role which determines the acceptance of direct and apparently more impolite utterances as politic behaviour. This conclusion seems to be corroborated by the fact that when defendants perform non-sanctioned requests which exceed their institutional role, as is the case in the pleading phase, they make a larger use of grounders to justify the challenging character of their utterances. Kryk-Kastovsky (2006) has suggested a different interpretation in her discussion of requests in 17th courtroom: she advocates a scale of politeness which increases along with the decrease of directness. In this respect she considers requests in the imperative or indicative mood (i.e. impositives and want-statements) as the most direct and least polite ways of performing requests on the part of defendants in the examination phase. By means of illustration she quotes two examples from the trial of Titus Oates (1685) where, in her view, the prisoner's structuring of the request reveals his power over the person interrogated and the Court:

> [Titus Oates]: Pray, my Lord, I desire to know what religion he is of.
> [Titus Oates]: But pray, my Lord, ask him, because it is a question here about a point of Time, whether he remembers, that within eight or ten days, he saw Ireland at Tixhall?

She explains what she interprets as a deviation from the formal politeness of the courtroom in terms of Oates's high social position and political and religious anti-Catholic orientation. Nonetheless, in my dataset, I have found several instances of defendants who, no matter what their social status and political/religious views, perform requests through imperatives and want statements without even providing grounders (which Oates does in the second example). This seems to confirm Culpeper and Archer's view (2008) that in the context of the evidence section the role of the defendant as interrogator was commonly recognised by the Court and as such there was no need to establish it linguistically to receive legitimation. Their conclusion also fits my findings regarding the different distribution of request strategies in the arraignment section. In that context, the imperative mood (maximum degree of imposition and directness) comes second after want statements, as defendants acknowledge that their requests fall outside the pleading script and mitigate them through indirectness.

– *Requests (a): want statements*

In order of frequency, the next category of requests which is utilised by defendants in the evidence phase is want statements. In many cases the prisoner words his requests to the judge by means of the verb *I desire/I wish,* which – following Kohnen (2002) – I interpret as closer to indirect requests.

1) [Mr Love]: I desire your Lordship to ask him this question, whether the supposed Narrative that he speaks of, that Alford said he brought over, and read at my House, was read at my house; or only by Alford, and so brought over as news. (1651)
2) [John Lilburne]: I desire you to ask him, whether I did not take notice or Cognizance of any of them first? Or whether they did speak to me before, before ever I said any thing to them? (1649)
3) [Lord Mohun]: My Lord I desire the witness may be asked how long after this Passage that she speaketh of, was it that he heard Murder cryed in the street. (1692)
4) [Colonel Sidney]: My Lord I desire you would ask Mr Edward Howard the same thing, what Discourse he had with my Lord Howard about this plot? (1683)

– *Requests (a): let-structure and will-you...?*

The last two structures adopted by defendants are *let*-constructions and *will you*+verb, which fall into the category of conventional indirect requests. The historical interpretation of *let*- provided by Kohnen suggests that the speaker is involved not so much in the act of requesting the addressee to do something but rather in the act of asking the H "to allow him/her or to cause him/her to experience the results of the requested action" (Kohnen 2004: 164). The historical sense of *let* as a main verb meaning "allow" or "cause" fits its usage in the evidence phase:

[Mr Love]: But let him prove how there was a correspondency on my part.

[J.Lilburne]: Pray let me answer the Thing: let me have fair Play above board. Sir I beseech you let me hold him close to the question.

The other type of indirect request is the *will-you*+verb structure. Most of the examples of *will-you*+verb form appear to be used by prosecution lawyers and judges (87% of the occurrences) either as invitation to defendants to ask witnesses questions or as a means of eliciting information:

[L.C.J.]: Well, will you ask this Witness any questions before he goes?

(Trial of Green, Berry and Hill, 1678)

[L.C.J.]: What will you ask her?

(Trial of Colledge, 1681)

[Mr Serj. Jefferies]: Pray, will you tell my Lord and the Jury what you had observed in particular, because I mentioned it in the time of Sir Robert Clayton; mention how that was.

(Trial of Pilkington, 1682)

[Mr North]: Pray Sir, will you give the Court an account of what you know of any Insurrection intended, and how they designed to carry it on.

(Trial of Colonel Sydney, 1683).

There are also cases in which professionals use *will-you* questions to commit or intimidate the witness as to the truthfulness of his testimony:

[L.C.J.] Will you undertake to say it was always in the door?

(Trial of Green etc. 1678)

[Recorder]: Mr Arnold, I would know one thing, will you undertake to swear positively that this Person was one of the Persons who stept before you? Will you take it upon your Oath that this Person, the Prisoner at the Bar, went before you?

(Trial of Thompson, 1682)

[Lord President]: Will you say that your heart is lifted up to God when your understanding is in your heels?

(Trial of Mr Love, 1651)

The few cases in which these structures are used by defendants document a form of dialogism between the professionals' discourse practices and the prisoners' discourse behaviour when acting as examiners:

> [Mr Giles]: Will you say that I am a Papist, Sir?

After illustrating the strategies through which defendants request judges to ask questions for them, it remains to be established whether judges actually do so. My data show that only in a few circumstances do they reword the question for the witness:

> [Col.Sidney]: My Lord I desire you would ask Mr Edward Howard the same thing, what Discourse he had with my Lord Howard about this Plot?
> [L.C.J.]: Mr Howard, Mr Sidney desires you to tell what Discourse you had with my Lord Howard about this Plot.
>
> (Trial of Colonel Sidney, 1683)

> [Lord Mohun]: My Lord, I desire this Witness may be asked, how long after this Passage that she speaketh of, was it that she heard Murder cryed in the street.
> [Lord High Steward]: You hear the Question, Mrs Bracegirdle, What say you to it?
>
> (Trial of Lord Mohun 1692)

In most cases the request to the judge is purely ritualistic and appears to have a mere symbolic value. In fact, the witness directly replies to the prisoner's request transforming a three party adjacency pair mechanism with A (making the request) B (granting permission and posing the question) and C (answering the question) into a more linear question-answer sequence: A(defendant)-C(witness).

> [Mr Turner]: pray ask sir Thomas whether I did not promise him to do all I could.
> [Sir Thomas Alleyn]: I pressed him hard, he said he would endeavour it.
>
> (Trial of Turner, 1663)

> [Mr Coleman]: Pray ask Mr Oates, whether he was not as near to me as this Gentleman is, because he speaks of his eyes being bad?

[Mr Oates]: I had the disadvantage of a Candle upon my eyes; Mr Coleman stood more in the dark.

(Trial of Coleman, 1678)

[Mr Love]: But let him prove how it was a correspondency on my part.
[Adams]: I did not say that Mr Love was one of the Correspondents, I deny that I said so, I said I conceived him to be so, but that is not, that he was so.

(Trial of Love, 1651)

– *Requests (b): want statements, performatives and obligation statement*

The second technique for framing questions in the form of requests is more linear as defendants simply ask the judge's permission to pose the question. The request is verbalised through want statements and performatives (with only one case of obligation statements). The former category is by far the most frequent.

[J. Lilburne]: I desire to ask him this Question whether...
[Mr Love]: I would ask him some questions and the first is ...
[Pilkington]: I desire to ask this Witness a Question, my Lord
[Lord Mohen]: My Lord, I desire to ask this Witness whether...
[Colonel Sidney]: I desire to know whether he was not...

Performatives occur in two trials only:

[Mr Turner]: I demand Sir Thomas Alleyn whether I did not...
[Mr Turner]: My Lord I ask Alderman Alley whether...

[J. Lilburne]: I ask you whether before the Things were compleat and perfect, your Forms were not both taken, and your Person seized upon?

It is worth pointing out that although Lilburne's questioning style is perceived as inappropriate by the judges ("You must desire us to ask him the Question and not you to demand it yourself"), twenty years later Mr Turner frames the question in a similar way without being reproached for it by the Commission. The different treatment may be due to the fact that the practice has become more acceptable throughout the years or to the different character of the trials: the first being a treason case where the defendant is tried by an extraordinary and special commission, the second being an ordinary trial for robbery.

3.2 Quantitative and qualitative analysis of representatives and directives

After this overview on the discourse practices adopted by defendants in the evidence phase of the trial, I intend to account for their distribution across my dataset. To this purpose I shall provide a quantitative analysis of the defendants' speech-acts drawing a distinction between representatives and directives. The former include accounts, descriptive statements, denials, confessions, answers to questions and comments. The latter concern direct questions addressed to the witnesses, requests to judges to pose witnesses questions or to grant defendants permission to ask the question themselves. The results of the analysis suggest that the examining practice began to develop not earlier than the second half of the century.

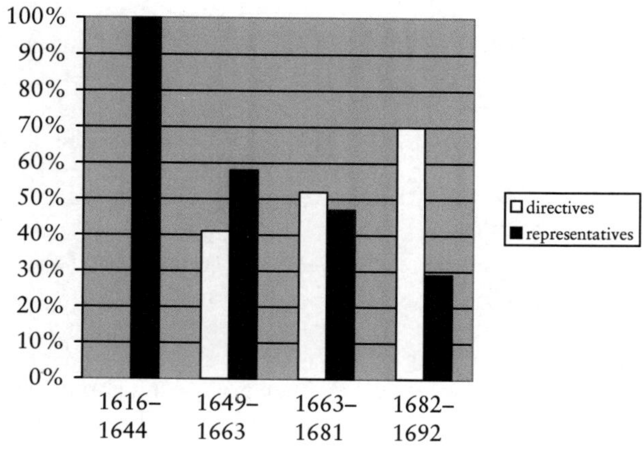

Figure 4. Distribution of directives and representatives across the 17th century.

I have subdivided my dataset into four periods of four trials each[13]. The sections are chronologically ordered and display the number of representatives and directives. The findings suggest that throughout the century defendants articulate their defence mainly through representatives, especially denials. Directives make their appearance only around mid-century though they show an increasing presence till the end of the century. They will drastically decline from 1692 onwards as a result of the introduction of the defence counsel who substitutes the defendant in witness examination. Representatives, on the other hand, show a descending cline from 1649, presumably under the effect of the defendants' increasing familiarity with the questioning practice used by professionals. The progressive shift from a monologic to an interactional structuring of the defence may be ascribed to a number of factors:

a) the growing familiarity with the questioning techniques used by professionals
b) the professionals' solicitation of defendants to prove their innocence via witness examination
c) the examples of previous trial cases where defendants were found guilty because their defence did not conform to the more effective interactive format.

---

13 The period from 1616–1644 contains the Trial of Lady Frances (1616), the Trial of Robert Carr (1616), Censure of Dr Bastwicke, Mr Burton and Mr Prynne (1637), the Trial of Lord Macguire (1644) and it amounts to 11,840 words. The period from 1649–1663 contains the Trial of John Lilburne (1649), the Trial of Mr Love (1651), the trial of Sir Henry Slingsby (1658), the Trial of Colonel Turner (1663) and it amounts to 32,400 words. The period from 1663–1681 contains the Trial of Edward Coleman (1678), the Trial of Robert Green etc (1678/79), the Trial of John Giles (1680), the Trial of Stephen Colledge (1681)and it amounts to 33,640 words. The last period from 1682–1692 contains the Trial of Nathanael Thompson (1682), the Trial of Thomas Pilkington, etc. (1682), the Trial of Algernon Sidney (1682), The Trial of Charles Lord Mohun (1692) and it amounts to 35,800 words. All the trials have been taken from the CED with the exception of the Trial of Lilburne, whose evidence phase has been taken from the State Trials, as it has not been transcribed in the CED.

In the first half of the century defendants came to Court unprepared to manage a defence, as a result their contributions essentially consisted of confutations of what other witnesses testified or of the presentation of different story versions. Defendants also experienced difficulties in having their answers accepted as true by judges. Given the strong prejudices held against them, laconic answers which did not fit judges' expectations were often read as unequivocal signs of the defendant's untrustworthiness. By means of illustration, in the extract below the maxim of informativeness (provide all the relevant information) clashes with the maxim of trustworthiness (say only what you know to be true) as a result of the judges' attempt to elicit the desired confession, no matter how far from truth this may be.

> [L.C. Justice]: It is all true that you say: but did you tell all that was true?
> [Mr Coleman]: I know no more, than what I declared to the Two Houses.
> [L.C.J.]: Mr Coleman, I'll tell you when you will be apt to gain credit in this matter: You say, that you told all things that you knew, the Truth, and the whole Truth. Can Mankind be persuaded, that you, that had this Negotiation in 74. and 75. left off just then, at that time vvhen your Letters vvere found according to their Dates? Do you believe, there vvas no Negotiation after 75. because vve have not found them? Have you spoke one vvord to that? Have you confessed, or produced those Papers and Weekly Intelligence? When you ansvver that, you may have credit; vvithout that, it is impossible: For I cannot give credit to one vvord you say, unless you give an account of the subsequent Negotiation.
>
> (Trial of E. Coleman, 1678)

As a confessed Roman Catholic, Coleman is treated with much suspicion. The judge, for example, reads his disclaimer "I know no more than what I declared" as a blatant flouting of the cooperative principle as well as an indicator of untrustworthiness. The defendant, on his part, insists that saying more than he knows to be the true (and abide by the maxim of informativeness) would mean being untruthful (and would break the maxim of trustworthiness). The judge counterattacks his defence showing that truth has no value insofar as it hampers cooperation and deviates from the reality version judges are eager to receive. Coleman's extract represents one of the several cases in my dataset in which judges adopt a "guilty but unwilling to confess" reality paradigm (Archer 2002) in order to invalidate the prisoner's innocence, no matter how convincing his defence may be[14].

In the next section I shall inspect the way in which defendants make use of representatives and questions in order to build up their defence. In those cases in which defence construction calls into play the notion of face attack and face damage, defence strategies will be analysed within an (im)politeness framework.

3.3 Defence strategies: challenge, redefinition and reconstruction

In their book *Reconstructing Reality in the Courtroom,* Bennett and Feldman (1981) analyse the strategic options available to the defence counsel to construct his/her client's version of the events. Although their study is based on contemporary American trials, the similarities existing between the discourse behaviour of present-day defence and 17th-century defendants suggest that the authors' classification may equally be applied to the analysis of EmodE courtroom discourse. Bennett and Feldman identify story telling

14 The notion of 'reality paradigm' comes from Archer (2002: 20). It is an umbrella term to refer to the many and varied 'particularised' mental perspectives of reality, which lawyers construct to support their own interpretation of the events. More recently Archer (2011c: 75) has defined reality paradigms as *truth* filters used by interlocutors to "interpret/make sense of their worlds". In this respect the notion is more specific to the individual than expectation frames, which more appropriately equate to schemas. At the same time, however, reality paradigms tend to overlap with representational frames described by Locher and Watts (2008: 99, n9) as way(s) in which interlocutors decide to "represent the character traits, ideas and opinions of and even statements made by others".

operations which make it possible to alter the interpretation of the prosecution story through challenge, redefinition and reconstruction of the story itself. Starting with the *challenge strategy*, they claim that:

> The challenge strategy usually involves some attempt to demonstrate that the key definitions of story elements are poorly supported by evidence or testimony; that the nature of the evidence permits definitions other than the ones the prosecution has assigned to it; or that the prosecution case has some obvious gaps or inconsistencies in it.
>
> (1981: 98).

In my dataset this is one of the most frequently used strategies to cast doubts on the witness's testimony. It is also found in combination with redefinition or reconstruction strategies and it is realised both in the form of representatives and directives. The latter take on the form and function of coercive questions which restrict the interlocutor's action-environment and acquire a controlling and occasionally accusing force. The most popular types of interrogatives with a challenging function utilised by defendants are:

- negative polar questions
- how (possible) questions

} both appearing in the form of direct interrogatives and (in)direct requests to judges

The *redefinition strategy* concerns the redefinition of particular elements in the story to show that a different meaning emerges when slight changes are made in the interpretation of the evidence. "Its success depends on the defence's ability to find a story element that is ambiguous enough to support another definition and, at the same time, central enough to the story to affect the meaning of the central action" (Bennett and Feldman 1981: 102). The 17th-century defendants actualise this in the form of informatives and directives or a combination of both. From the 1660s onwards this strategy tends to be framed more through questions than through informatives as defendants come to realise the necessity of proving their points via witness examination.

Finally, *the reconstruction strategy* generally occurs when the defence finds it difficult to challenge or reinterpret the prosecution story and as a result tells a story of its own. Under this strategy the defendant may introduce his/her own evidence in order to tell a completely different story about his/her behaviour. The reconstruction option is actualised in the form of informatives and questions. In the first half of the century this strategy generally takes the shape of a denial followed by an alternative version of the events presented in a monologic style following the prosecution evidence (cf. Trial of Lord Macguire 1644). This practice, however, was not particularly effective as by that time the jury had already formed a negative opinion of the defendant. In the second half of the century the growing familiarity with questioning strategies led defendants to reconstruct the witness's evidence as the trial unfolded.

3.3.1 Challenge strategy

The examples selected for analysis are taken from the Trial of Mr Love dated 1651 and from the trial of Edward Coleman. Christopher Love was a Welsh Protestant preacher and a supporter of Presbyterianism during the Civil War. He was involved in a treasonable correspondence with the Scottish covenants to restore Charles II and was arrested on 7 May 1651. During the trial, evidence against him revealed that a certain Colonel Titus was commissioned by Scottish Presbyterians to carry letters to Charles I's wife, Henrietta Maria, in France. Her replies were read at Love's house, together with other letters coming from Scottish supporters of Charles II. Love was tried by the High Court of Justice under the presidence of Richard Keble and condemned to be executed for High Treason. In the extracts below the defendant examines hostile witnesses in order to construct his evidence by discrediting their testimony.

- [Mr Love]: But let him prove <u>how</u> it was a correspondency on my part.
- [Adams]: I did not say that Mr Love was one of the correspondents, I deny that I said so, I said I conceived him to be so, but that is not, that he was so.

(Trial of Mr Love 1651)

85% of the occurrences of how(possible)-questions in my dataset belongs to judges and lawyers. The remaining 15% belongs to defendants who, in all probability, attempted to emulate the discourse practices of professionals in the witness-examination phase. Indeed how-questions were exploited by lawyers as effective tools to undermine the witness's credibility (casting doubt on the logical possibility that the events/actions reported actually took place the way the witness claims) and were equally suitable to the construction of both the prosecution and the defence evidence. What is more, they allowed accusation to be framed indirectly, while at the same time neutralising the potential offence under the claim that the speaker was simply posing an information-seeking question as his job required. The systematic use of how-questions at crucial points in the trial is responsible for their collocation within Archer's *ambigious-to-speaker-intent* zone.

In Love's trial, the how-question verbalised as an indirect request to the judge seems to be implicitly aimed at accusing Adams of lying. The face threatening force of the utterance is conveyed by the assumption that the defendant ultimately knows that the response requested is face damaging to the witness uttering it and, therefore, advantageous to his own cause. In this sense, Love's turn can be defined as a case of "response seeking challenge" which – as Bousfield claims – causes 1) negative face damage insofar as it attempts to force the witness to respond in a highly restrictive and face aggravating way and 2) positive face damage as it carries an underlying criticism of Adam's behaviour (Bousfield 2008: 132). Even so, it is worth pointing out that Love is acting within his insitutionally sanctioned role of examiner and in the utterance there are no overt markers of impoliteness. In this sense although the defendant is personally involved in the outcome of the trial and his questions are (theoretically) more likely to be laden with hostile feelings than is the case with professionals, he nonetheless maintains a degree of formality which apparently neutralises the challenging force of the utterance. The witness's response is of the defensive type and suggests that although a certain degree of offence has been taken at the implied challenge, the utterance still falls within Archer's *politic zone* (2011a).

The second example provides another instance of response seeking challenge. In this case the attack on the witness's negative face is stronger, as we can see from the prisoner's direct reference to his contradictory testimony.

- Mr Love: He said, if I have taken him rightly, and if not, I desire your Notaries to inform me better that Mr Love did not agree to such a summe as forty pounds and afterwards he said, that all there said it was convenient. <u>Now I would ask *how* these two can agree together</u>?
- President: You are right for the thing of the agreement he disclaimed totally.
- Mr Love: Then I did not agree to it
- President: No, nor any else
- Mr Love: But afterwards he sayes, that they did conceive it was convenient. <u>Now I pray ask him *how* he knew that I thought it was convenient?</u>
- Jaquel: I cannot say anything that Mr Love did say it was convenient; but it was not dissented from, nor spoken against by any, as I remember.

(Trial of Mr Love 1651)

The coercive force of the question is reinforced by its repetition which determines an escalation of face damage. Nonetheless, even in this case, the defendant's behaviour may be considered politic, i.e. appropriate to his discoursal goals and social role in cross-examination. As a result his face attack appears closer to forms of sanctioned aggression than impoliteness. The witness perceives the face threat inherent in the challenge, however he is skilful enough to evade it, justifying his evidence on the assumption that silence implies consent. The extract shows that although the defendant struggles to obtain a response which can help him to prove his innocence, he still lacks the coercive power to shape the witness's reply so as to achieve his discoursal goal (Archer 2005). In this sense perplexities remain as to his actual role and involvement in the conspiracy.

The last example is taken from the trial of the English Catholic Coleman who was falsely accused by the minister Titus Oates of conspiring the death of the king and the subversion of the Protestant religion. In the evidence phase Mr Oates reported testimony of the correspondence between Coleman and other Jesuits where arrangements were made for the propagation of the Catholic religion and for the assassination of the king. Although there was no proof of a real connivance on the part of Coleman (except the testimony of Oates and Bedlow, the former being later found a perjurer), the jury found him guilty of high treason (see Kenyon 1972).

In the extract below the challenge strategy is actualised in the form of a representative (i.e. an informative). The defendant highlights a clear contradiction in Oates's testimony saying that when he was examined before the Council, Oates was unable to recognise him, though now he is ready to report plenty of (false) evidence of their acquaintance. Coleman denounces the inconsistency as follows:

> [Att. Gen.]: If the prisoner at the bar be minded, he may ask him any Question.
> [Prisoner]: I am mighty glad to see that Gentleman Sir Thomas Dolman in the Court, for I think he was upon my Examination before the Council, and this man that gives now his Evidence against me. There told the king, he never saw me before; and he is extremely well-acquainted with me now, and hath a World of Intimacy. Mr Oates at that time gave such an Account of my concern in this matter, that I had orders to go to Newgate, I never saw Mr Oates since I was born, but at that time.

This challenge seems to differ from the others in the use of positive and negative impoliteness markers, such as the distancing term "this man", rather than title and last name, and the sarcasm inherent in the emphasisers "extremely well acquainted" and "a World of Intimacy" which reveal the prisoner's intent to discredit the witness for his inconsistent account. Even so Coleman's facework may be said to equate with institutionally sanctioned aggression rather than prototypical impoliteness. Indeed, given that the defendant knows that Mr Oates is overtly lying and inflicting on him the maximum of face damage, one would expect (even justify) a more direct and unmitigated counter-attack on his part. The fact that he opts for off record strategies suggests that his primary aim is to discredit the witness's story in the attempt to save his life rather than to insult his individual face for some personal sense of spite and maliciousness. In this regard, it is also worth noticing that although some offence is present in the defendant's words, the witness does not seem to take it. In his reply he simply justifies the inconsistency without any clear attempt to reciprocate the face attack. Oates's mildness, however, might be also due to his bad faith.

> [Mr Oates]: My Lord, when Mr Coleman was upon his Examination before the Council Board he saith, I said there that I never saw him before in my Life: I then said I would not swear that I had seen him before in my Life because my sight was bad by Candle-light, and Candle-Light alters the sight much, but when I heard him speak I could have sworn it was he, but it was not then my Business. I cannot see a great way by Candle-Light.

3.3.2 Redefinition strategy

In the first example selected for analysis the redefinition strategy is actualised through a set of declaratives which frame a different version of the events. For this reason I have adopted Halliday's transitivity model ([1985]1992) which allows for an account of the defendant's reconceptualisation of the evidence in terms of participants' roles[15]. The example is taken from the trial of Slingsby

15 Halliday's transitivity model concerns the transmission of ideas, i.e. how people encode in language their experience and conceptualisation of the world. Transitivity has therefore a very important role in the analysis of the ideational function, which is actualised in semantic processes expressed in the clause. Each process has three components: the process itself, expressed by the verb phrase, the participants involved in the process and the circum-

dated 1658 where the defendant was accused of plotting the return of the king with the help of a considerable army. Lieutenant Thomson – a witness for the State – provides a narrative where the prisoner is conceptualised as the main instigator of the conspiracy. Slingsby is in fact encoded as the "sayer" of all verbal processes related to the organisation of the conspiracy:

> [Lieutenant George Thomson sworn.][Being asked what Officer he was, he answered,] I am a Lieutenant to Major Waterhouse, I was desired to go and see <u>Sir H Slingsby</u> 16 April, <u>who told me</u> that he had great confidence in me, I said to him, why? <u>He told me</u> he thought I had good thoughts of the King; <u>his Son told me</u> he heard the King was to come in, and to bring in a considerable Army, but knew not when. Next day I went again to Sir H. Slingsby and asked him if he would walk on the Leads, which he did, and there I told him I had been pondering on the words <u>he last spoke to me</u>, <u>who then hugging me said</u>, I have a great deal of confidence in you, there is a design in agitation to bring in the King with a considerable Army, but he did not know how soon it would be, <u>but told me</u> I should have notice of it, and <u>said</u> that the King had promised pardon to all Officers but the Lord Protector and Lord Bradshaw.
>
> (Trial of Sir Henry Slingsby 1658, my emphasis)

By comparing this story version with the defendant's narrative reported below we can see how modifications in the transitivity network determine a completely different ideational representation of the events. The defendant attributes the role of do-er to a third person – Major Waterhouse – and presents himself as the target or recipient of the instigation process. In so doing he attempts to mitigate responsibility for the engendering of the material and verbal actions connected to the plotting.

---

stances associated with the process. Processes are classified as material, verbal, mental and relational. In the extracts reported for analysis the two predominant processes are the material and the verbal. Material processes represent actions and have two participants: the actor, i.e. the do-er of the process and the goal, which represents the person or entity affected by the process. Verbal processes are processes of communicating, telling, reporting. The participant roles are that of sayer: the individual who is speaking and the target: the addressee to whom the process is directed.

> [Sir H Sl.] I confess such like discourses; but Waterhouse spoke to me that I would speak to Thomson to try whether he would be assistant, but I told him I would not, least he should not accept it, and then turn him out of his place. Waterhouse pressed me to go to Thomson, and M Waterhouse invited us to his house to Dinner, after Dinner he spoke to Thomson to go with me on the Leads to shew me the Guns, we walked about, and came down again, then said Waterhouse to me, did not you speak to Thomson? I said not: you had a good oportunity, said he. At last Thomson came to me, and I had some discourse with him about it.
>
> (Trial of Sir H. Slingsby 1658, my emphasis)

The redefinition strategy can also occur in the form of conducive questions which are equivalent to assertions and serve to bias the jury's interpretation of the evidence in a way favourable to the defendant. The second example is taken from Coleman's trial. The judge intervenes to summarise the evidence and presents Mr Oates's testimony as sufficient proof of Coleman's conspiracy in the murder of the king:

> The Court asked Mr Oates how he should come now to charge you with all these matters of poisoning and killing the king, and yet he mentioned you so slightly at the Council Table; but it is said by Sir R. Southwell he did charge you with five thousand pounds (for poisoning the king) to be added to the ten thousand pounds, and he charged you expressly with it at the Council-Table.

The prisoner repeats his own story version and appeals to the Court's reasonableness in the attempt to challenge and redefine Mr Oates's testimony.

> (Mr Coleman): The charge was so slight against me by Mr Oates, that the Council were not of his Opinion…I humbly ask whether it was a reasonable thing to conceive that the Council should extenuate the punishment, if Mr Oates came with such an amazing account to the Council.

Coleman draws the Court's attention towards a crucial story element which is ambiguous enough to elicit a re-interpretation of the events and cast doubt on the trustworthiness of Oates at the Council and in Court. The point is that if Oates had had much evidence against him, his punishment would not have been extenuated. Unfortunately for Coleman, at the time the Court was engaged in a witch-hunting which explains their willingness to ascribe blame to whoever happened to be brought to their attention for his political and religious orientation. Furthermore, Lord Chief Justice William Scroggs has gone down in history as a person of coarse and violent manners in life as well as on the bench. Chronicles report that he treated the prisoners denounced by Oates with characteristic violence and sarcasm (see Roscoe and Roscoe 1825: 174; Hostettler 2006: 34).

3.3.3 Reconstruction strategy

In the first half of the century the reconstruction strategy was primarily articulated through denials of the prosecution evidence. There was no witness examination but only statements with an informative purpose supported by no better evidence than the defendant's word. Below I report an extract from Macguire's trial (1644). The defendant was accused of seising Dublin Castle in the attempt to raise a Catholic rebellion in Ireland against Protestant England. Witnesses for the prosecution testify his presence in Dublin, his breaking into the Castle as well as the murder of many Protestants. When Macguire was captured by the authorities he admitted all the material facts that he then retracted in the trial

> Then the Lord Macguire proceeded to make his defence, wherein he first of all denied his Examination (although testified as before by so many credible witnesses) and said that he knew no such Examination. That at the time of his apprehension at Dublin, he came about his own particular occasions, as his Estate was in danger if he did not follow it: That because he was found about the City, he was therefore apprehended; That his lodging was not within the City, but he lodged without the City; that he did lodge at Mr. Nevils House formerly, but not at this time: That for some of the places mentioned, where he should be about the Conspiracy, he had not been there a year before, he was certain of it. For the number of Protestants that were mentioned to be slain, he said he did not think there were so many Protes-

> tants in the whole Kingdome. That he was continually either at his owne House, or at Dublin, and knew nothing of the Plot but by hear-say.
> (Judge) You confesse in your Examination, when the day was for the rising, that you were in the conspiracy, and appointed for the taking of Dublin Castle; and that you were taken when you came about it. Also you rode about it, and provided Armes.
> (Macguire) I was in the house in the Cock-loft where I was taken, I did not know where any Army was!
> (S.W.) My Lord Macguire does forget himself what he acknowledges under his own hand.
> [Then the Examination being shewed him he said;] Theres my name but not my hand.

The prisoner's defence is reported in third person by the scribe who intervenes with negative comments on Macguire's credibility. The defendant's reconstruction technique sounds totally unconvincing to the jury, all the more so given his open denial of the signed confession. His case is indicative of the desperate situation of many defendants, who were often deprived of the right to call their own witnesses, who lacked counsel and who were brought to the bar with no better preparation than what their instinct dictated.

The second example is taken from the trial of John Giles and takes place in the second half of the century (1680). Giles was accused of the murder of a member of the House of Commons. This time, the defendant's reconstruction of a different story version is entrusted to a set of conducive questions with a challenging function.

Mr Bridge is the witness for the prosecution and is called to the bar to discredit Giles as supporter and defender of the Papists' plot against the king.

> [Mr. Bridges] I had some Discourse with him concerning the Papists, he said that it was the best Religion, and that those that were not of that Religion should be Damn'd: I alledged against him, and told him the contrary: I thought not. Can it be such a Religion said I, that will Act such things against the King and the Government? Says he, If any says there is such a Plot against the King or the Government, he is a Rogue, and a Thief.
> [...]

> [Giles] My Lord, I beseech you I may speak to this man, Do you hear, Sir, Were not these the words that I said when you charged me to be a Papist, That I knew of no Popish Plot, and they that said I was a Papist, or knew any of the Plot, were Rogues or Whores, or worse.
> [Bridges] You said thus, That the Papists were the best Religion, and that those that were not of that Religion were Damn'd.
> [Giles] Have not you been a Papist Sir?
> [Bridges] I am not now.
> [Giles] Will you say that I am a Papist?
> [Bridges] I say you defended it so much I thought you were. Said I, I wonder it being such a good Religion, that they would offer to Act such a thing against the King and Government. Said he, He that says this Plot is Acted by the Papists, is a Rogue and a Thief. (Trial of John Giles)

Instead of using a denial, Giles attempts to reconstruct a different version of the events by attaching his reported speech to the polar negative interrogative with a seeking confirmation function: "were not these the words that I said… that I knew of no Popish plot and they that said I was a Papist, or knew any of the Plot, were Rogues or Whores, or worse". The controlling force of the conducive question however is not enough to gain the desired confirmation as the witness resists intimidation and restates his previous testimony. At this point the prisoner changes tactic and tries to discredit the witness for his Catholic past. The polar negative interrogative "Have not you been a Papist, sir?" functions as an indirect accusation which reveals the prisoner's intention to damage the witness's reputation in front of the jury. The defendant's linguistic behaviour recalls the professionals' leading questions used with the intent to cause face-damage while still preserving the illusion to be acting in line with their primary aim to seek and establish the facts of the case. Unlike professionals, however, defendants cannot disguise their face threatening intentions under the pretence that they are seeking information, since they already have a direct knowledge of the events. In this sense the challenging character of their utterances is harder to downplay or neutralise. Giles's question, for example, uncovers a primary intention to harm the witness by reciprocating his FTA. Indeed, at the time prejudices against Papists were so diffused that any accusation of Catholic sympathies was sufficient to incriminate an individual or at least to attack his/her credibility for ever (Cecconi 2010). Even so the lack of boosters of impoliteness in the utterance and the defendant's appropriate framing of the accusation in the form of a question prevent us from classifying his behaviour as an instance of prototypical impoliteness. Again, I would claim that his offensive behaviour originates as a by-product of the interaction, where the defendant's primary aim is to prove his innocence and escape death.

The escalation of the witness's intimidation continues in the next yes/no question: "Will you say that I am a Papist". The defendant uses a *will-you*+verb question which is commonly adopted by prosecution lawyers in the attempt to put the witness on the spot. Indeed the polar question solicits a verbal response from the addressee which may be either favourable to the defendant's counter-narrative or self-incriminatory in the case that the witness cannot prove the truth value of his statement. Given that witnesses under an oath risked an incrimination for perjury if they were found to have lied, the implied face threatening force of the *will-you* question was deeply felt. The witness manages to evade the threat inherent in a yes/no reply by means of an elaborate answer where he ultimately confirms his version of events "I say you defended it so much I thought you were". The verbal duelling between examiner and examinee does not have a positive outcome for the defendant, despite his emulation of professionals' questioning strategies. This seems to be due to the fact that in the 17th-century courtroom the coercive questions used to challenge, redefine or reconstruct evidence are really effective only in those cases where a legally sanctioned right to ask them combines with a recognised position of authority in the courtroom, which is exactly what defendants lack (see Archer 2008).

3.4 Conclusion

In this chapter I have investigated some of the major defence strategies adopted by prisoners. Although in the first half of the century defendants were still reluctant to appeal to their questioning rights to shape their defence, from the 1650s onwards we register an increase in the number of questions in witness examination. Throughout the century questions and declaratives coexist as a means of challenging, redefining and reconstructing the prosecution evidence. The analysis has revealed that defendants take inspiration from the professionals' examining practices and borrow some of their major questioning techniques to cast doubts on the witness's testimony or to exercise forms of intimidation. In this regard we have considered the use of

- how (possible) questions
- polar negative questions (did you not…?/ask him whether he did not…)
- yes/no questions (e.g. will you say…?)

Although on several occasions professionals and defendants appear to share the same discourse behaviour, there is a considerable difference in the outcome of their turns, no matter how similar they may be from a syntactic and semantic point of view. Defendants, in fact, have the power to ask questions but lack the institutionally recognised position of authority which allows them to coerce witnesses and shape their testimony. As a result the illocutionary force of their questions is rarely accompanied by the desired perlocutionary effect, despite their emulation of the professionals' expertise.

Another interesting point concerns the facework dynamics characterising the defendants' questioning of hostile witnesses. These in fact differ from the professionals' discourse behaviour. When prosecutors, for example, adopt how-questions or polar questions which may be perceived as challenging, their role enables them to justify their conduct as consistent with their truth-seeking purposes. Their utterances are constructed so as to strategically oscillate between the professional's aim to elicit information and a more malicious intent to aggravate the witness's face. When defendants, on the other hand, utilise the same challenging questions, their attitude is clearly face aggravating since their primary aim is to defend their version of the story by attacking that of the interlocutor in the attempt to prove their innocence. This task, however, is institutionally recognised and their face threats are generally closer to the incidental category, overlapping with the politic zone.

In some circumstances defendants borrow too much from the professionals' discourse practice and abuse their questioning rights. One case in point is their attempt to intimidate witnesses by reminding them that they are under oath. Consider the following example:

> [Mr Turner (defendant)]: I would ask all this back again, you are upon your Oath, Mr Alderman

This is a very common face aggravating practice among judges and prosecutors but it falls outside the defendant's institutional position and power, hence the judge's reproach:

> [Lord Justice Hide]: You need not tell him that he is sworn, the Court and Jury understand it so.
>
> (Trial of Colonel Iams Turner 1663)

Given their lack of competence and assistance, 17th-century defendants rely on the surface imitation of the professionals' model, apparently unaware that the effectiveness of examining strategies is measured against the institutional authority of the speaker and its public acceptance by all courtroom participants. In this regard it is significant that in the 16 trials considered for analysis there are only two cases of acquittal (the trial of Lilburne, 1649, and the trial of Lord Mohun 1692).

Part two

The representation of defendants in treason cases

Chapter 4

Representation of defendants as a form of political propaganda

4.1 Object and aims of the analysis

In this chapter the focus of analysis shifts from the interactional role of defendants to their representation at the author-readership discourse level. In this regard, I examine three famous court cases for high treason taken from the *ST*: the trial of Thomas Wentworth, earl of Strafford (1641), the trial of the Duke of Hamilton (1649) and the trial of William Laud, Archbishop of Canterbury (1644). For the purposes of the analysis, I have ordered the three trials according to their telling mode rather than chronologically. Even so the dates testify to their importance in the history of Stuart England, covering the major phases of the Civil War, from its preparation to its outcome. The three political prisoners were all tried for their alignment with Charles I's Personal Rule and the accounts of their trials are all Royalist in stance though they vary in terms of their reporting mode. In fact, while the trials of Strafford and Hamilton have been written by an external recorder who presents himself as an eye-witness to the proceedings, the trial of Laud has been recorded by himself *a posteriori*. The analysis focuses on the representation of the defendant, be it in the form of other-presentation (trial of Strafford and Hamilton) or self-presentation (trial of William Laud). This requires an in-depth investigation of the discourse strategies adopted by the author in order to elicit and gather consensus with respect to the Royalist personage[16].

16 Since the compilers of the ST combine different authorial sources in their texts, the notion of authorship becomes problematic. In the analysis I shall

In the context of the Civil War and at a time when the power of the press was decisive in biasing the public opinion, a convincing ideological framing of the defendant could prove as precious as a victory on the battlefield. While Parliamentarians took full advantage of their control of the judicial system and exploited the courtroom as an arena for sanctioning their opponents' defeat, Royalists counterattacked by re-enacting the proceedings in print for a wider audience outside the courtroom. Indeed, in line with the rapid expansion and circulation of printed accounts, readers assumed an increasingly authoritative role in the socio-political circles of Stuart England. They were usually referred to as "judges" or "jury", two epithets which acquire an added significance in a period when structures of power were subject to questioning and "when judicial procedures were exposed to public scrutiny"(Sauer 2005: 21). By staging their trials by print Royalists involved public opinion in the exercise of judgement and inflicted their strongest attack on the legitimacy of the Parliamentary procedure. As Sauer claims "the interaction of literature [pamphleteering], writers and the court of public opinion produced a culture of debate and political dissent and a war of words that fuelled the civil war." (2005: 36).

The three trial texts differ from the court proceedings previously examined in three main respects: 1) they are mostly reported in the indirect mode (especially the trial of Strafford and Hamilton) 2) they share features of pamphlet literature 3) they contain several markers of evaluation. The study of evaluation is extremely important in critical discourse analysis. Thompson and Hunston (2001: 6) identify three main functions of evaluation which make it an object of interest to the linguist:

- to express the speaker's or writer's opinion, and in doing so to reflect the value system of that person and their community

---

use the word author to refer to the reporting voice in the text, though I am aware that the trial text contains more than one authorial source.

- to construct and maintain relations between speaker or writer and hearer or reader
- to organise discourse.

Evaluation is actualised in discourse through a set of lexico-grammatical markers which have attracted the attention of many linguists over the years. Biber and Finegan define stance markers as "the lexical and grammatical expression of attitudes, feelings, judgements or commitment concerning the propositional content of a message" (1989: 93). Three types of stance have been identified in discourse construction:

> 1) epistemic stance, commenting on the certainty, reliability or limitation of a proposition, including comments on the source of the information;
> 2) attitudinal stance: conveying the speaker's attitudes, feelings or value judgements;
> 3) style stance: referring to the manner in which the information has been presented.
>
> (Conrad and Biber 2001: 57)

These markers of stance will be systematically scrutinised in my analysis as they shape the author's representation of the defendant and his opponents in the trial. Within the category of style stance and attitudinal stance I shall also examine reported speech dynamics, especially instances of heteroglossia (i.e. the parodic rendering of the adversaries' speech) and forms of slipping from one mode of speech presentation to another implying emotional distance or closeness (see Mc Hale 1978; Leech and Short 1981; Bakhtin 1981). Reported speech has an enormous significance for pragmatics, since its formal varieties cannot be fully understood without reference to contextual factors. Collins has recently discussed the context-sensitivity of speech representation in a historical perspective, extending its attestedness to earlier stages of the language. In particular, he has shown how:

> the choice of strategy is oriented to the intended interpreter in the reporting situation. Speakers and writers choose the form they perceive as potentially most effective for what they want to communicate and, concomitantly, for

> how they intend to organize their texts. Their perceptions are socially grounded – based on the experiential knowledge of how a specific kind of audience goes about interpreting the discourse in particular contextualizations and in particular genres.
>
> (Collins 2001: xiv)

Special attention will also be given to cases in which the author performs structural operations in the report, such as amplification or condensation, so as to enhance the force of the defence or downplay that of the accusation. Before proceeding to the stylistic investigation of the reporter's voice, I shall provide a brief overview of each of the political prisoner and I shall outline the history of their trial and the literature available on it.

4.2 The trial of Thomas Wentworth, earl of Strafford (1641)

The entire life of Thomas Wentworth testifies to the tension existing between parliamentarian forces and Royal service in the years preceding the Civil War. Since his early career as a member of Parliament, he soon learnt the importance of finding mediation between the popular leaders and the Crown. To this purpose, he strongly supported the Petition of Rights, which attempted to limit the power of the king. Nonetheless when Charles – albeit reluctantly – accepted it, he acknowledged the Royal authority as fundamental to the maintenance of order and government. While on the one hand, this diplomatic manoeuvre gave rise to resentment among Parliamentarians, on the other it won him the title of Baronet Wentworth. In 1628 he became Viscount Wentworth and was made president of the Council of the North where he proclaimed his intention to do his best to keep the Crown and the liberties of its people united. Unfortunately his tactics were the same as those he would later adopt in Ireland and for which he would be charged with tyranny and abuse of power against the kingdom. In the meantime the hostilities between king and Parliament led to the final breach. Wentworth could no longer maintain his position of mediator between the parties and was forced to take a definite position. He opted for the king's side and became one of the strongest supporters of Charles I's Personal Rule, using all his energy and domineering temperament to repress any act of revolt againt the old constitution. During the absolute monarchy, along with William Laud, he acted as a faithful advisor of the king.

As Lord Deputy of Ireland, Wentworth ruled the country with a certain harshness and brutality. Convinced of the inferior character of the Irish, he adopted autocratic and extreme means to convert them to English customs in matters of religion, law and social habits. His firm-handed measures, however, enhanced the strength of the Royal administration and contributed to the realisation of his ambitious design to turn a Popish land into a prosperous Protestant English colony. Recalled to England in 1639, he was appointed earl of Strafford and became the king's chief advisor in the delicate matters of bankruptcy and the war against the Scottish Covenanters. Being in favour of military action against the rebels, Wentworth did his best to secure subsidies both in England and in Ireland. Once appointed Lord Lieutenant of Ireland, he returned there and raised a Catholic Irish army to be used against the Presbyterians in the coming war. This met with opposition from the Commons who were against a possible invasion of Scotland and refused to grant the king funds. Given the urgency of the situation, Strafford saw no other choice but to vote for the dissolution of Parliament. This was taken as an act of treason against the institution and when it was again summoned in 1640, its main objective became the elimination of Strafford. Charles gave him his full support promising that he "should not suffer in his person, honour and fortune" but things took an unexpected course. The original impeachment against Wentworth for high misdemeanours issued by the Commons soon turned into a charge of high treason for attempting to subvert the fundamental laws of the kingdom. An utterance claimed to be spoken by him was demagogically exploited to substantiate the accusation: "You have an army in Ireland you may employ here to reduce this Kingdom". Strafford was sent to the Tower and on 31 January 1641 the accusations were presented in detail (see Wedgwood 1961; Merritt 1996).

4.2.1 Charges against Strafford

Strafford's impeachment for high treason was based on nine general articles. Having served both as President of the Council of the North and later as Lord Deputy of Ireland, his prosecutors were able to accumulate a great number of accusations concerning crucial issues such as justice administration, fiscal policy and the Scottish war. The most grievous charge was that the earl had taken advantage of his offices both in England and in Ireland in order to subvert the fundamental law of the land and establish an arbitrary and tyrannical government above the law. This was the essence of the first, and arguably most significant, article:

> ...Thomas earl of Strafford had traiterously endeavoured to subvert the fundamental Laws and Government of the Realms of England and Ireland, and instead thereof to introduce an arbitrary and tyrannical Government, against Law, which he hath declared by traiterous Words, Counsels and Actions, and by giving his Majesty Adivice by Force of Arms, to compel his Loyal Subjects to subvert thereunto.

The second article blamed the earl for having assumed "Regal power over the Lives, Liberties, Persons, Lands and Goods of his Majesty's Subjects, in *England* and *Ireland*" as a result of the people's "Subversion and Undoing". The third article accused him of having robbed the king of his revenues to use them for his personal purposes while he was Lord Deputy of Ireland in the 1630s. The fourth article charged him of connivance with the Papists to carry on his "malicious and tyrannical Designs". The fifth article impeached him for having instilled "Enmity and Hostility between his Majesty's Subjects of *England* and those of *Scotland*". The sixth held Strafford responsible for the defeat of the English army against the Scots with the final loss of Newcastle and the resulting, dangerous hostility in the relations between England and Scotland. The seventh article was related to Strafford's responsibility in the dissolution of the Short Parliament and purported that the earl had "laboured to subvert the Right of Parliaments... and by false and malicious Slanders to incense his Majesty against the Parliament" so as to create a damaging division between them. The last two articles stated that all the offences reported occurred during the period in which Strafford was Lord Deputy of Ireland, Lieutenant General of the Royal Army and Lord President of the North and that the prosecution reserved the right to add further articles and proof against Strafford during the trial.

The seven general charges were subsequently articulated into 28 specific articles, each of them was discussed, testified and answered to in the courtroom. The trial started on 22nd March and lasted till mid-April, the earl having personally replied for 15 days. On 13th April Strafford resumed his defence speaking with great eloquence as reported in the chronicles. He was able to take advantage of the weak points of the accusation and the Lords appeared to be influenced in his favour. In the meantime, the Commons realised that Strafford would never be condemned for high treason in the name of the Law and therefore elaborated and passed a bill of attainder according to which Strafford could be executed regardless of the crime but simply because it was the will of the Parliament that he should die. They also insisted that the trial should be suspended and that Strafford's counsels should not be heard but the Lords resisted the requests. The counsels were therefore heard though the Commons did not go to hear them, "saying it was beneath their dignity to dispute with lawyers" (see Guizot 1856).

On 8th May the bill of attainder was sent to the Lords who – for fear of the insurrections of the mob and of continuous attempts to get the earl out of prison – voted Strafford guilty of high treason upon the 15th article, for levying money in Ireland by force of arms, and upon the 19th article for imposing an oath upon the subjects in Ireland that they should not protest against any of the king's commands. The king was required to sign the bill. On account of Strafford's loyal service, Charles was reluctant to sign his death warrant though a refusal to comply with the Parliament's will would put the monarchy in great danger. It was Strafford himself who released the king from his conscience by declaring his willingness to reconcile the king with his subjects. Charles gave his assent to the execution on 10th May and two days later Strafford was beheaded. The state trial ends with the reporting of the defendant's speech upon the scaffold followed by an additional paragraph devoted to the king's revocation of the bill of attainder and the name list of all the Straffordians posted on 3rd May 1641:

> for all which Causes, be it declared and enacted by the King's most Excellent Majesty, by and with the Advice and Consent of the Lord's Spiritual and Temporal, and Commons in this present Parliament assembled, That the Act entitled *An Act for the Attainder of* Thomas *Earl of Strafford of High Treason,* and all and every Clause and Article, and Thing therein contained, being obtained as aforesaid, is now hereby repealed, revoked and reserved.
>
> (ST vol. I, 764)

4.2.2 Literature on Strafford's trial

Strafford's trial has been one of the most controversial treason cases in the history of England. Over the centuries important sources – both within and outside the kingdom – have described the proceedings as a manifestation of abuse of power over the political figure of the earl. The *Histories* of Thomas May, Edward Hyde earl of Clarendon and the French Francois Guizot have all depicted the defendant as a great man victim of the unjust manoeuvres of the king's enemies and of their political ambitions:

> But now a great actor is brought upon the stage, Thomas Wentworth earl of Strafford, lieutenant of Ireland, a man too great to be let escape; no sooner accused but surprised, and secured for a trial.
>
> (Thomas May, [1647] 1854: 86, book 1)

> Then they childishly concurred with the greatest enemies their nation and religion had, in the conspiracy against the life of the earl of Strafford, lord lieutenant of that Kingdom, by whose wisdom and government that Kingdom had reaped great advantages ... and in the end procured the miserable (and never to be enough lamented) ruin of that great person.
>
> (Clarendon: [1717] 1826: 9)

> Strafford applied all his efforts to dispossess them [charges] of this character, speaking with magnanimity of his imperfections, of his frailties, opposing a modest dignity to the violence of his adversaries, and proving, without contumely, the passion-born illegality of their proceedings.
>
> (Guizot: [1826] 1856: 101)

Toward the end of the 20th century the Royalist mystification around the person of the earl and his accusers began to be rethought in light of new historical evidence and of deeper research on 17th-century legal theory. This has led to a division between scholars of pro-Strafford orientation, who insist on the unprecedented nature of the proceedings and on the unsupported character of the accusation, and scholars of an anti-Strafford stance who consider the charges as falling within commonly accepted definitions of treason and therefore as legitimate. In his recent book *From Treason and the State: law, politics and ideology in the English Civil War* (2002), Orr takes stock of the situation comparing modern historians' opposite opinions about the substance of the accusation of treason. He starts off from the consideration that:

> Strafford stood his trial for his role in Charles I's personal rule of 1629–1640 and his impeachment represented more than simply a political vendetta of a leading faction within the Early Long Parliament. The proceedings against Strafford were an indictment of the methods, practices and policies of Charles I's government during the personal rule both in England and in Ireland.
>
> (2002: 61)

The most authoritative representative of the anti-Strafford argument is the famous historian Conrad Russell. In his 1965 article "The theory of Treason" he claims that the earl's impeachment for high treason lay on "accepted doctrines of law and political theory" and in particular on that tradition of treason law – presumably of Roman origin – according to which the making of a division between the king and the people constituted an act of treason (1965: 30–31).

A similar position was held by J.H. Timmis who asserted that the 15th and 23rd articles against Strafford – the former accusing him of devising and contriving, by Force of Arms, to subdue the subjects of Ireland to his tyrannical power and the latter imputing him of having advised the king to employ the Irish army to quell England – fell within the statutory definition of treason as a levying of war against the king. The two articles later consituted the basis for the bill of attainder which, according to Timmis, was not maliciously issued to disguise the legal weakness of the accusation but simply because the proof of the 23rd article were not sufficient in matter of fact (1978: 680).

The pro-Strafford school, on the other hand, is represented by Wedgwood who, in her 1961 biography of the earl, considered the whole trial an abuse of power on the part of the Commons and W.R. Stacy who, following Wedgwood, insisted that the case against Strafford was based "on an unprecedented theory of accumulative treason". He further claimed that the bill of attainder was essentially issued for fear that the Lords would not vote against the prisoner, given the frailties of the impeachment both in matter of law and fact. In this regard Orr reports a relevant passage from Stacy's argument:

> Throughout the trial and attainder the key charge against Strafford was that through an accumulation of lesser offences, he had endevoured to subvert law and government and thereby divide the king and his people. This amounted to an unprecedented theory of accumulative treason, and the arguments of the prosecution advanced to support and supplement this charge were indeed novel and severely strained the law.
>
> (1985: 324)

By and large Orr laments the fact that both pro- and anti-Strafford arguments rely on statutory laws to establish and comment on the (il)legality of the proceedings, while disregarding the ideological component which is crucial in the interpretation of the law. In fact, he argues "the statutes themselves are subject to interpretation as expressions of ideological positions concerning the nature of political authority" (2002: 63). As a result he claims that the case needs to be examined and assessed in relation to the range of ideological positions concerning the relationship between sovereignty, state and public authority in the 17th century. By refining Russell's argument, Orr comes to the conclusion that the idea of treason against the kingdom – at the basis of Strafford's impeachment – was not an unprecedented innovation but rather fell within the accepted practices of English Treason Law: "Extra-statutory treasons did exist and were known in 1641. The Roman Law conception of treason [including the plotting of a division between ruler and ruled] was not only a common place but stood largely in conformity with accepted English Law" (2002: 64).

Though illuminated by interesting considerations on the historical and ideological context, Orr's argument does not resolve the controversy around the justice of the proceedings. Perplexities remain as to the motives which led to the elaboration of the bill of attainder and recent scholars still maintain that the manoeuvre was solicited by the threat that the earl could be released for lack of evidence (see Kilburn and Milton 2002, Sauer 2005). In Sauer's words:

> Threatened by the prospects that the Lords might vote against them, the Commons replaced the impeachment for treason with an act of attainder, which extinguished the legal rights of the accused. Thus the Court would declare Strafford's guilt despite the lack of legal Evidence.
>
> (2005: 45)

Another fertile branch of literature on Strafford's trial studies the unprecedented resonance that the court case had on contemporaries thanks to the wide circulation of newsletters, pamphlets, rumours, rhymes and parliamentary speeches before, during and after the trial. In their article "The public context of the trial and execution of Strafford" Kilburn and Milton interestingly notice that:

> The proceedings against Strafford in the Long Parliament were being very consciously played out before a wide and intrigued public audience – either assembled in the public galleries, or petitioning outside Westminster Hall, or conversing in the streets and squares of London, or sitting at home in the provinces, anxiously devouring news of events at the centre of the kingdom. (2002: 230)

A similar point is made by Cressy (2006) who, commenting on the impact of Strafford's trial soon after his execution, reports the words of a correspondent: "everything sells that comes in print under his name; therefore he is everyday apparelled with an idle pamphlet or other bearing the affection of the true author, either in favour or against him" (1888: 282). Though an under-researched area, the continuous discovery of an impressive number of printed texts and manuscripts has given rise to important studies on the impact of the printed word in the public assessment of the Strafford episode. Literary critics, such as M. Heinemann (1982) and M. Butler (1987) have analysed pamphlet-plays of a pro-parlamentarian stance, R. Wilcher (2001) has examined different genres from newsbooks to poems of pro-royalist orientation, Kilburn and Milton (2002) have concentrated on parliamentary speeches printed before, during and after the court case and Elizabeth Sauer (2005) has examined the complex relationship between courtroom drama, printed culture and public opinion as the fuel/amplifier of dramatic tensions and ruptures culminating in the Civil War.

The early speeches anticipating the trial were all intended to attack Strafford as the incarnation of the Personal Rule and, as a result, as the cause of all the evil which had lately damaged the kingdom[17]. Their public circulation in printed format was fos-

17 Kilburn and Milton however point out that most of the speeches proposing Strafford's impeachment were published only several months later, when the trial was underway (2002).

tered with the intent to shape public opinion and create a hostile climate for the earl. During the trial, however, things did not proceed as smoothly as expected for the Commons. Strafford's defence was eloquent and convincing at a number of crucial points and the accusers had to replace the impeachment for treason with an extrajudicial act of attainder. The debate around the elaboration of the bill led to a proliferation of publications relating to Strafford. Along with the printing of official speeches there was an increase in the number of pamphlets advocating Strafford's execution. They were part of a larger political campaign "designed not only to manipulate and inflame popular political opinion, but also to counter any attempt to secure Strafford's release" (Kilburn and Milton 2002: 237). At the time the strong impact of the anti-Strafford literature was in all probability enhanced by the limited publications in favour of the prisoner's defence. This might be ascribed to the more or less overt political pressure to prevent a pro-Strafford argument in print. As Kilburn and Milton make clear the fact that "tacitly understood official censorship and fears of parliamentary censure and reprisal tied the hands of printers during the period of the prosecution... cannot be lightly dismissed" (2002: 239).

In the aftermath of the trial pamphlets began to be produced with several editions of Strafford's last dying speeches. The speech upon the scaffold was portrayed as a theatrical performance played in front of an audience. As Sharpe (1985) explains, the event was laden with important ideological values as it represented the public occasion in which the criminal acknowledged the justice of the judicial system and the State by confessing his crime and repenting. In this regard, Kilburn and Milton define Strafford's speech as a real *coup de théatre* for its unexpected deviation from the traditional pattern of last dying confession. Far from admitting his faults, in fact, the earl confirmed his innocence in matters of religion and politics with considerable eloquence and truthfulness which favourably impressed the multitude. This gave the anti-Strafford campaign an unexpected blow. His opponents attempted to obviate the damage by publishing their own printed version of his last speech in the period after the execution. Kilburn and Milton argue that since they could not substitute a speech which had been so widely heard by the public, they decided to frame a new one, which – they claimed – had been made by the earl *before* the scaffold. In this revised version Strafford behaved according to the 'script', recognizing the justice of the proceedings and accepting his execution.

After Strafford's death, the competing accounts of his last speeches, along with the emergence of the Royalist party, made their way into the public sphere, promoting opposing portrayals of the earl's public image. Kilburn and Milton interestingly conclude that:

> the continuing public trial of Strafford was one that both sides were happy to encourage, but was also one in which neither the Parliamentary managers nor Strafford's defenders had control over the final verdict. They were competing advocates in the court of a public opinion that seems, within limits, to have been capable of a certain autonomy of judgement.
>
> (2003: 251)

4.2.3 The Royalist account in the ST

The account given by the Royalist author in the ST is indebted to several sources including the *Histories* of Thomas May (1647) and Edward Hyde, earl of Clarendon (1704), John Rushworth's *The Tryall of Thomas Earl of Strafford* (1680), and Lord Somers' *Tracts* (1748). Unlike professional scribes hired to provide a verbatim transcription of the proceedings, especially in the second half of the century, the reporter of this trial forges his account adopting an indirect presentational format with evaluative comments, digressions and descriptions. This, obviously, does not mean that there are no concessions to mimetic renditions. In fact there are crucial points at which the author withdraws from the text in order to let other participants speak by themselves. This is particularly the case with the prisoner, whose defence is reported in the direct format so as to increase the emotional impact of his words for persuasive purposes. Even here, however, the author occasionally manifests his underlying presence through insertions, signalled by square brackets, where he summarises or comments on the defendant's speech.

(1) I shall proceed in repeating my Defences, as they are reducible to these two main Points of Treason: and for Treason against the Statute, (which is the only Treason in effect) nothing is alledged for that, but the fifteenth, two and twentieth, and twenty seventh Articles. [Here he brought the Sum of all his Replies made to these three Articles before, and almost in the same Words as before; only that Testimony of Sir Henry Vane's, because it seemed pressing, he stood up on it, and alledged five Reasons for the nullifying thereof] ...
The Articles contain Expressions and Actions; my Expressions either in Ireland or England, my Actions either before or after these late Stirs. [In this Order he went thro' the whole Charge, from the first Article to the last, in an excellent Method, and repeated all the Sums and Heads of what was spoken by him before...]

(I, 755)

The trial record collocates within a wide range of pro-Strafford literature of Royalist orientation following the earl's death. In this respect, it is part of the author's primary task to guide the readership in the desired interpretation of the prisoner's defence. Along with the consistent mimetic rendition of Strafford's speech both in the courtroom and on the scaffold, there are also instances of sudden slipping from indirect to direct speech and back to indirect speech again, where the author never completely withdraws from the text but rather signals his narrative presence through brackets with third person reference and the reporing tag:

(2) For Sir Henry Vane's and Northumberland's Testimony, about persuading of an Offensive War, he [the defendant, *my insertion*] said, he remembered it very well, and thought it as free for him to give his Opinion for an Offensive, as they for a Defensive War: Opinions, said he, if they be attended with Obstinacy or Pertinacy, may make an Heretick, but that they ever made a Traitor, he never heard it till now; not (under favour) should I be an Heretick either (<u>said he</u>) for as I was then, so am

> I now, most willing to acknowledge my Weakness, and correct my Errors, whereof no Man hath more, or is more sensible of them, than I myself; yet if that Opinion of mine had been followed, it might perhaps have spared us some Money (said he) and some Reputation too, of which we have been prodigal enough.
> For the last, about the Ships, it proves nothing: but he would willingly confess, that some ships were there detained, and that by himself, and his own direction...
>
> (vol. I, 748, my emphasis)

In the passage while the first bracket (under favour) is a parenthetic expression belonging to the defendant, the next two (he said) clearly belong to the recorder and are used in order to instruct the reader as to the sudden shift from third to first person. The narrative slipping from one mode of speech presentation to the other takes on significant, evaluative connotations in the text. Indeed foregrounding Strafford's words through direct speech (DS) as well as backgrounding his opponents' statements through narrative report of speech act (NRSA) or omission reveals the writer's aim to draw the readers' sympathies towards the former while enhancing emotional and ideological distance from the latter.

Unlike what happens in other trial proceedings where the defendant indulges in verbal duelling with the judges, Strafford's court case was designed according to a 'script' intended to guarantee the predictability of the outcome and the political approval of an audience, beyond the House of Parliament. There were however a number of occasions during the trial in which the courtroom drama deviated from the playtext prepared by the trial managers (Sauer 2005). Some of these deviations concerned the unexpected eloquence and incisiveness of the prisoner's defence and acted to the detriment of the 'directors' of the trial text. Other deviations were cunningly exploited by the opponents in order to construct a negative image of Strafford. One case in point is when Strafford [allegedly] *accidentally* refers to some hostile members of the House of Commons by means of the derogatory expression "malicious Enemies":

> (3) To this the Noble Lord replied, That he wished his Innocence might not be taken for Impudence; that he hoped shortly to clear himself of all those foul Aspersions which his malicious Enemies had cast upon him; and he was very confident that he should give the Honourable Houses full Satisfaction concerning his Life hitherto, and thought of nothing more hereafter than to retire himself from all publick Employments.
>
> Mr Pym gave at this a great Shout, and desired the House to take notice what an Injury he had done to the House of Commons, in calling them malicious Enemies.
>
> Whereupon the Lieutenant falling down upon his Knees, humbly besought them that they would not mistake him; and withal gave a large Panegyrick of their most just and moderate Proceedings, protesting that if he himself had been one of the House of Commons (as he had the Honour once to be) he would not have advised them to have done otherwise against his dearest Friend: but withal told them, that he might justly say he had his own Un-friends, which he hoped in time to make known.
>
> (vol. I, 737)

Mr Pym cunningly takes advantage of the offensive character of the expression "malicious Enemies" and constructs it as a case of intentional positive face attack against the entire category of the Commoners. By shifting the referent of the derogatory term from a small group of individuals to the House of Commons as a legal and political authority, the accuser manages to cause individual and public face damage to the defendant in a way that is difficult for him to repair. Conscious of the face aggravating resonance of Mr Pym's words, Strafford opts for pleading as an extreme counter-strategy to sort out the misunderstanding. Given the strong and tyrannical character of the earl, his act of supplication reveals the effect that his new, powerless position has on his relational behaviour with the authorities. Along with the copious use of politeness strategies (e.g. show approval: "a large Panegyrick of their most just and moderate Proceedings" and avoid disagreement: "if he himself had been one of the House of Commons… he would not have advised them to have done otherwise against his dearest Friend"), Strafford rephrases the original derogatory expression with the more diplomatic descriptor "Un-friends". His pleading entails an annihilation of his person in terms of positive and negative face wants which can only be explained in terms of the socio-political reversal of power relations between a Royalist and the Commoners on the eve of the Civil War.

4.2.4 Midway between court records and news pamphlet style

The account of Strafford's trial differs from ordinary court transcriptions in maintaining features of 17th-century news pamphlet literature. These can be seen in:

1) the use of interactive I-you pronominal forms, indicating strong authorial presence and the awareness of a reader.
2) authorial comments which function as a guide to the interpretation of facts
3) claims to empirical fidelity, as pamphleteers recognised the undercurrent of distrust around their works and vigorously resisted the imputation that they manufactured "fabulous lyes".
4) aspects of realistic reportage with precise details of time, place and participants.
5) the record of information with an emotional and attitudinal dimension
6) the report of different opinions, though those ideologically closer to the author are given primary attention and are foregrounded by end-focus position.

The last three features – i.e. factuality, emotional dimension and the report of different opinions – are classified as persuasive content features of the journalistic style (van Dijk: 1988: 85) and are all significantly present in the trial account for propaganda purposes. Below, I shall provide examples of each of the six features in order to show how the author exploits the audience's familiarity with the pamphlet style so as to forge public opinion.

4.2.4.1 *The use of interactive I-you pronouns*

The I-you pronouns establish a conversational style in discourse which is crucial to the ideological construction of consensus. As Fowler claims:

> The personal voice is a necessary but accepted illusion...The basic task for the writer is to word institutional statements in a style appropriate to interpersonal communication, because the reader is an individual and must be addressed as such. The task is not only stylistic but also ideological: institutional [political] concepts have to be translated into personal thoughts.
>
> (1991: 47)

On a number of occasions the author stresses his presence by means of the I pronouns in order to express his epistemic, emotional and style stance. Particularly interesting are those cases in which he speaks in the first person so as to a) legitimate the veridicity of his account, b) prove his willingness to impartiality and c) beg the reader's pardon for any bias that his emotional involvement in the events may cause. In the following passage the author stresses his position as direct eyewitness to the events, which is one of the basic conventional conditions of truth (see van Dijk 1988: 86).

> (4) I have been a daily Hearer of these Proceedings against this great Personage now upon the Stage, therefore do presume I can give a reasonable account thereof.
>
> (I, 738)

After Strafford's defence, the author reassures the reader about the veridicity of the words reported through the following metadiscoursive comment:

> (5) You have his very Words as near as I can remember, only with so much loss and detriment as hath perished by transcribing the Copy from his own Mouth. But you desire Impartiality, and indeed you have it, and with some Grains too of Allowance; for I was so afraid of my own Affection to the Gentleman, that I rather bowed to the other Extremity, and therefore have set down his Defences rather to his Disadvantage by

> my rude Pen, than in the native Colour, to his eternal Glory, and the confusion of his Enemies.
>
> (I, 757)

The entire passage follows a rhetorical pattern whereby the author – by mentioning his concessions to the opposite party so as to counterbalance his sympathies for the earl – does the very opposite, that is he highlights and confirms his pro-Strafford orientation.

4.2.4.2 Authorial comments

On crucial occasions the author strategically substitutes the verbatim report of the opponents' speech (DS) with his own ideologically-laden account of the speech-event (NRSA). Diegetic modality facilitates the inclusion of evaluative lexico-grammar patterns through which the author intends to negatively bias the reader's impression-formation of the accusers. By means of illustration, after Strafford's defence, the accusation repeats all the charges against him and concludes with the Aggravation of the Offence outlined by Mr Pym. Since Pym's words occur in end-focus position and could exert a strong persuasive power over the audience, the author takes care to omit them, leaving room for his authorial comments on the clumsy manner of Pym's speech-delivery.

> (6) The Aggravation of the Offence, he said, he had left to Mr Pym who here spake that Speech which is now in print. It was a Sport to see how Mr Pym in his Speech was fearfully out, and constrained to pull out his papers, and read with a great deal of Confusion and Disorder, before he could recollect himself; which failing of his Memory was no small Advantage to the Lieutenant: because, by this means, the House perceived it was premeditated Flash, not grounded upon the Lieutenant's last Answer, but resolved on before, whatsoever he should say for his own Justification. But the Lieutenant was not suffered to reply a Word, either to Glym or Pym because the last Word must be theirs. And so with Tuesday ended the Matter of Fact.
>
> (vol. I, 757)

The omission of Pym's speech is cunningly justified by the fact that it is now in print and those who are interested can buy a copy and read it. The aim of the Royalist author, on the other hand, is to cast a more indiscreet and critical glance on the *how* of the speech, which reveals the manufactured nature of the proceeding. It is interesting to see how the author guides the reader's interpretation of events not only through his evaluative comments on Pym's behaviour in Court ("it was a Sport to see how Mr Pym in his Speech was fearfully out") but also venturing into an account of the MPs' perceptions ("the House perceived it was premeditated Flash…"). This inner viewpoint is quite unrealistic given the author's position of external observer and can only be explained as a narrative strategy exploited to forge public opinion by fostering the readers' identification with the House's stance. In this regard, even the use of the lexico-grammatical expression "it was a Sport to see" deserves some consideration. The pattern *it+link verb+noun group+infinitive clause* is used as a linguistic means to express evaluation (Hunston and Sinclair 2001). Its importance in persuasive discourse relies on the fact that it disguises the evaluative stance of the author and verbalises it in an impersonal/ objective format which elicits common agreement on Pym's ridiculous attitude: "it was (for everybody) a Sport to see". By means of the evaluative expression, the author assumes solidarity with his readership and makes sure that they interpret the evidence in the desired way.

4.2.4.3 Claims to empirical fidelity

Claims to authorial reliability have already appeared when discussing the interactive character of the trial account and in fact the two features generally combine. The author usually enters the discourse as "I" when he needs to defend the authenticity of his evidence. It was very common for the propagandist to camouflage his political stance by insisting on the reliability of the facts reported. Here are some examples where the author discredits the opponents' reports by appealing to his eye-witness testimony:

(7) ...therefore let Fame pretend what it please about the Malice and Discontent of the Multitude, *that if he [Strafford] pass the Stroke of Justice, they will tear him in Pieces;* yet I see there is more in Rumour than in Sight and Appearance.

(I, 736)

(8) There was a Report that the Parliament of *Ireland* had sent a Protestation against the Act made last Year, for the King's Supply in his Expedition against the *Scots*; as a thing which was violently in part, and in part surreptitiously obtained from them; but I have learned this to be an Untruth.

(I, 737)

4.2.4.4 Realistic reportage

As happens in news pamphlets and newsbooks, the Royalist author emphasises the factual nature of events in order to foster people's acceptance of the account as true and, consequently, gather consensus around his pro-Strafford argumentation. In the trial text factuality is articulated not only through the usual reference to date and time of the court sessions and through an allegedly complete rendering of the words spoken but also in the form of direct and detailed description of the setting and participants. This can be seen especially at the beginning, when the recorder describes the courtroom with his camera eye and takes care to signal all the movements of the Royal family.

(9) The Place appointed for the Trial was the great Hall in *Westminster* where there was a Throne erected for the King, on each Side there of a Cabinet enclosed with Boards, and before with a Terras. Before that, were the Seats for the Lords of the Upper House, and Sacks of Wool for the Judges; before them ten stages of Seats, extending further than the midst of the Hall, for the Gentlemen of the House of Commons: at the End of all was a Desk closed about and set apart for the Lord-Lieutenant and his Counsel.
[...] The King, Queen and Prince came to the House about nine of the Clock, but kept themselves private within their Closets, only the Prince came out once or twice to the Cloth of the State; so that the King saw and heard all that passed, but was seen of none.

> [...] The Queen went from the House about eleven of the Clock, the King and Prince staid still the Meeting was dissolved, which was after Two.
>
> (vol. I, 736)

Attention is also given to the report of the numbers of people involved in the transportation of the defendant from the Tower to Westminster. The rhetoric of news and persuasive discourse, in fact, suggests truthfulness by the implied exactness of figures though, as van Dijk makes clear, "it is not so much the precision of the numbers that is relevant but rather the fact that numbers are given at all" (1988: 88):

> (10) *March 22. Monday* Morning about seven of the Clock he came from the *Tower*, accompanied with six Barges, wherein were one hundred Soldiers of the *Tower*, all with Partizans, for his Guard, and fifty Pair of Oars. At his landing at *Westminster* there he was attended with two hundred of the Trained-Bands; and went in, guarded by them, into the Hall.
>
> (I, 736)

Once the reporter has proved his closeness to the events (and has presumably gained the reader's trust), he ventures into a description of the multitude which discredits the general opinion that people were against Strafford. It is precisely at this point that the rhetoric of factuality is put to the service of politics and propaganda:

> (11) The Croud of People was neither great nor troublesome; all of them saluted him, and he them, with great Humility and Courtesy, both at his Entrance and at his Return; therefore let Fame pretend what it please about the Malice and Discontent of the Multitude ...yet I see there is more in Rumour than in Sight and Appearance.
>
> (I, 736)

By denying the common assumption that a tumultuous multitude was against Strafford, the account assumes strong ideological connotations. These are further enhanced by the schematic opposition between the impersonal and abstract voice of "*Fame*" (spread by the Parlamentarians) which "pretends" and the personal voice of the author who observes.

4.2.4.5 The emotional dimension

In order to highlight the emotive impact of the earl's personality on the readership, the author indulges in descriptive and evaluative accounts of his behaviour and attitude during the trial. Most of the evaluative lexical markers suggest the image of a man whose strength and courage reside on the confidence in his innocence. Emphasis is also given to his moderation as opposed to the excess and fervour of the opponents. This topos will also be found in Hamilton's and Laud's trial.

(12) The Lieutenant with no less Moderation and Wisdom than the other with Heat and Passion, spake to his own Defence; and that with such a Measure of Eloquence and Livelyhood, that his very Enemies were affected with it, and do marvellously report of it.

(I, 736)

(13) He hath all this time carried himself courageously, to the Admiration (and withal so moderately that it is to the great Satisfaction) of his very Enemies; so that he seems neither dejected with Fear, nor to affect Boldness with Confidence, but to carry himself with that Constancy and Resolution, which his Innocency and brave Parts do promise.

(I, 737)

Once again, it is hard to establish the reliability of the passage. In fact, foregrounding the opponents' approval of the defendant seems to be a *leitmotiv* of Royalist trial accounts, as is also documented in the Duke of Hamilton's trial:

(14) But the Duke's Carriage and Discourse that day gained much on all Spectators, being so serene and calm, that his very Enemies did applaud it.

(II, 2)

The positive encoding of the interpersonal relationship between the defendant and his opponents serves the first-order function of linguistically construing a corresponding empathy between Strafford and the readers, no matter what their political orientation or spatio-temporal positioning.

4.2.4.6 *The report of different opinions*

The truthfulness of the events is also enhanced when opinions of different orientations are given, though those which are shared by the author receive particular prominence through reference to their larger consensus and through end-focus positioning.

> (15) The Expectations are exceeding various and different about the Event of this great Action: some think it will be impossible to escape the many and great Accusations laid to his Charge; others, and that the greater Number too, are of Opinion that he will be in no Hazard of his life, and that it will not be possible to bring him into the Compass of Treason;
>
> (I, 737)

The two opposing opinions are followed by a conclusive comment of the reporter who anticipates the dramatic end of the proceedings: "His adverse Party is so great and so far interested both in Point of Safety and Honour against him, that *flectere si nequeunt Superos &c.* nothing will be left unessay'd, that may accellerate his ruin".

The presence of the Royal family was another controversial point in the trial and was much discussed among the multitude. The reporter takes care to record the various opinions and gossip circulating at the time, reserving the end-focus position for his privileged view.

> (16) Some give Reason of this, from the received Practice of *England* in such Cases: Others say, that the Lords did intreat the Keing either to be absent, or to be there privately, less Pretensions might be made hereafter, that his being there was either to threaten, or some otherwise to interrupt the Course of Justice: A third sort, That the King was not willing to be accessary to the Process till it came to his part, but rather chose to be present, that he might note and understand what Violence, Rigour, or Injustice happened.
>
> (I, 736)

The reference to the violence and unjustice that the king should control is intended to denounce the Parliamentarians' premeditated manoeuvres to incriminate the defendant. In this sense, its end-focus encoding can be read as an anticipatory cue to the negative outcome of the trial.

4.2.5 Stance markers

Van Dijk distinguishes 3 types of stance: attitudinal, epistemic and style stance which are conveyed through features of lexis and grammar. Stance has already emerged in the previous extracts, where the author provides explicit metadiscoursive comments on the authenticity of the account (epistemic and style stance) or evaluates the situation and the defendant's behaviour (attitudinal stance). My aim in this section is to pinpoint the most common stance markers to be found in the text and see how they combine to form lexico-grammar patterns which enhance the author's viewpoint.

4.2.5.1 Attitudinal stance markers

Attitudinal stance markers are the most frequently used in the text. Evaluation is primarily carried out by means of descriptors and speech-style and manner adverbs/adverbials, as we can see in the following examples:

- The Lieutenant with no less Moderation and Wisdom than the other with Heat and Passion, spake to his own Defence; and that with such a Measure of Eloquence and Livelyhood, that his very Enemies were affected by it
- He modestly recounted his Service
- He mentioned himself as the most weak and meanest Instrument with a wonderful Prudence
- He hath all this time carried himself corageously to the Admiration (and withal so moderately that it is to the great Satisfaction) of his very Enemies.

- To this the Noble Lord replied
- The Lieutenant, falling down upon his Knees, humbly, besought them that they would not mistake him
- To this he replied without the least Semblance of Passion
- At this the Lieutenant rose, and humbly intreated the Lords no Evidence should be received against him upon an article of such Importance
- The Lieutenant modestly answered
- He went thro' the whole Charge from the first Article to the last, in an excellent Method
- Master Glyn bitterly replied
- It was bitterly replied by Master Glyn

As far as descriptors are concerned, it is worth noticing that Strafford is never referred to as "the defendant" or "the prisoner" but rather through noun phrases which foreground his professional and social status: "the Lieutenant", "the noble Lord", "brave Gentleman". This testifies to the author's intention to eclipse the man's role as defendant in the trial in order to highlight his dignity and respectability as Stateman. The same strategy will be used in the duke of Hamilton's trial where the man will be consistently referred to as "the Duke". Most of the nouns in the adverbials are premodified either by intensifiers (so, such), superlative expression (the least) and adjectives (wonderful, excellent) which enhance their evaluative meaning. The adverbs and prepositional phrases referring to Strafford all have positive connotations. The only two occurrences of a negative speech-style adverb ("bitterly") are attributed to Mr Glyn, Strafford's leading accuser. The adverbial constructions contain several nouns which are markers of the author's stance and carriers of 17th-century socio-pragmatic values. They can be grouped into two opposite semantic fields: moderation vs passion. While the former is praised as a virtue and is referred to the earl, the latter equates with impoliteness and rudeness, and is attributed to his accusers.

> The Lieutenant: Moderation, Wisdom, Measure of Eloquence, Livelyhood, Constancy, Resolution, Life and Grace
> Accusers: Heat and Passion

Evaluative adjectives premodifying nouns are less common. Here are some examples:

> Lieutenant: brave Parts, Noble Lord, excellent Method, Inimitable Life and Grace, brave Gentleman
> Accusers: mortal Enemy, Back Friends

Lexis is not the only means through which the author expresses attitudinal stance. In some cases, in fact, he relies on the use of logical connectors acting as internal evalutation devices such as *but, yet, tho' (though), negation* (see Labov and Waletzky 1967). I shall focus on the linker *though* which is one of the most commonly used and occurs in the following lexico-grammatical patterns: though + Np/ though + Adv. + VP/ though + VP. Given the subordinate value of the proposition expressing a parenthetical authorial consideration, the *though pattern* is generally put in brackets or between commas. From a semantic point of view, the *though-clause* marks a contrast between a state of affairs and what should be reasonably expected in a particular situation. Here are some examples:

– *though + NP*

> The Lord Cork (tho' his mortal Enemy) was now examined and admitted as a witness. (I, 739)

The implicit authorial assessment is that the examination of this witness is contrary to what should be expected in a just and lawful procedure, as a result the Court is acting illegally.

– *though + Adv. + Vp*

> Nor did he all this time speak one bitter word against Mr Pym, tho' justly incensed, which hath infinitely advanced his Reputation (I, 738)

The implicit authorial evaluation is that it would have been reasonable and understandable for the earl to reciprocate his accuser's rudeness. The fact that he did not do it enhances his moral superiority. In this example the *though-clause* co-occurs with *negation* which is put in prominent position in order to intensify the contrast between Pym's exacerbated challenge and Strafford's moderation.

– *though + Vp*

> But for all this, the Witness was received, because in Matter of Treason a Man's Enemy may witness against him *pro Domino nostro Rege*, tho' I suppose, the king's advice was never asked for the present. (I, 738)

In the example above, the author combines attitudinal and epistemic distance from the source of the Law ("though/I suppose") by reserving the end-focus position to the presumed abuse of power on the part of the authorities.

There are other lexico-grammatical patterns carrying attitudinal stance in the text and they occur in the following combination:

– *it + link verb + adj. Group + clause*

> It will be a very hard Matter for him to expect every Man's Testimony, and to give his Answers. (I, 737)

– *it + link verb + NP + clause*

> It was a Sport to see how Mr Pym in his Speech was fearfully out, and constrained to pull out his Papers. (I, 757)

In both cases the author encodes his subjective stance within an impersonal construction which assumes and builds up general consensus around his assessment of the defendant and the prosecution.

I conclude the analysis of attitudinal stance by examining instances of parody as a form of internal evaluation. Parody is defined by Bakhtin as a double-voiced discourse where two voices and two ideological orientations – that of the original speaker and that of the author – enter a dialogic confrontation within an utterance. Double-voiced discourse is a form of heteroglossia, which is classified as "***another's speech in another's language,*** serving to express authorial intentions but in a refracted way" (Bakhtin 1981: 324). Bakhtin explains:

> (17) [Double voiced discourse] serves two speakers at the same time and expresses simultaneously two different intentions: the direct intention of the [original speaker] and the refracted intention of the author. In such discourse there are two voices, two meanings and two expressions. And all the while these two voices are dialogically interrelated...it is as if they actually hold a conversation with each other.
>
> (322)

In the examples below it is interesting to see how the author takes hold of the lexico-grammatical features which are laden with the socio-ideological intentions of the accusers and compels them to serve his own distancing, almost satirical purposes. The result is a hybrid construction where two opposite viewpoints – the Royalist and the Parliamentarian – enter the arena of confrontational discourse. This time the author gives voice to his pro-Strafford propaganda not ***in*** language but ***through*** language, i.e. through the stylisation of the opponents' speech. Consider the following examples:

> (18) It is impossible to call to Mind all the Hyperboles, the Flashes, and superlative Expressions that he [Mr Pym] used; the main Points were, that it was Treason far beyond the Reach of Words, that he the Lieutenant, a native Subject and a Peer of England, the prime Governor of Ireland, the Commander of his Majesty's Forces, and a Protestant in Religion, should have in such an impious and gross Manner recompensed his Majesty's Favours, abused his Goodness, and drawn all his Dominions into Hazard and Peril of their Religion, Lives, Goods and Privileges: That one of these Faults alone had been enough, and too much, for the fulfilling of the Exorbitancy and Wickedness of any one Man; and that no Punishment could be thought upon, sufficient to expiate Crimes of such a trascendent Nature.
>
> (I, 736)

(19) Mr Glyn after a large Flourish, on Wednesday, told the Lords That the Lord Strafford was impeached, not with simple, but accumulative Treason: For tho' in each particular Article, such a monstruous Crime could not be deprehended, yet when all was conceived in the Mass and under one View, he should be undoubtedly found the most wicked and exorbitant Traytor that ever was arraigned at the Bar.

(I, 738)

(20) Upon Wednesday Whitlock charged thus: That the preceeding Articles were of so high a Consequence, and of so Trascendent a Nature, that nothing wanted to make up the perfect Measure of the most horrid Treason, and monstruous Attempt that ever, by a Native was indeed against his King and Country …

(I, 750)

The author parodies the bombastic as much as void character of the accusers' rhetoric through the repetition of:

- intensifiers: such, so, far beyond, too much
- adjectives in the superlative form: the most horrid Treason and monstruous Attempt, the most wicked and exorbitant Traytor
- adjectives and nouns semantically denoting "excess/extreme negativity": impious and gross Manner, a trascendent Nature, Wickedness, Exorbitancy.
- Accumulation of phrases in a listing format for aggravation's sake, which is a standard rhetorical device:

he the Lieutenant, a native Subject and a Peer of England, the prime Governor of Ireland, the Commander of his Majesty's Forces, and a Protestant in Religion/ recompensed his Majesty's Favours, abused his Goodness, and drawn all his Dominions into Hazard and Peril of their Religion, Lives, Goods and Privileges.

(I, 736)

The analysis of the three extracts above also reveal interesting forms of intertextuality in the speeches of the accusers (Mr Pym, Mr Glyn and Whitlock) which testify to the premeditated and manufactured character of their framing of the defendant:

> (Mr Pym) Exorbitancy and Wickedness of any one Man; and that no Punishment could be thought upon, sufficient to expiate Crimes of such a trascendent Nature
> (Mr Glyn) he should be undoubtedly found the most wicked and exorbitant Traytor that ever was arraigned at the Bar
> (Whitlock) and of so Trascendent a Nature /the most horrid Treason.

Parodic discourse can be considered a *speaker-based* strategy (Lakoff 1984: 483–84) in which the author gives readers little of the responsibility for sense-making (in this case, evalutation of the validity of the accusation). As a matter of fact, the interference of his voice is such that readers receive the information already biased from his Royalist point of view. In this sense, although the readership is commonly framed as an impartial judge to the events narrated, it is worth pointing out that this is a mere discourse illusion created by the writer to camouflage his communicative goals. The Royalist author consistently acts as an interpreter imposing his meaning on the evidence by using different degrees of explicitness.

4.2.5.2 Epistemic stance markers

The next stance category regards epistemic markers. These are not as numerous as those expressing attitude. They are usually actualised in the form of verbs expressing "metaphorized modality" and modality (see Toolan 1998): "The Point seemed exceeding Weighty", "do I presume I can give a reasonable Account"; "I suppose the king's advice was never asked for the present". Particularly interesting for the propaganda purposes of the court record are those cases in which the author commits himself to the truthfulness of the defendant's words, while keeping his distance from the pretentiousness of the hostile witness's allegations. In fact, while the choice of neutral reporting verbs introducing Strafford's speech shows the unchallenged character of his saying (said, replied, answered), the propositions referring to the opponents' testimony are modified so as to highlight their unreliability in terms of quality and quantity of the information given. Consider the following examples:

- lexical verb choice

  Then *Cork* [a hostile witness] alledged That he had advanced a Groom of his to be a Preacher (I, 739)

- post-modification of the lexical verb by means of adverbs or prepositional phrases

  And yet they [his Back-friends] proved very little but what they took upon Hear-says. (I, 741)

- restrictive adverbs

  For the last, which were the most dangerous Speeches (about reducing of the Kingdom) there was only Sir *Henry Vane's* Testimony; who declared only thus, That he had heard either those words or the like... (I, 748)

This last example is particularly relevant as it regards the kernel of the whole accusation. Sir Henry Vane was in fact the only witness who could incriminate Strafford for high treason. Since according to the Law, the testimony of less than two witnesses is not sufficient to accuse or condemn a man for high treason (Statute *Hen* 7.12 and *Edw.* 6.5), the Royalist author stresses the limitation of both the source (one single man and one of Strafford's enemies) and his utterance so as to denounce the partiality and injustice of the proceedings.

4.2.5.3 Style stance markers

Style stance is articulated in the form of 1) external metadiscoursive comments on the rendering of the information, 2) content omission 3) distancing speech-presentation through NRSA instead of the usual IS, 4) slipping into DS to create emotional involvement

- Metadiscoursive comments

  It is impossible to call to Mind all the Hyperboles, the Flashes and superlative Expressions that he [Mr Pym] used. (I, 736)

  You have his very Words as near as I can remember, only with such loss and detriment as hath perished by transcribing the Copy from his own Mouth. (I, 757)

- Omission of the accuser's speech-content

  The Aggravation of the Offence, he said, he had left to Mr Pym, who here spake that Speech which is now in Print. (I, 757)

- Distancing speech-presentation

  The Repetition of the Charge did not spend much time; they proceeded orderly Article by Article, in the very same Words and Matter as before.

Content omission and NRSA when the accusation speaks acquire relevance in relation to instances in which the author indulges in a more mimetic rendering of the speech-event, either through DS, IS or free indirect speech (FIS). In one case the author overtly manipulates the evidence deciding for the reader what is not worth reporting (maximum degree of imposition), in the other case he gives the reader greater responsibility for the interpretation of the evidence (minimum degree of interference). Even in this latter case, however, caution is in order since the hearer's interpretative act continues to be under authorial control. The choice of a higher degree of mimetic speech, in fact, seems to be dictated by the author's assumption that his readers share the right background to interpret the information the same way he does (Clark and Gerrig 1990: 793). By means of illustration, Mr Glyn's closing speech is reported with no overt evaluative markers, after several instances of negative metadiscoursive comments such as: "His adverse Party is so great and so far interested... that nothing will be left unessy'd, that may accellerate his Ruin", "It is impossible to call to Mind all the Hyperboles, the Flashes and superlative Expressions that he [Mr Pym] used" and evaluative reported speech like: "Master Glyn bitterly replied...", "it was replied by Mr Glyn (for all of them spake as occasion served)", "it was bitterly replied by Mr Glyn". Below is an extract from the accuser's speech, oscillating between IS and FIS with minimum interference from the author:

> He [Mr Glyn] closed; that throughout all his [Strafford's] Defence he had pretended either Warrants from the King, or else the King's Prerogative: and what was this else but to draw up a Cloud, and exhale the Vapour of the eclipsing of the bright Sun, by the Jealousies or Repining of his Subjects, if the strength of his Piety and Justice should not dispel all these Mists, and send them down to the Original? That the very standing and falling of these three Kingdoms stood upon this Process; all of which do conceive their Safety so far interested in his just Punishment, that no feeling of their Peace or Quiet could be expected without this...
>
> (I, 757).

– Slipping into DS to create emotional involvement.

> The Lieutenant went on thus:
> *My Lords,*
> This Day I stand before you charged with High Treason, the Burden is heavy, yet far the more, in that it hath borrowed the Patrociny of the House of Commons; if they were not interested, I might express a no less easy, that I do a safe Issue and good Success to the Business, But let neither my Weakness plead my Innocence, nor their Power my Guilt. (I, 754–55)

Slipping into DS is the last technique adopted to articulate style stance and occurs when the earl verbalises his defence. In this case the DS creates a sense of drama and vividness which enhances the reader's emotional involvement in the illocutionary force of the earl's words. What is more, by using DS the recorder puts the reader on an equal footing with himself, in the position of a witness who must evaluate the represented speech-event autonomously. It is interesting that this interpretative freedom is attributed to the readers only after the author has made sure that they have received the necessary instructions as to how to make sense of the events in a Royalist perspective. Thus the author withdraws from the text only when he can assume solidarity with his readership and trust their pseudo-autonomous judgement.

As we have seen throughout the analysis, the Royalist's foregrounding and backgrounding of the information is consistent with value judgements which are ultimately indicative of the author's propaganda purposes in the text. By and large, all the strategies adopted at the micro and macro discourse level are directed toward the construction of events where the inhibiting role of the defendant – as framed by his accusers in the courtroom – is revitalised through its representation in the printed trial. As a result, while the prosecution is consistently represented as involved in cunning and illegal manoeuvres to confound the multitude and incriminate the earl, the defendant is framed within the reality paradigm of the innocent whose eloquence and moderation undermine the baseness of the prosecution and move people's hearts. In this regard, though the partiality of the state trial compromises the authenticity of the actual events, the text still merits scrutiny as an example of the ideological position from which the Roylalists attacked the Parliamentarians' treatment of Royalist prisoners.

4.3 The State Trial of James Duke of Hamilton and earl of Cambridge (1649)

James Hamilton came from one of the most powerful families in Scotland. When his father died he became third Marquis of Hamilton and second earl of Cambridge. In 1628 King Charles appointed him Master of the Horse – a post which had remained vacant after the assassination of Buckingham and which brought him directly into the king's entourage. He was later appointed to the Privy Council and soon became Charles's chief adviser in Scottish affairs except for religious matters, which were the province of William Laud. After the outbreak of the Scottish revolt against the imposition of common worship, the king made Hamilton Commissioner in Scotland to negotiate with the Covenanters. He tried hard to invite the king to moderation and compromise but unsuccessfully. The Covenant Assemby continued to meet in defiance of the Royal authority and despite Hamilton's announcement of its dissolution.

On the eve of the Civil War the duke took Charles on his last visit to Scotland in an attempt to reach an agreement with the covenanting earl of Argyll against the English Parlamentarian forces. The result was that Hamilton and Argyll were forced to flee from Edinburgh on the discovery of a plot to assassinate them, while the king left Scotland, persuaded to have its support against Westminster. When things precipitated, Hamilton was sent back to Scotland to prevent the intervention of the Scots in the approaching Civil War. He was however unable to hinder the formation of an informal Scottish Parliament which began to collaborate with Westminster. The king held him responsible for the failure of the negotiation and he fell into disgrace.

After his imprisonment and subsequent liberation, the duke returned to the king who was being kept in semi-captivity by the Scottish army in Newcastle. He was re-admitted to his favour and renewed his involvement in Scottish affairs, which led him directly to the final capitulation. In 1647 the king and the Scottish commissioners signed the Engagement, according to which, the king would confirm the Solemn League and Covenant in the English Parliament and in return the Scots would send an army to England in support of Charles in case Parliament refused cooperation with him. The Parliamentarian concessions were rejected by the Scots and Hamilton was given the command of the Engager Army which invaded England in July 1648. The duke showed complete incapacity in military command and his troops were dramatically defeated by Oliver Cromwell at the battle of Preston.

Hamilton was imprisoned and tried by the High Court of Justice in February 1649 as the Earl of Cambridge. The title, in fact, proved him an Englishman and as such triable under the High Court's Jurisdiction. He was charged of having "traitorously invaded [England] in a hostile manner, and levied War to assist the

King against the Kingdom and People of England", of having "committed sundry Murders, Outrages, Rapines, Wastes, and Spoils, upon the said People" and finally of "having [near Preston] made War, joined Battle and fought against the Forces of the Parliament, and therein murdered and killed Colonel Thornley and others". Most of the debate around the legitimacy of Hamilton's trial concerned his status as Englishman or Scotsman. While the duke insisted that he was born in Scotland, before his father's naturalisation and could not be tried in England, the prosecution used every possible stratagem to prove that he was *post-natus* and therefore triable for treason by the High Court of Justice. Hamilton was found guilty along with four other English Royalists and executed on 9 March 1649 (see Rubenstein 1975; Scally 2004).

4.3.1 The Royalist account in the ST

The compilers of Hamilton's trial in the ST favoured two sources of Royalist orientation: Gilbert Burnet's *Memoirs of the Dukes of Hamilton* ([1677] 1852) and Edward H. Clarendon's *History of the Rebellion and Civil Wars in England* (1717). In particular, the first part of the proceedings is much indebted to Burnet's account, which is said to be drawn "partly from the journal of the court and partly from notes of what passed taken by eyewitnesses" (1852: 488). Despite Burnet's claim to accuracy and impartiality, his trial description pervasively reflects his ideological stance.

As happens in Strafford's trial, the account is in indirect reported speech with significant instances of slipping either forward into direct discourse or backward into NRSA. Examples of mimetic foregounding occur in two crucial and dramatic moments in the trial: 1) when the prosecutor frames his accusation through an objection-rebuttal sequence and 2) when the defendant gives his emotionally-charged speech before the execution. Both passages occur in the second section of the trial, when the reader has already been instructed as to how to interpret the evidence. The first section, on the other hand, presents interesting cases of authorial interference in the form of backward shifts from IS to NRSA. By and large the orchestrating strategies adopted in the text are the same as the ones activated in Strafford's trial and serve to enhance the audience's ideological distance from the Parliamentarians and promote its empathic closeness to the duke. What distinguishes this proceeding from the former is the author's *a posteriori* restructuring of the speech-events, not only through the partial omission of more controversial speeches (as was the case with Strafford's trial) but also through the addition of stretches of discourse which were not originally spoken in the trial (see also Laud's trial in this regard). I shall provide examples of the "adding" operation in the course of the analysis.

4.3.2 Features of news pamphlet style

As was the case with Strafford's trial, the court record of the duke contains several features of the news pamphlet style which reveal the ideological position of the Royalist author and his communicative aims. I shall focus on three of them: authorial comments, claim to empirical fidelity and emotional dimension.

The author introduces the arguments of the defence counsels through a set of evalutative comments on their speech-performance:

> (1) Then the Counsel began to plead, and all four spoke on several Heads of the Plea. Mr *Heron* spoke cursorily and elegantly but not very materially: Mr. *Parson*, a young Man, spoke boldly, and to good purpose: Mr *Chute* the Civilian spoke learnedly and home: and Mr *Hales* (since the much-renowned Chief Justice of the King's Bench) elaborately and at length. The Heads of their Arguments follow.
>
> (II, 5)

The authorial stance is actualised in the form of speech-style adjuncts and adjectives which enhance the good qualities of the Pro-

Hamilton counsels. In a similar fashion, the pleading of the Parliamentarians is negatively framed through the use of adjuncts, intensifiers, prepositional phrases and adjectives which express the incompetence and impudence of the accusers:

> (2) ...the Counsel for the People pleaded by so poorly, that all who heard them were ashamed: But they had one Advantage, that neither the Duke nor his Counsel were allowed to speak after them, nor to discover their impertinent Allegations, which made the Duke's Counsel obviate all they could imagine they might say, though they said a great deal so far out of the way of Reason, that none could have thought of it; and yet it was so weak, that it needed neither to be obviated, nor replied to.
>
> (II, 6)

Authorial comments also occur in parenthetical insertions where the writer interrupts the diegetic account in order to give voice to his political interpretation of the events. In particular, he hints at Commissions which were ignored by the Parliament as they would not conform to the Court script fabricated by the accusers and he also refers to the subjection of the Houses to the earl of Essex's interests against the duke.

> (3) But before Sentence, Bradshaw the president resumed all, and spoke long for aggravating of every particular, justifying everything the Counsel had pleaded, as if it had been all both good Law and good Reason. Then he caused to be read the Earl of Essex's Commission, to shew how little power was given him: (*But spoke nothing of Fairfax or Lambert their Commissions, which had been more pertinent, but the reason was they were ampler; and yet the Parliament had never refused to ratify any articles Essex gave*).
>
> (II, 16)

Claims to empirical fidelity are based on the direct observation topos (i.e. the author is eyewitness to the events) and reference to notes taken by defence counsels. Below is an example of the latter mode which enables the author to report stretches of discourse which have never been spoken at the trial but which serve to enhance the persuasiveness of the duke's defence in the account:

(4) Yet at the end of every Branch of their Pleading, I shall add the Answers against them, as they are set down in some Notes taken by the Duke's Counsel.

(II, 6)

The metadiscoursive comment prefaces a textual manipulation of the original proceedings prompted by the fact that the defence was not granted permission to object to the charges directly during the trial. By reporting the counsel's notes, the author gives the defence the right to speak the final word. This "additive" strategy will be examined in the section devoted to the author's style stance.

As far as the emotional dimension is concerned, the Royalist author adopts two main devices to appeal to his readership's feelings: 1) the use of the reality paradigm showing enemies who applaud the defendant, 2) the direct report of the duke's speech before the execution.

(5) The Court adjourned to the next day without giving him any satisfactory Answer. But the Duke's Carriage and Discourse that day gained much on all Spectators, being so serene and calm, that his very Enemies did applaud it.

(II, 2)

(6) I know you that are here to be true and faithful to me, I will therefore, in your hearing, say somewhat in order to myself and to my present condition, and give you also this Copy of it, which, after I am gone, may, perhaps, be thought necessary to be published as the last testimony of my Loyalty to my King, for whom I die, and of my Affection to my Country, for the pursuance of whose pious and loyal Commands I am now to suffer.

(II, 16)

The next paragraph is devoted to an analysis of stance markers at the micro discourse level.

4.3.3 Stance markers: attitudinal, epistemic and style stance

The Royalist author manifests his stance through a set of lexico-grammatical features and narrative patterns. In the course of the analysis we have already come across a set of lexical devices – in the form of speech-style adjuncts and adjectives – which are carriers of attitudinal stance. As far as descriptors are concerned, on the other hand, Hamilton is never represented as "the defendant/prisoner" but as "the Duke" and even his counsel is qualified as "the Duke's Counsel" rather than as "defence counsel" so as to downplay the negative connotations inherent in the role of "prisoner".

In this section, I shall concentrate on inner evaluation devices in the form of logical connectors (but, though, if, yet), comparators (negation) and quantifiers (all) which are equally important in biasing the reader's impression formation of the trial (see Labov and Waletzky 1967). By means of illustration, in the following examples the coordinators highlight the unmotivated hostility of the Court against the prisoner.

(7) The Duke expressed a deep Resentment of this Injury done on him by the Governour, who wounded his Honour so much, which he valued above all earthly things...; adding that if he were not a Prisoner, he would desire Right of the Governour for that Scandal cast on him, and chuse no other place for it but *Westminster-Hall*. But to all this the Governour made no Reply; only the President said, that though he could not blame the Earl of Cambridge for what he said, yet for all that the Governour was not to be discredited.

(II, 3)

(8) He [Hamilton] desired a Warrant for bringing some Gentlemen, then Prisoners in Whitehall, who were his material Witnesses: but the Court adjourned, and promised to consider that Motion in the Painted Chamber; yet they granted it not.

(II, 3)

(9) Whereupon he and his Counsel moved, That if what he said and proved was not satisfactory for the Avernment of his Plea, he might

> answer the Charge exhibited, which he had not yet done. But to this, neither the Court nor their Counsel, would yield, tho they gave no Reason for it, save only that it implied a Desire of Delay: but the Reason, as was said, was That they knew had they yielded to that, the Charge had been overthrown, since the Law of England does not admit that to be Treason which they charged on him, that he had assisted the King against the Kingdom and People by levying War.
>
> (II, 4)

(10) But the Counsel answered, That it was impossible for them to undertake it, and discharge their Consciences to their Client, having so short a time allowed to them; there being divers Records for Precedents, which required a competent time, as had been allowed in former Cases. But the Court refused to promise it, only they said they would take it into consideration.

(II, 4)

The way in which the author frames the Court-prisoner confrontation by means of the adversative conjunctions *but* and *yet,* the *negation* (referring to something which did not happen, in contrast to the expectations of justice), and the concessive *though* illustrate his indignation at the hostile reactions of the Court to the legitimate requests of the prisoner.

Along with connectors, narrative slipping is another evaluative strategy which signals shifts of ideological perspective. By taking IS as the norm in the account, instances of shifts into NRSA show a stronger authorial discourse control, which has the ultimate purpose to alienate the opponent's speech in the eyes of the audience. By means of illustration, in the passage below the defendant's plea is reported in the indirect mode, whereas the aggravation of the charges on the part of the accusers is rendered with a sudden shift into a distancing NRSA. The result is that the audience is given a clear and detailed rendition of what the defendant said in his defence but is not given an equal account of the prosecutor's evidence against him, with a consequential alienating effect.

(11) His Plea consisted of three Heads: First, He pleaded that his undertaking that Employment was by Command of the Parliament, and Supreme Authority of the Kingdom of Scotland, for such Ends as he conceived were good and justifiable, and in no way derogatory to the Peace and Happiness of these Dominions: That he did earnestly endeavour to decline it, but that not being accepted of, he could not disobey their Commands without incurring the severst Censures. Secondly, That he was born in Scotland before the Naturalization of his Father in England, therefore he conceived himself an Alien, and not triable in England. Thirdly, That he had rendered himself Prisoner upon Capitulation and Articles with those who had Major-General Lambert's Commission; and that by these he was first a Prisoner of War... Upon this the Counsel for the People caused the Act of his Father's Naturalization to be read, and spake a little to aggravate and set out his Fact: but he desired a convenient time to procure Papers, Witnesses and other Evidences material to his Plea, which he said was seldom denied to any in that condition. (II, 1)

With respect to indirect speech, it is hard to establish to what extent the words reported are the ones actually spoken by the duke and to what extent they reflect the author's interference as *a posteriori* reporter. Given the ideological closeness between the two voices, it is very likely that an overlapping of idiolect and stance occurs in the passage. In this sense, the indirect reported speech of the duke would represent a case of double-accented speech, manifesting a dialogic interlacement between the intentions of the defendant in the here and now of the courtroom and the refracted, propaganda intentions of the Royalist author in the new Republican England. Consider the next example where the emphatic rhetorical discourse of the defendant seems to converge with the propaganda purposes of the author:

(12) He desired them to consider, how sacred Articles of War were reputed in all Places, and among all Nations, and how inviolably they were kept, all Princes and States being most careful to observe them[...] adding the following instances. *Elijha* the Prophet would not suffer the King of Israel to kill the *Syrian* Captains, saying *Wouldst thou smite those whom thou hast taken captive with thy Sword and thy Bow?* The Blood of *Abner* lay on *Joab*'s head, who killed one that had the

> King's Safe-Conduct. The *Gibeonites* also, though they used *Joshua* deceitfully, yet were preserved according to the Articles given them ... That Prince *Robert* and the Lord *Cottington*, tho excepted from Life or Pardon by Act of Parliament, were notwithstanding that upon the Articles of the Rendition of *Oxford*, permitted to go beyond Sea, and never questioned for Life: and the like Justice was done to the earl of *Bristol* and the Lord *Paulet*... therefore he did not doubt the like Justice would be done on him.
>
> (II, 3)

In the second part of the trial the author unexpectedly opts for the direct reporting of the accusation's speech and leaves only little room for the objection of the defence:

> I [the Attorney General] shall first answer the material Objections which I conceive made by the Counsel on the other side, before I offer any thing positively to assert the Invalidity of this part of the Plea.
> Obj: *It hath been said, The Proof is not clear for the Earl of Cambridge's being* a Post-natus; *viz one born after King James's Access to the Crown of* England; *and that being but a* non liquet in favorem vitae, *the most favourable Construction is to be taken for the Prisoner.*
> Answ. First, I deny that the Proof amounts to no more in this Particular than a *non liquet*; for there is one positive Witness that speaks directly to the Earl's Birth after King *James*'s coming to the Crown of *England* [...].
>
> (II, 8)

The choice of DS in this context can be justified by the fact that the Royalist author has already schooled the reader as to the illicit character of the trial and can therefore indulge in an unmediated account of the opponents' words. In the first part of the proceedings, the author consistently adopts speaker-based discourse strategies through which he evaluates the participants' behaviour for his readers: speech-style and manner adjuncts ("so poorly", "impertinent", "weak", "far out of the way of reason"), inner evaluation devices ("but", "though", "yet", "all", "only") and evaluative reporting verbs ("study", "labour", "make it appear", "aggravate"). In light of this, the use of DS in the second part of the record may be regarded as a by-product of the reporter's desire not to analyse what he considers as self-evident. In other words the writer can refrain from interference in the text as he is sure about the reader's ideological response to the speech event.

Epistemic stance also plays an important role in the court-record. On several occasions, in fact, the propaganda character of the account emerges through the author's distance from the truthfulness and reliability of the opponents' propositions. In the court-record the main markers of epistemic stance are lexical verbs referring to the manufactured and treacherous character of the Parliamentarians' allegations and the restrictive adverb *only* stressing the limitation of the accusation. Both are present in the first part of the account.

– Evaluative speech act verbs: *labour, study, allege, make it appear, aggravate, justify*
   a) The Court objected the time they had already granted, and alledged this was a mere Delay. (II, 2)
   b) Yet even that was not clearly proved, tho it was much laboured. (II, 3)
   c) And Proof was brought, that notwithstanding Articles were given, yet some had been forced to take the Negative Oath; and thereby they [accusers] studied to evince that the Parliament did not hold themselves bound to stand to Articles. (II, 3)
   d) They began with Alienage, and studied to make it appear, that though he was a *Scotchman* born, yet he was no Alien. (II, 6)
   e) But before Sentence, *Bradshaw* the president resumed all, and spoke long for aggravating of every particular, justifying every thing the Counsel had pleaded, as if it had been all both good Law and good Reason. (II, 16)

– Restrictive adverb: *only* + lexical verb *hear* denouncing the hear-say character of the opponents' evidence
   a) but as the Letters proved no Conjunction, so it did not appear that they were his Letters; only *Peters* assterted they were like his Hand. (II, 3)
   b) The Governor deposed, That the Duke said to him he needed not fear his Escape, he would be a true Prisoner, and not go away though the Gates were opened. The Marshal said, he only heard this from the Governor. (II, 3)

The evaluative tagging process used for the accusation's speech is particularly interesting when compared with that used for the defendant's. The duke's words, in fact, are introduced by semantically general *verba dicendi*, such as "told" and "spake" which enhance the objective and factual character of his saying as opposed to the fictitious plots of his rivals.

In the entire court record there is only one clear manifestation of style-stance and it occurs when the author signals his additive, structural operation in the text. As previously argued, the *a posteriori* manipulation is intended to obviate the defence's impossibility of objecting directly to the accusers' plea.

> Yet at the end of every Branch of the Pleading, I shall add the Answers against them, as they are set down in some Notes taken by the Duke's Counsel.
>
> (II, 6)

The author ensures the reliability of the defence's answers by claiming to have copied them directly from the notes of the counsel. In order to distinguish the *a posteriori* addition from the words actually spoken in the courtroom, he reports them in italics. Below is an example:

> They also urged his being Post-natus, which must be held true, since he brought no Evidence to the contrary, and it being so, his Tie of Subjection was as great in England as in Scotland: That Allegiance was only due to the King and not to the Kingdom; That there was a King, and when he entred into England, and that though he was secluded from the Government, yet all Writs were issued in his Name; so that his Expedition was a Breach of the Allegiance he owed to the King. *This was the oddest Part of all their Plea, since his Charge was, That he assisted the King against the Kingdom; and now they plead he owed no Allegiance to the Kingdom, but to the King, whom they had so lately murdered; the Duke's coming with his Army being only to relieve him from the barbarous Usage he had met with.*
>
> They also urged at large, That an Englishman's Children, in what place of the World so ever they were born, were Denizens of England, and cited many Precedents. *But the Mis-application of them was gorss and palpable, those being of Persons who were Englishmen before their Children were born; whereas the Duke's Father was naturalized after he was born; so that he could not communicate that Privilege to him, which he did indeed transmit to his Children born after his Naturalization.*

> [...] They added, That Scotland belonged to the Crown of England, and so was to be look'd on as some of the Countries of England. *But Scotland had no Subjection to the Crown, but only to the King of England, whom they had murdered, and so they had no Power to judge any Scothman.*
>
> (II, 6)

It is worth pointing out that although the author claims that the answers are taken from an official source and as such speak the counsel's mind in a professional way, there are some evaluative expressions which suggest his enunciational interference. Consider for example the value judgements: "This was the oddest part of their Plea", "the Mis-application of them was gross and palpable" or "whom [the King] they had so lately murdered". In this sense the original, monologic character of the accusation's speech is not only turned into a *fictional,* dialogic confrontation between accusers and defence but it is also charged with the orchestrating voice of the Royalist author, who rearranges discourse in such a way as to highlight the wickedness of the Parliamentarian arguments and steer the reader's ideological consensus towards the defence counsel's version of the events.

In some cases, the objection of the defence deserves some considerations as to the mitigating strategies adopted by the counsel to soften the illocutionary force of the accusers' utterances. As Danet points out "defendants can mitigate *the form* of their utterances by using a rhetorical device to soften the impact of some unpleasant aspect of an utterance on the speaker or the hearer" (1980: 524)[18]. In the example below it is interesting to notice how the author blames the accuser Mr Cook for his demystified interpretation of the Law, while the defence relies on exactly the same deceptive devices:

> Cook, by a strange Subtilty, said, The Articles only secured his Life during Imprisonment; so that his breaking of Prison, and being retaken, put an end to the Obligation of the Articles, *Though he broke not Prison, but went out at the Door and Gate, which was no Crime.*
>
> (II, 7)

18 Danet, B. "Language in the Legal Process" in *Law and Society Review,* vol. 14, n. 3, 1980.

The lawyers' verbal duelling unfolds along a set of opposing reality paradigms which have the ultimate purpose to construct a representation of the (secondary) reality that corresponds to the facts *as they see them* (Archer 2002: 26).

4.3.4 Conclusion

The analysis of the duke of Hamilton's trial has documented the use of discourse strategies which are similar and at times identical to the ones found in Strafford's trial, notwithstanding the different charisma of the two figures. This seems to suggest that Royalist authors tended to conform to a set of discourse practices which were primarily consistent with the propaganda purposes of their ideological community. As a result the representation of the defendant was carried out through formulaic patterns whose popularity rested on their repetitiveness. Both the earl and the duke were depicted as innocent victims of the Parliament's manoeuvres. Both were described as courageous, modest, eloquent to the point of eliciting their enemies' approval and in both cases their defence was enhanced while the authoritativeness of the accusation was downplayed. This prompts considerations on the extent to which both Parliamentarians and Royalists appealed to scripts in order to bias and forge public opinion. While the former forced the prisoner within a Court script which was necessarily detrimental to his cause, the latter relied on a "trial script by print" which ensured the prisoner's rehabilitation both as person and as Stateman.

4.4 The State Trial of William Laud, Archbishop of Canterbury (1644)

The history of William Laud encompasses the history of both Church and State in Stuart England. Laud became Archbishop of Canterbury in 1633 and as one of the king's favourites he received many other ecclesiastical and academic preferments and honours in the following years. This increased his power in both religious and state matters, making him one of the major actors on England's political stage. Like Charles I, he strongly believed in the uniformity of worship practices, the value of ceremony and obedience to political and religious superiors. Radical Puritans recognised in these values the manifestation of a "papal" power and accused Laud of being aligned with the Church of Rome aganist the authority of both the king and the Parliament. Resentment against the Archbishop became stronger after the English government proposed the introduction of the new prayer book and canons in Scotland in 1637. In that same year William Prynne (the future barrister at Laud's trial) along with John Bastwick and Henry Burton were tried and imprisoned for seditious libels, in particular for vilifying episcopacy and condemning Laud. During their imprisonment, their ears were cropped and their cheeks branded. These extreme measures were justified by Laud on account of national security but it was precisely this uncontrolled power that soon brought him to ruin. The mishandling of the three conspirators, the reinforcement of censorship and Laud's recording of his personal trials in the *Diary* were the major actions which 'set the stage' for his charge of high treason in 1640 and his imprisonment the next year (see Carlton 1987, Trevor-Roper 1988).

As Orr (2002) points out, behind Laud's impeachment lies a conflict of interpretation around the notion of supremacy in altering and determining the doctrine and discipline of the Church. The ideological position of Laud's prosecutors in the trial is consistent with Erastianism, i.e. the view according to which "the power to determine doctrine and exercise of discipline over the established church rested ultimately with the secular magistrate, whether that be king, parliament or king-in-parliament, rather than with any ecclesiastical body" (Orr 2002: 102). For Laud and his followers, on the other hand, their power was legitimised as it came directly from God by apostolic descent: it was *iure divino*. Prynne and the other barristers read Laud's claim to *iure divino* as proof of his popish alignment and equated it to an exercise of power greater than that of the king and his Parliament. Hence the central thrust of the charges against Laud was that during the Personal Rule he had usurped a jurisdiction greater than that properly belonging to the king or king-in-parliament and had further claimed to hold this jurisdiction *iure divino* (Orr 2002: 107).

4.4.1 Laud' s impeachment and charges

The proceedings against Laud were extremely long, spanning over three years and taking place in an atmosphere of "indifference and intense hatred that fed on the memory of wrongs done long before" (Carlton 1987: 216). The immense delays which characterised the trial were due to the fact that from 1642 the Long Parliament was engaged in the Civil War and the attention of Parliamentarians was addressed to the time-consuming business of "baronial revolt" (see Orr 112 note 51). In all probability the trial of Laud would have been deleted from the magistrates' agenda if it had not been for the pressure exerted by the Scottish allies.

Laud's impeachment was articulated in two sets of articles: one consisting of 14 charges in 1641 and the second comprising ten additional articles brought up in 1643 after the outbreak of the Civil War. In contrast to Strafford's and Hamilton's trials the charges did not always report the precise instances in which Laud's words and actions could be equated to treason. Furthermore while the original articles were based on a charge of high treason, the second set of articles contained both the charge of treason and of other high crimes and misdemeanors, thus posing the problem of distinguishing the original charge from the others.

Prefaced by a fervent exchange of "paper contestations" between Antilaudians and bishops, the trial of Laud began on 12 March 1644. John Maynard, one of the counsels at Strafford's arraignment, headed the prosecution. The main burden of the defence fell on the Archbishop, who, despite his hopeless situation, provided a better quality defence than that of his friend Strafford (Orr 2002). As Sauer claims "Laud's ability [in managing his defence] undermined the parliamentary 'show trial' which – as in Strafford's case – ultimately 'failed to demonstrate what it had intended to prove'" (Sauer 2005: 52). Carlton reports that Laud did most of the legal research for his defence and the notes taken by the scribe of the Parliament shows that the trial version reported by Laud in *The History of The Troubles and Tryal...of William Laud* was "fairly accurate, even if he tended to embellish and improve his statements while doing the opposite to those for the other sides" (1987: 218).

The trial began with the reading of the first article, according to which Laud had "traitorously endeavoured to subvert the fundamental laws and government of the kingdom, and instead thereof to introduce an arbitrary government against law". It continued that the Archbishop had advised the king "that he might at his own will and pleasure levy and take money of his subjects, without their consent in Parliament" and that he said that this "was warrantable by the law of God". It is possible to see similarities here between Strafford's and Laud's charges in matter of subversion of the law and proposal of extraparliamentary taxation.

The second original article concerned the promotion and publication of "divers sermons and other discourses...in which the authority of parliaments, and the force of the laws of this kingdom are denied, and an absolute and unlimited power over the persons and estates of his Majesty's subjects is maintained and defended". As Orr points out, the charge was not only related to "the maintenance and promotion of power above the law but [also to] the clerical assumption of that power" (2002: 115). The second additional article derived from the original article and charged Laud of endeavouring "to advance the Power of the Council Table, the Canons of the Church, and the King's Prerogative, above the Laws and Statutes of the Realm". Again the charge was aimed at denouncing the clerical usurpation of sovereign power intended as the power of king-in-parliament. As Orr makes clear, in fact, for the Erastians of the Long Parliament the legal authority of the king was intended as the authority of the king-in-parliament and not king-in-convocation (2002: 116).

The third and fourth general articles were similar in that they both accused Laud of subverting the ordinary course of justice. The former charged that Laud "by letters, messages, threats, promises...hath endeavoured to interrupt and pervert, the course of justice, in his Majesty's Courts at *Westminster*". The latter emphasised the manoeuvres of the Archbishop to corrupt the justice system by selling "justice to those that had causes depending before him, by colour of his ecclesiastical jurisdiction, as Archbishop, High Commissioner, Referee, or otherwise".

After several delays the hearings resumed on 16th April with the fifth and sixth original articles and the ninth additional article. The fifth and ninth articles were similar in that they both concerned the legality of the 1640 canons. The fifth article charged Laud with composing, publishing and putting into execution Canons without authority, "in which Canons many Matters are contained contrary to the King's Prerogative, to the fundamental Laws and Statutes of the Realm, to the Right of Parliament, to the Property and Liberty of the Subjects..."(vol. I, 869). The ninth article differed from the fifth in that there was no mention of the Canons being contrary to the king's prerogative, but only the assertion that the canons were "contrary to the Laws of the Realm, the Rights and Privileges of Parliament and Liberty and Property of the Subject...". Laud noticed the contradiction inherent in the two articles and asked how he could be accused of favouring the king's prerogatives and yet writing canons against it. The fact is that while the fifth article was drawn in the period before the Civil War, when king and the Parliament still represented a single body at Westminster, the ninth article reflected the situation after the outbreak of the war, when every member of the Long Parliament could be accused of usurping the king's Prerogative power of war and peace. For this reason the prosecution decided to eliminate the controversial mention of the king's prerogatives, maintaining the position that the canons should be subject to parliamentary approval.

The seventh original and seventh additional articles concerned the ecclesiastical innovations introduced by Laud's Personal Rule such as the setting of the communion table altarwise, the wearing of copes, the presence of a crucifix and images in places of worship. According to the seventh original Laud had "traitorously endeavoured to alter and subvert God's true religion by Law established in the Realm; and instead thereof to set up Popish superstition and idolatry". The seventh additional article continues in a similar vein, accusing Laud of receiving and harbouring popish priests. The primary concern in the trial was to establish whether the Archbishop held the authority to carry out the programme of ecclesiastical reforms that he introduced during the 1630s. Again the notion of clerical supremacy was strongly challenged.

The eight, ninth, tenth, eleventh and twelfth original and the sixth additional articles all refer to the ecclesiastical policies of Laud's Personal Rule and his alleged manoeuvres to enhance them. The thirteenth article charging Laud of having "maliciously and traitorously plotted, and endeavoured to stir up war and enmity betwixt his Majesty's two kingdoms of England and Scotland" was laid aside under the Act of Oblivion. The fourteenth article was the last issued and accused Laud of having "laboured to subvert the rights of Parliament and the ancient course of the parliamentary proceedings; and by false and malicious slanders to [have] incense[d] his Majesty against Parliaments" so as to avoid answering for his actions. The charge echoes the seven articles against Strafford thus increasing the association between the two. Nontheless while

Strafford continued to believe in the power of Parliaments and their role in the kingdom, Laud was legitimately considered as one of the Parliament's most fervent opponents, questioning its usefulness and necessity in the monarchy.

Laud was accused of having usurped the Royal supremacy by creating an ecclesiastical state within the state. The legitimacy of the prosecution rested on their claim to be acting for the preservation of the king's authority. The irony of the dispute lies in the fact that while Laud had always acted under Charles I's consent, the Parliament had been at war with the king for two years and this despite their pretence to be supporters of his supremacy (Orr 2002: 139–140).

4.4.2 Literature on Laud's trial and execution

The resonance of Laud's trial and execution on public opinion is evident from the number of pamphlets and broadsides which followed his death. Laud was conscious of the power that the printed word would have in vindicating him. Before the execution, he handed a copy of his last dying speech to his chaplain, so as to make sure that the public shorthand writer would publish the true and authentic version of his sermon. After his death, his speech was promptly reported by two rival newsbooks of the time: *Mercurius Aulicus* and *A Perfect Diurnall.* While the former lamented the act of "studied Murther" against Laud, the latter celebrated the fairness of the trial and criticised the Archbishop's speech for its fallacies, omissions and misleading comparisons of the Scritpures. The pro-Parliamentarian account of Laud's final moments was counterattacked in various pamphlets including Heylyn's *A Briefe Relation of the Death and Sufferings of ... Canterbury* (1645), where the author bestows the events with tragic contours: "It is a preposterous kinde of writing to beginne the story of a great mans life, at the houre of his death; a most strange way of setting forth a solemne *Tragedie...*".

Far more interesting is the way in which pamphlet literature prefaces and frames Laud's trial and its tragic outcome. The most accomplished exponent of such trial propaganda was Laud's fierce enemy William Prynne. Just in time for the official opening of Laud's trial, Prynne published a series of papers, which he declared he had found in the Archbishop's chamber in the Tower and entitled them *The Popish Royal Favourite* (London: 1643). His most cynical blow, however, was yet to come. In 1644 Prynne published his manipulated edition of Laud's *Diary*, which apperared in print the same day that the Archbishop appeared before Parliament (2nd December 1644). As Peacey argues the publication of Prynne's *A Breviate of the Life of William Laud* was intended "to influence not merely the public's perception of Laud but also the very members of Parliament he was about to address" (2004: 262–263)[19]. Further evidence of the way in which the printed word piloted the trial is offered by Prynne's subsequent publication of *Hidden Works of Darkeness* (December 1644). The work was aimed at assisting the process of convincing the Lords to agree to pass an ordinance of of attainder, which they finally did on 4th January 1645, thus authorising the Commons to proceed to Laud's execution six days later. Prynne was finally assigned the task to print the trial's epilogue in his famous work *Canterburies Doome* (1646), containing and altered version of the Proceedings. As Orr claims, it is foolish to read this tainted source as a "historically accurate depiction of the actual events", even so the text merits scrutiny as a document of the ideological position from which Laud was attacked during the trial (2002: 121). In the account Prynne seises every opportunity to reveal the damage done by Laud's *Oratory, Subtlety, Protestations and*

19 Prynne's *Breviate of the Life of William Laud* (1644) was defined by Henry Wharton as a corrupt and barbarous version of Laud's *Diary*. In order to redeem the figure of the Archbishop Wharton subsequently published a corrected version as an introduction to his edition of Laud's self-defence, *The History of the Troubles and Tryal of .... William Laud* (1695).

verball Apologies and exploits every possible detail to unmask his popish intentions.

The paper-contestations centred around the trial and execution of William Laud documented "the practices of textual revolt and collective identification that generate[d] alternative interpretative communities ... and intensifi[ed] the social and political dramas on the [17th-century] English stage" (Sauer 2005: 56). In order to win the battles consumed on the print market, the rhetoric of persuasion became crucial and Laud proved to be fully aware of it when he produced the account of his own trial.

4.4.3 *The analysis of authorial stance*

The proceeding of William Laud differs from that of Strafford and Hamilton in the telling mode. Laud is in fact both defendant and reporter of his own trial. The compilers' intervention is visible only in occasional additions taken from other sources, mainly Rushworth's *Historical Collections* (1692) and Prynne's *Canterburies Doome. A Complete History of Laud's Trial* (1646). The insertions are written in italics and put in square brackets so as to distinguish them from the authorial voice of the Archbishop. As was the case with the trials of Strafford and Hamilton, Laud's account is informative, argumentative and persuasive. It is informative in that the author claims to provide the reader with a truthful report of what happened in the courtroom; it is argumentative and persuasive in that his primary aim is to counter-attack the propaganda manoeuvres of his accusers and convince the readership of his innocence.

Laud re-enacts his trial in the paper and invites the reader to take on a judicial function in the dispute between the parties. To the 'social drama' performed in the courtroom and directed by his opponents, Laud replies with his own staging. If, on the one hand, his direct involvement in the case undermines the objectivity of the account, on the other hand it solicits an examination of the discourse strategies adopted to bias the opinion of the multitude. All of Laud's words both as experiencing and reporting I are audience-oriented. This means that even in cases where the Archbishop (as reporting I) re-enacts the words spoken to the Lordships (as experiencing I), his speech addresses two tenors simultaneously: the original recipient at the time of the event, and the readership at the time of narration. Insofar as the audience is expected to assume the same role as his examiners, it is easy to imagine how Laud's persuasive appeal to the Lords combines with his stronger appeal to the audience:

> For Mr Bond [a witness], he begins with somewhat that I should say at the Council Table; as namely, that he must seal a Bond of two thousand Pounds to brew no more with Sea-Coal. Now this argue, if I did so speak, that it was in delivering to him the sense of the Board; which Office was actually put upon me... <u>And your Lordships may here again see what Envy hath followed me upon that which I could not decline</u>.
>
> (I, 858)

Laud's viewpoint in the text is expressed through a set of external and internal markers of stance which will be examined as usual in terms of Conrad and Biber's distinction between epistemic, attitudinal and style stance. I shall start with an analysis of style markers since the most salient evaluative operations in the text are structural.

4.4.3.1 Style stance

Before beginning the account of the trial, Laud ventures into a long digression where he establishes an intimate relationship with his future readers. In particular he provides them with a lens through which they will be called to interpret and make sense of the events narrated. All the information given in this introductory session is ideologically oriented in the sense that it is intended to denounce and create common disapproval with respect to: 1) the partiality and corruption of the court 2) the hostile, almost inhuman treatment of the prisoner 3) the disadvantage inherent in a system of evidence which relegates the defence at the very end of the entire accusation 4) the art of instructing witnesses to the prisoner's detriment.

> And now being ready to enter upon the Hearing and the Trial itself; I hold it necessary for me to acquaint the Reader with some general Things before that begin: partly to the end he may see the Course of this Trial, and the Carriage which hath been in it; and partly to avoid the often tedious Repetition, which else must necessarily be of some of them; and especially that they may not be mingled either with the Evidence or my Answers to it, to interrupt the Carrent, or make any thing more obscure... Now for the Method, which I shall hold in the History of my Trial, it shall be this: I will set down the Evidence given on each day by itself and my Answer to it. But whereas all the Evidence was given together, and so my whole Answer after, to avoid all looking back and trouble of turning Leaves to compare the Answer with the Evidence, I will set down each particular Evidence and my Answer to it, and so all long that the indifferent Reader may, without farther Trouble, see the Force of the one, and the Satisfaction given in the other, and how far every particular is from Treason. And if I add anything in my Answers in place, either it is because in the Shortness of time then given to me to make my Answer, it came not to my present Thoughts; or if it did, yet I forbear to speak it with that Sharpness, holding it neither fit nor fare, in my Condition, to provoke either my Accusers or my Judges. And whatever is so added by me in either of these respects, the Reader shall find it thus[a] marked in the Margin as here it stands in this.
>
> ‘
‘ } a
‘
>
> (vol. I; 838–839).

In the preface Laud accounts for two crucial structural manipulations of the original proceeding which inevitably affect the shape of the trial and its impact on the reader.

1) He reports his answer immediately after the accusation. This determines a dialogic, confrontational structure which is advantageous to the defendant. His immediate rebuttal in fact allows him to invalidate the force of the evidence before it settles in the audience's mind.

2) He adds stretches of defence which were not spoken during the trial. This has the effect of making his argumentation far more convincing in the eyes of the reader.
3) He omits parts of the trial on the basis that they are "tedious" repetitions which bring nothing new to the evidence.

Regarding the first organisation device, Laud fictionally constucts an accusation-answer sequence in such a way that the accusation is reported indirectly by means of IS or through the more distancing NRSA, whereas his answer is given in free direct speech (FDS). The absence of the reporting tag enhances the dramatic immediacy of Laud's words and their persuasive potential. Consider the following examples:

> And Mr Prynn [one of his accusers from the House of Commons] witnessed very carefully, That this Book was found in my own Study, and given me by Bishop *Montague*. And what of this? Doth any Bishop print a Book, and not give the Archbishop one of them? Or must I answer for every Propostion that is in every Book that is in my Study, or that any Author gives me? And if Bishop *Montague* be of opinion that Tythes are due by Divine Right, what is that to me? Your Lordship know many men are of different Opinions in that Difficulty; and I am confident you will not determine the Controvery by an Act of Parliament.
>
> (I, 877)

> Here the Charge is bowing *versus Altare* [...]. And first Dr *Jackson* says, the bowing was versus Altare; so not *to* but *toward* the Altar and Dr *Blechenden* says, it was the Adoration of the high Majesty of God, to whom, if not Altare were there, I should bow. Dr. Jackson says this bowing was to his grief. Strange! I avow to your Lordhips and the World, no Man did so much approve all my Proceedings in that Church, as he.
>
> (I, 891)

> In this particular Mr *Genebrand*, Brother to his Almanack-Maker, witnesseth, that the Queen sent to me about this new Almanack. If her Majesty did send to me about it (as 'tis probably she would disdain the Book) is that any Crime in me? Could I prevent her Majesty's sending, who could not know so much as that she would send? He says his Brother was acquitted in the High Commission, but charged by me, that he made a Faction in the Court. If I did say so, surely, My Lords, I saw some practising by him in this new-found

> Way. He says the Papists bought up a great Number of these Almanacks and burnt them. It seems he could not hinder that, nor I neither; unless it shall not be lawful for a Papist to buy an Almanack: for when he hath bought him, he may burn him if he please.
>
> (I, 903)

> The fourth Charge was Mr Mountague's Preference. The Parliament (they say) called him in Question, and the King called in his Book, yet in Affront to the Parliament, that he was preferred by me. No, it was then publickly known in Court (whether now remembered or no, I cannot tell) that he was preferred by my Lord Duke.
>
> (I, 905)

Rhetorical questions, exclamations and ironic comments are some of the basic ingredients of Laud's defence and will be analysed in depth in the section devoted to attitudinal stance. At present, suffice it to notice how Laud's slipping from the diegetic to the mimetic mode in relation to the alternation of accusation and defence enables him to exercise authorial control on the evidence while foregroung the argumentative strength of his rebuttal. It is not easy to establish now whether the words reported in FDS are those actually spoken in the trial (though later on at the end of the charges) or reflect the reporting I's interference at the time of narration. Given the fragmentation of the original defence into snippets and their new collocation as second pairs of a fictional accuser-defendant interaction, it is very likely that the original wording has undergone some changes. By Laud's own admission, the sharpness of his argumentation was downplayed during the trial so as to avoid performing FTAs which could be further detrimental to his cause and person. Even so, the centrality of (F)DS is not so much the fidelity to the original but rather the perlocutionary effect that it has on the interpreters. As Collins claims, "the quintessence of DS … is not *mimesis* but *methexis* ("participation"), to adapt a term from Platonic and early Christian philosophy – an act that, in accordance with culturally determined interpretative conventions, allows the audience to participate both in the new event (the re-creation) and, vicariously, in the prior event, real or imagined, that is being represented" (2001: 74).

With respect to the second organisational device, i.e. the addition of defence which Laud could not give during the trial, the text features a high number of interpolations which have no other purpose than to convince the reader of the prisoner's good faith through the force of the extended argumentation. Here is an example

> 'But tho' I was not allowed there to make any further Answer in defence of these Canons; nor 'can hold it fit to insert here so long an Answer as these Vote require; I humbly desire the 'Corteous Reader, if he please, to look upon the Answer which I made to a Speech of Mr '*Nathaniel Fiennes,* in the House of Commons against these Canons [...] However I cannot but 'observe this in present. The Words in the Sixth Original Article are ... that the late Canons 'contain Matters contrary to the King's Prerogative, the Laws, etc. But in the Ninth Additional 'all the rest of the Exceptions are in against them, but these Words about the King's Prerogative 'are quite left out. I would fain know, if I could, what is the Reason of this Omission in these 'added Articles: is it for Shame because there was a purpose to charge me (as Serjeant Wild did 'in his Speech the first Day) that I laboured to advance the King's Prerogative above the Law? 'To advance it, and yet made contrary Canons against it; which is the way to destroy it. What 'pretty Non-sense is this? Or is it because the Framers of these Additionals (whom I conceive 'were some Committe with the help of Mr Prynn) though the time was come or coming which 'the King should have no more Prerogative? Or if there be a third Reason, let them give it 'themselves.
>
> (I, 871)[20]

Laud is interested in uncovering the wickedness and treacherousness of his accusers to the eyes of the readers. He does so by guiding them through a set of reflections about the contradictory behaviour of the Commons. His argumentation is constructed through a combination of alternative yes/no questions (is it for ... or is it because?) which is highly face damaging to his interlocutors and thus is given only *a posteriori*. At first he suggests that the discrepancy between the original article and the additions is due to the ill faith of his accusers who (from the first day) were labouring to charge him of advancing the king's will above the Law and therefore could not longer maintain that he had acted against the king's Prerogative in the additional articles. Then he maximises his face-

20 The opening inverted comas at the beginning of each line indicate that the paragraph was inserted by Laud at a subsequent stage of writing and was not part of his original speech in the trial.

attack by suggesting the possibility that they were wilfully denying the existence of Royal prerogatives, which would make them (and not him) the real traitors of the kingdom. In either case, Laud attempts to undermine the reliability of the Commons so as to create consensus around his self-presentation as victim of their envy and maliciousness. He concludes his argumentation by inviting his opponents to justify their actions but since no answer follows, the validity of his claims appears self-evident.

The next interpolation ('...') shows how Laud takes advantage of his favourable position as *a posteriori* narrator in order to integrate his on-line defence with more meditated considerations:

> 'For I never justified the making or having of that Picture. For Calvin's Rule that we picture that 'which may be seen is grounded upon the Negative, that no Picture may be made of that which 'was never seen. And to ground this Negative, is the Command given by Moses, Deut. Iv. 15–16 '*Take good heed to yourselves.* For what? That you make not to yourselves this Picture. Why? '*For that you saw no Manner of Similitude in the Day that the Lord spake unto you out of the 'midst of the Fire*...Exodus. xx. 21. So no Picture of him, because no Similitude ever seen. And 'this Rule having ever possessed me wholly, I could not justify the having of it'. I said indeed 'that some Men in later superstitious Times were so foolish so as to picture God the Father, by 'occasion of that place in *Daniel:* But for myself I ever rejected it...
>
> (I, 895)

The rhetorical questions *(for what?, why?)* are addressee-oriented and serve to foster the audience's involvement in the strength of the argumentation. Laud's defence here turns into an occasion for preaching so as to enhance the force of his Protestant creed and persuade the reader of his good faith. In this regard, the precise reference to the Holy Scriptures is given as showing his strict adherence to biblical teaching and as ultimately revealing of his truthfulness of heart.

The third manipulation of the original proceeding concerns the omission of repetitions of charges and answers which have already been given. Time and again the reader is invited to refer to previous or subsequent sections of the account where the same accusation or answer has been provided. Laud's preference for linearity in the telling opposes the redundant style strategically promoted by his adversaries to gather consensus among auditors who changed everyday.

> 'This Business was left by the Serjeant to Mr Maynard, who made the most that could be out of 'my Diary against me: And so did Mr Browne, when he came to give the Sum of the Charge 'against me, both before the Lords and the House of Commons. And therefore for avoiding of 'all tedious Repetition, and for that the Arguments which both used are the same, and because I 'hold it not fit to break a Charge of this moment into divers Pieces, or put them in different 'Places, I will set down the whole Business together and the Answer which I then gave.
>
> (I, 888)

> 'And this hath been their Art all along, to run over the same Thing twice and again..., to the end 'that as the Auditors changed, the more of them might hear it; and that which wrought not upon 'some, might upon others. In all which I patiently referred myself to my former Answers, 'having no other way to help myself.
>
> (I, 893)

Although contemporaries reported the benevolence of 17th-century Court towards defendants (Beattie 1986: 345), Laud's re-structuring of the trial suggests how detrimental the entire procedure was to his cause.

4.4.3.2 Epistemic stance

Laud systematically indulges in evaluative comments on the partiality and unreliability of the witnesses for the prosecution. He does so by overtly stating that:

1) they are single and in their own cause
2) they are great enemies to him
3) they have been instructed by the prosecution
4) they speak with the sole purpose of aggravating the accusation.

It is possible to identify a general pattern of witness-introduction in Laud's account which features 1) the name of the witness 2) one of the above comments 3) the evidence reported. Consider the following examples:

After this Man's Testimony, comes *Mr Prynn* himself in his own Cause. He made a long Relation of the Business, and full of Bitterness against me. This I doubt not was puposely done to represent me as odious as he could to the Lords and the Hearers...First then he says...

(I, 856)

The first [witness] is *Grafton* in his own Cause: And 'tis much if he cannot tell a Plausible Tale for himself. He says first that...

(I, 862)

The next Witness is *Mr Ward*; and he is an angry witness, for his Cause before mentioned about Simony. That which he says is...

(I, 866)

The third Witness is *Mr Talboyes*, (who, it seems, will not be out of anything which may seem to hurt me). He says that...

(I, 875)

The sixth Instance concerns the putting of one Mr Grant out of his Right. He says, (but he is single, and in his own cause) that...

(I, 877)

The second Charge was laid on me by *Sir Arthur Hafelrig... Sir Arthur* being single and in his own Cause says...

(I, 879)

Then I was accused for setting old Popish Canons above the Laws. *Mr Burton* is the sole Witness. He says, it was...

(I, 877)

The third Witness was *Mr Anthony Mildmay;* a Man not thought on for a Witness until I called for his Brother *Sir Henry.* But now he comes laden with this Brother's Language. He says...

(I, 897)

The Witnesses, the two Church-wardens, *Colliar* and *Wilson*; two plain Men, but of Great Memories: for this Business was when I was Bishop of *London*, and yet they agree in every Circumstance, in every Word, tho' so many Years since. Well, what say they?

(I, 875)

In some cases Laud discredits the witnesses after their evidence. His value judgements are often coloured with a distancing irony, which is a salient feature of his attitude in the trial:

> Then about taking down of a Pew in a Church in London, which Pew was set above the Commission-Table...that they came to me to have an Order for it; and that thereupon I should say, *You desire an Order of Court, that you may have it to shew, and get a Prohibition; but I will break the back of Prohibitions, or they shall break mine.* And this is jointly witnessed by Mr Pocock and Mr Langham: and this they say was thirteen or fourteen Years ago. Excellent Memories that can punctually swear Words so long after!
>
> (I, 865)

The following comment is marked as an insertion intended to denounce the strong partiality of the Court. As a result it functions as an additional defence provided *a posteriori*:

> 'For Mr Wakerly, he is a *Dutchman* born; and how far the Testimony of an Alien many be of 'Force by the Law, I know not: And a bitter Enemy to me he hath ever shewed himself, since I 'complained to the King and the Lords that a Stranger born and bred should be so near a 'Secretary of State, and all his Papers and Cyphers, as he was known to be to Mr Secretary 'Coke. A Thing which few States would endure. And how far the Testimony of such a canker'd 'Enemy should be admitted, let the World judge. Admitted he was.
>
> (I, 916)

In the last example below Laud exploits the interactional structure of his telling to downplay the reliability of the witness's proposition:

> He adds that if he remembers well, the Alteration was drawn by me. But if he do not remember well, what then? Surely here's no Evidence to be grounded upon *ifs*.
>
> (I, 916)

This strong authorial interference responds to Laud's design to bias the readers' impression-formation of the hostile witnesses so as to ensure the rejection of their reported claims.

4.4.3.3 Attitudinal stance

Laud's attitude is expressed through the three paradigms of humility, Christian mercy and distancing irony. Each attitudinal position emerges as a result of its opposition to the accusers' discourse behaviour. In this sense, his humility/patience has to be read in relation to the opponents' violence/foolishness, his mercy as opposed to their maliciousness/wickedness and his irony/sarcasm as a counter-attack to their plotting. Laud's self-representation is carried out through a combination of telling and showing. This means that at times his attitude in the Court is communicated to the reader by means of evaluative lexis (basically adverbs), while in other cases it manifests itself in his discourse behaviour and has to be worked out by the reader. The value judgements about his accusers' conduct are conveyed through overt comments and evaluative lexis.

I shall start with an analysis of the humility/patience *vs* violence/foolishness paradigm. In Laud's trial there are more than 100 occurrences of the style adjunct "humbly" used as modifiers of the defendant's speech acts addressed to the Court. I report some examples:

I humbly petitioned
I humbly desired
I humbly thank their Lordships
I humbly prayed
But do most humbly pray
I humbly craved
I humbly conceived

Although it is a common practice for defendants to mitigate their requests through the adverb "humbly" as a conventional marker of deference, on more than one occasion Laud juxtapposes the adverb ***humbly*** with words referring to the violence and coarseness of his opponents' manners so as to stress the attitudinal clash between the two. In this way, the collocation of ***humbly*** contributes to the construction of ideologically biased discourse. Consider the following example where the adversative conjunction ***but*** highlights the attitudinal and ideological contrast between the Christian patience of the defendant and the bombastic style ("he grew higher and higher") and violent attitude of the accuser :

> When I came to the Bar Mr Nicolas began with great Violence, and told the Lords, the Business grew higher and higher against me. What the Business did will after appear; but I am sure he grew higher and higher: and from this time forwards, besides the Violence of Expression gave me such Language, as no Christian would give a Jew. But God, I humbly thank him, blessed me with Patience; and so I made my Ears obedient.
>
> (I, 905)

In order to denounce the uncontrolled rudeness of his accuser Mr *Nicolas*, Laud indulges in the use of intensifiers ("extremely", "insomuch that", "many and gros", "over and over again") which are intended to elicit the readers' disapproval of the accusation and encourage their distancing from the unacceptable procedure:

> Here Mr *Nicolas* fell extremely foul upon me, insomuch that I could not but wonder at their Patience which heard me. Among other Titles bestowed upon me, many and gros, he called me over and over again *Pander to the Whore of Babylon*. I was much moved and humbly desired my Lords, that if my Crimes were such as that I might not be used like an Archbishop, yet I might be used like a Christian. (I, 915)

The next attitudinal paradigm concerns the mercifulness of the Archbishop *vs* the malevolence of the accusers. On more than one occasion Laud adds an interpolation where he demonstrates his mercy towards those who are maliciously acting against him. This may be read as a subtle strategy engineered by the Archbishop in order to disguise his moral criticism of the accusers under the pretence of being benevolent and merciful to them. The only target of this ***a posteriori*** paradigm is the reader who is led to approve of Laud's Christianity as opposed to the witnesses' amorality.

> 'As for Mr *Greece* [a witness] who hath laboured much against me in all this Business, God 'forgive him; and while he inherits his Father's ill Affections to me, God preserve him from his 'Father's End.
>
> (I, 891)

> Yet the second Witness, Mr *Tomlyns*, says also, that I justify this Picture. 'God forgive him the Malice or Ignorance of this Oath, be it which it will.
>
> (I, 894)

> The first Witness for this was *Quaterman,* a bitter Enemy of mine; God forgive him.
>
> (I, 901)

> … so soon as he came, fell to his wonted railing, and asked aloud, *What the Lords meant, to be troubled so long and so often, with such a base Fellow as I was? They should do well to hang me out of the way.* I heard the Words with Grief enough and so left them and him in the Hands of God.
>
> (I, 905)

In the last example the reference to divine judgement makes the expression particularly indeterminate as to Laud's real intentions. Indeed the force of the propostion appears to oscillate between mercy (as Laud restrains from judging them) and open threat, in line with the view of God as an implacable and righteous judge. By and large it can be argued that Laud exploits the politeness paradigm of mercifulness as a means of engaging in 'impolite civility' (Johnson and Clifford 2011). Put simply, he uses a "masking merciful attitude" to "varnish" otherwise (theoretically) blameworthy attacks on his adversaries.

Laud's use of irony/sarcasm as a countermove to his opponents' plotting is the third and last paradigm which characterises his attitudinal stance. By and large distancing irony and sarcasm are used as a means of reciprocating the hostility of his accusers without sinking in their excesses. Consider the following examples:

> And the House of Commons, by their Order, agreed to the Lords, that should have Copies of any of the Papers for the Defence taken from me, but it should be at my own Charge. Wonderful Favour this, and as much Justice! My Estate all taken from me and my Goods sold, before ever I came to Hearing; and then I may take Copies of my Papers at my own Charge
>
> (I, 834)

> The second Proof was my procuring from the King such Impropriations in *Ireland* as were in the King's Power, to the Church of Ireland. [Which Mr *Nicolas* (in his gentle Language) calls Robbin' of the Crown]
>
> (I, 877)

The positive evaluative lexis *(wonderful, favour, Justice, gentle)* is here charged with clear hostile intentions so as to mean the opposite of what is said. In all probability even his exclamation in the previous extract (Wonderful Favour this, and as much Justice!) has been added at the time of narration thus creating an interesting interplay between the Commons – defendant and the defendant – reader discourse levels.

On several occasions the Archbishop's ironic attitude detemines a systematic shift of pragmatic meaning in a group of evaluative lexemes with positive semantic value. By means of illustration, the words *carefully* and *diligent* when collocating with the names of the accusers (*Mr Prynn* in four cases out of five) automatically assume a negative connotation which extends to the entire proposition. In so doing the Archbishop creates a representational frame where the notion of *care* (when referred to the adversaries) is encoded as synonymous with treacherousness and labour performed with the only purpose to damage both his personal and institutional face[21].

> The third Witness was Sir *Nathaniel Brent* (now absent but coming the next day). He says I was esteemed popishly-affected in *Oxford*; and he gave three instances very carefully to prove it.
>
> (I, 917)

> Mr *Nicolas* added That this was seconded by Bishop *Mountague's* Book [Mount. Orig. Eccles. p. 464] which Mr *Prynn* (carefully) witnessed was found in my study and licensed by Dr *Bray*. Is this Argument come again that Bishop *Mountague's* Book was in my study?
>
> (I, 914)

> [And that is true; some Impediments there were, no doubt, or else I had come sooner to Hearing. And as a conceive a chief Impediment was there was not a Man whose Malice would make him diligent enough to search into such a forsaken business till Mr *Prynn* offered himself].
>
> (I, 840)

---

21 Representational frames equate to the way(s) in which interlocutors opt to 'represent the character traits, ideas and opinions of and even statements made by others' (Locher and Watts 2008: 99, *f*.9).

> The third Witness was Mr *Prynn*. He says He had taken a Survey of the Windows at *Lambeth* and I doubt not his Diligence.
>
> (I, 887)
>
> In this diligent and curious Search (from Mr *Prynn*'s Malice made it) they found some Papers concerning Parliaments...
>
> (I, 905)

The construction of this reality paradigm is consistent with Laud's *a posteriori* invectives against the politically biased character of the accusation:

> '...and whether this do not look like a Thing plotted by the Faction so much imbittered against 'me, let understanding Men judge].
>
> (I, 867)
>
> 'That's only the Construction made on't at the Bar; which, as it is without all Proof for any such 'Intention, so I am confident they shall answer for it at another Bar, and for something else in 'these Proceedings.
>
> (I, 865)

The analysis has brought to light some of the discourse strategies adopted by Laud in the attempt to convince the reader of his innocence. The notion of representational frames has proved crucial in this regard as it has enhanced our understanding of the devices used by the Archbishop in order to frame himself as victim of the cunning manipulations of the Commons. The persuasiveness of the text has been fostered by strategies activated at the level of style (discourse organisation, reporting modes, evaluative interpolations), epistemology (e.g. through repetitive patterns for discrediting witnesses) and attitude (basically expressed through the construction of representational frames which oppose the defendant's good-faith to the accusers' maliciousness). As recorder and protagonist of the trial, Laud has privileged mimesis for his self-representation, so that rather than evaluating his conduct for the readers (as was the case when referring to his accusers), he has left them the task of sense-making and interpretation. Obviously the readership has only been given the illusion of autonomous judgement, as all the time reality comes to them filtered through the ideological stance of the author.

4.5 Conclusion

Prominent political trials were one of the favourite propaganda forms exploited both by Royalists and Parliamentarians in coordination with other political manoeuvres. Indeed, as Peacey points out, the publication of trial proceedings was intended to

> affect public opinion regarding individuals who were perceived to hold sway over the popular imagination, and whose judicial treatment was likely to provoke political unrest and civil disorder, as well as in support of everyday political activity and the work of key parliamentary committees.
> (2004: 266)

Strafford, Laud and Hamilton stood charged for their roles in Charles I's Personal Rule and for their unlawful acting against the kingdom. The three trials extend through a period which encompasses the most salient phases of the Parliament's revolution from 1641 (pre-civil war phase with the trial of Strafford) through 1644 (central phase with the trial of Laud) up to 1649 (concluding phase of the civil war with the trial of Hamilton). While Hamilton was basically tried for his military invasion of England to assist the king, against the kingdom and his people, Strafford and Laud were respectively indicted for their constitutional and clerical usurpation of the sovereign power in the 1630s. If at the time of Strafford's trial the king's political and personal body were still conceived of as a unity, in Laud's and Hamilton's proceedings the charge of treason was grounded on the separability of the king's two bodies. In this way the accusation was able to frame the Royalist prisoners as guilty of treason against the Crown despite their acting under the king's authorisation. Paradoxically, this new ideological framing represented Parliamentarians as the only supporters of the sovereign power thus corroborating Friggis's claim that [Commoners] "pretended that the Parliament took up arms against the person of the King, but in support of his authority". (Orr 2002: 109).

The three documents in the State Trials are all propaganda texts of Royalist stance intended to construct and promote consensus over the defendants through different forms of ventriloquy. In this sense they share several similarities in terms of discourse construction. Nonetheless, the different positioning of the recorders – two being Royalist observers and one being the protagonist of his own trial – also determines differences concerning event-representation. In this concluding section I shall resume my findings by first providing a list of similarities among the texts and then discussing some of their differences related to the external *vs* internal authorial stance of the recorder.

All three trials emphasise the prisoner's defence by

- foregrounding the eloquence of the defendant (either through DS or evaluative lexis) despite the Commoners' attempt to cast him in a rigid and prefabricated script
- omitting some of the accusers' speeches or reporting them through NRSA so as to downplay their effect
- commenting overtly on the accusers' linguistic violence and maliciousness
- denouncing the premeditation of the accusation
- modifying the original trial script so as to expand the prisoner's defence with additions
- ridiculing the accusers' speeches through parody or irony
- discrediting the hostile witnesses' testimony.

The three trials however also differ in important respects. In the trial of Strafford and Hamilton, for example, the external perspective of the reporters favours a higher use of evaluative lexis for representing the prisoner or his counsel so that the reader is provided with a ready-made interpretation of their attitude ("Measure of Eloquence and Livelyhood", "a wonderful Prudence", "corageously", "moderately", "in an excellent Method", "boldly", "learnedly", "elegantly"). This is not the case in Laud's trial where the Archbishop privileges a self-representation through *showing*, so that, with the exception of the formulaic adverb "humbly" and a few cases of "patiently", there are no overt evaluative markers of his behaviour. In this regard, however, it is worth bearing in mind that although the reader is given the illusion that s/he is making his/her own judgement of the qualities of the defendant, the interpretative process is constantly guided by the authorial control.

Another major difference between Laud's trial and the other two regards its larger use of overt comments on the injustice of the proceedings and the unreliability of the accusation. As a matter of fact, while the Royalist authors attempt to preserve an aura of neutrality by favouring internal evaluation devices such as explicatives (though, because, since, even so), negation, impersonal lexico-syntactic patterns of evaluation (it + link verb + adj. phrase + clause) and forms of veiled parody, Laud takes full advantage of his authorial and authoritative voice to discredit the counterpart overtly by means of interpolations and evaluative comments.

The analysis of the three trials has revealed the importance of the defendants' representation in the courtroom both in the form of other-representation (trial of Strafford and Hamilton) and self-representation (trial of W. Laud) for the propaganda purposes of the author. Several discourse strategies are used by the reporters in order to vindicate the subservient role of the defendant through his framing in the *a posteriori* account. By means of illustration, the rigid court script which has proved to be necessarily detrimental to the prisoner undergoes interesting structural changes in the Royalist renditions. As a result the defendant is given more opportunity to make his claims and expand his defence and the reader is scrupulously guided in the interpretation of the accusers' premeditated conduct against the defendant. Evaluative lexis and overt comments do the rest, foregrounding the good-faith of the prisoner and eliciting the audience's ideological consensus on his person and institutional status. In this way, while the role of defendant in a high treason trial would cast him in a no-win situation from the onset of the proceeding (e.g., through an assumption of guilt, the imposition of an unfavourable pleading script, very restricted use of counsel, no opportunity to reply to the charges until the end, admission of single and unreliable witnesses), the printed trial ensures his rehabilitation in the collective memory. This was a priority among Royalists, who were about to witness the collapse of the monarchy under the attacks of the Parliament. In a few years England would become a Republic.

Bibliography

Corpora

A Corpus of English Dialogues 1560–1760. 2006. Compiled under the supervision of Merja Kytö (Uppsala University) and Jonathan Culpeper (Lancaster University).

OBP (*Old Bailey Proceedings Online*) *The Proceedings of the Old Bailey, 1674–1913*. <www.oldbaileyonline.org> (accessed 7 March 2010).

ST (*State Trials*). *A Complete Collection of State Trials, and Proceedings for High Treason, and Other Crimes and Misdemeanours; From the Reign of King Richard II to the Reign of King George II*. <http://www.constitution.org/trials/ccst1742/ccst1742.htm> (accessed 7 March 2010).

Primary Sources

Burnet, G. ([1677] 1852) *The Memoirs of the Lives and Actions of James and William Dukes of Hamilton and Castle-Herald*. Oxford.

Campbell, John (1849–1857) *The Lives of the Chief Justices of England. From the Norman Conquest to the Death of Lord Tenterden*. In three volumes. London: John Murray.

Clarendon, Edward, Hyde earl of (1702–1704) *The History of the Rebellion and Civil War in England, begun in the year 1641. With the precedents passages, and actions, that contributed thereunto, and the happy end, and conclusion thereof by the king's blessed restoration, and return upon 29th of May in the year 1660*. Oxford.

De Veil, Thomas (1748) *Memoirs of the Life and Times of Sir Thomas Deveil, Knight*. London.

Guizot, F.M. and W. Hazlitt ([1826] 1856) *History of the English Revolution of 1640: from the accession of Charles I to his death*. London: Savill and Edwards printers.

Hawkins, William (1721). *A Treatise of the Pleas of the Crown.* Vol. 2. London.

HMC, *12th Report, The Manuscript of the Earl Cowper...Preserved at Melbourne Hall, Derbyshire,* (1888), ii. 282.

Hawles, John Sir (1689) *Remarks upon the Tryals of Edward Fitzharris, Stephen Colledge, count Coningsmark, the lord Russel, collonel Sydney, Henry Cornish, and Charles Bateman: as also the earl of Shaftsbury's grand jury, Wilmore's Homine replegiando, and the award of execution against Sir Thomas Armstrong.* London: Printed for Jacob Tonson.

Heylyn, Peter (1645) *A briefe relation of the death and sufferings of the most reverend and renowned prelate the L. Archbishop of Canterbury.* London.

Laud William, Henry Wharton, Edmund Wharton (1695) *The History of the Troubles and Tryal: the second volume of the remains of the most Reverend father in God, and blessed martyr, William Laud, lord arch-bishop of Canterbury.*

May, Thomas ([1647] 1854) *The History of the Parliament of England.* Oxford: Oxford University Press.

Prynne, William (1644) *A Breviate of the Life of William Laud, Arch-bishop of Canterbury: Extracted (for the most part) verbatim out of his owne Diary, and other Writings under his owne Hand.* London.

Prynne, William (1646) *Canterburies Doome. Or, The First Part of a Complete History of the Commitment, Charge, Tryall, Condemnation, execution of William Laud Late Archbishop of Canterbury.* London.

Roscoe, Henry and Thomas Roscoe (1825) *Westminster Hall or Professional Relics and Anecdotes of the Bar, Bench and Woolsack.* Vol. III. London: John Knight and Henry Lacey.

— (1646) *Canterburies Doome. Or, The First Part of a Complete History of the Commitment, Charge, Tryall, Condemnation, Execution of William Laud Late Archbishop of Canterbury.* London.

Rushworth John (1680) *The Tryal of Thomas Earle of Strafford upon an impeachment of high treason.* London.

Rushworth, John (1692) *Historical Collections,* vol. III: 1639–1640. London.

Somers, John (1748) *A Collection of Scarce and Valuable Tracts on the most Interesting and Entertaining Subjects: but chiefly as relate to the History and Constitution of these Kingdoms.* London.

References

Aijmer, Karin (1996) *Conversational Routines in English: Convention and Creativity.* Harlow: Longman.

Archer, Dawn E. (2002) "'Can Innocent people be guilty?' A Socio-pragmatic analysis of examination transcripts from Salem Witchcraft Trials", *Journal of Historical Pragmatics,* 3: 1: 1–30.

Archer, Dawn E. (2005) *Questions and Answers in the English Courtroom (1640–1760): A Socio-pragmatic Analysis.* Amsterdam: John Benjamins.

Archer, Dawn E. (2006) "(Re)initiating strategies. Judges and defendants in Early Modern English courtrooms". *Journal of Historical Pragmatics,* 7: 2: 181–211.

Archer, Dawn E. (2008) "Verbal aggression and impoliteness: Related or synonims?". In D. Bousfield and M. Locher (eds.). *Impoliteness in Language. Studies on its Interplay with Power in Theory and Practice.* Berlin, New York: Mouton de Gruyter, 181–207.

Archer, Dawn E. (2011a) "Facework and im/politeness across legal contexts: An Introduction". *Impoliteness and facework across legal contexts – Special Edition of the Journal of Politeness Research,* vol. 7: 1–19.

Archer, Dawn E. (2011b) "Libelling Oscar Wilde: The case of Regina vs. John Sholto Douglas". *Impoliteness and facework across legal contexts – Special Edition of the Journal of Politeness Research,* vol. 7: 73–99.

Archer, Dawn E. (2011c) Lawyers, facework and *the adversarial courtroom. Journal of Pragmatics* vol. 43 (13): 3216–3230.

Austin, Paddy (1990) "Politeness revisited: The dark side". In Allan Bell and Janet Holmes (eds.). *New Zealand Ways of Speaking English.* Philadelphia: Multinlingual Matters, 277–293.

Baker, John H. (1990) *An Introduction to English Legal History.* London: Butterworths.

Bakhtin, M.M. (1981) *The Dialogic Imagination,* trans. by C. Emerson and M. Holquist, Austin: University of Texas Press.

Beattie, John M. (1986) *Crime and the Courts in England 1660–1800.* Oxford: Clarendon Press.

Bennett, W. Lance and Martha S. Feldman (1981) *Reconstructing Reality in the Courtroom.* London and New York: Tavistock Publications.

Bertuccelli Papi, Marcella (2000) "Is a Diachronic Speech Act Theory Possible?" *Journal of Historical Pragmatics* 1 (1): 56–66.

Biber, Douglas (1988) *Variation Across Speech and Writing.* Cambridge: Cambridge University Press.

Biber, Douglas and Finegan, Edward (1989) "Styles of stance in English: lexical and grammatical marking of evidentiality and affect". *Text*, 9: 93–124.

Biber, Douglas and Finegan, Edward (1992) "The linguistic evolution of five written, speech-based English genres from the 17th to the 20th centuries". In M. Rissanen, O. Ihalainen, T. Nevelainen and I. Taavitsainen (eds.). *New Methods and Interpretations in Historical Linguistics*. Berlin: Mouton de Gruyter, 688–704.

Blum-Kulka, Shoshana (1982) "Learning to say what you mean in a second language: a study of the speech-act of performance learners of Hebrew as a second language". *Applied Linguistics* 3(1): 29–59.

Blum-Kulka, Shoshana (1987) "Indirectness and politeness in requests: Same or different?" *Journal of Pragmatics* 11: 131–146.

Blum-Kulka, Shoshana (1989) "Playing it safe: The role of conventionality in indirectness". In Shoshana Blum-Kulka, Juliane House and Gabriele Kapser (eds.). *Cross-cultural Pragmatics: Requests and Apologies*. Vol. XXXI. Advances in Discourse Processes. Norwood NJ: Ablex, 37–70.

Blum-Kulka, Shoshana, Brenda, Danet & Gherson, Rimona (1985) "The language of requesting in Israeli society". In Joseph Forgas (ed.). *Language and Social Situation*. New York: Springer Verlag, 113–141.

Blum-Kulka, Shoshana, House, Juliane, & Kasper, Gabriele (eds.) (1989) *Cross Cultural Pragmatics: Requests and Apologies*. Vol. XXXI. Advances in Discourse Processes. Norwood NJ: Ablex.

Bousfield, Derek (2008) *Impoliteness in Interaction*. (Pragmatics & Beyond New Series 167) Amsterdam and Philadelphia: John Benjamins.

Bousfield, Derek and Locher, Miriam A. (2008) *Impoliteness in Language. Studies on its Interplay with Power in Theory and Practice*. Berlin, New York: Mouton de Gruyter.

Brown, Penelope and Gilman, A. (1960) "The pronouns of power and solidarity". In T.A. Sebeok (ed.). *Style in Language*. Cambridge, MA: MIT Press, 253–276.

Brown, Penelope and Gilman, A. (1989) "Politeness theory and Shakespeare's four major tragedies". *Language in Society*, 18: 159–212.

Brown, Penelope and Levinson, Stephen C. (1978) "Universals in language usage: Politeness phenomena". In E.N. Goody (ed.). *Questions and Politeness: Strategies in Social Interaction*. Cambridge: Cambridge University Press, 56–289.

Brown, Penelope and Levinson, Stephen C. (1987) *Politeness: Some Universals in Language Usage*. Cambridge: Cambridge University Press.

Brownlees, Nicholas (2005) "'Sir, I am not an ordinary prisoner': terms of address and self-presentation in the trial of Charles I". In Bertacca A. (ed.). *Historical Linguistic Studies of Spoken English*. Pisa: Plus, 175–183.

Brownlees, Nicholas (2005) "Spoken Discourse in Early English Newspapers". *Media History* 11(1/2): 69–85.

Brownlees, Nicholas (2006) "Gerrard Winstanley and Radical Political Discourse in Cromwellian England". In M. Dossena and I. Taavitsainen (eds.). *Diachronic Perspectives on Domain-Specific English.* Bern: Peter Lang, 19–39.

Brownlees, Nicholas (2011) *The Language of Periodical News in Seventeenth-Century England.* Newcastle upon Tyne: Cambridge Scholars Publishing.

Butler, Martin (1987) *Theatre and Crisis 1632–1642.* Cambridge: Cambridge University Press.

Carlton, Charles (1987) *Archbishop William Laud.* London: Routledge and Kegan Paul.

Cecconi, Elisabetta (2011) "Power confrontation and verbal duelling in the arraignment section of 17th century trials". *Impoliteness and facework across legal contexts – Special Edition of the Journal of Politeness Research,* vol. 7: 101–121.

Cecconi, Elisabetta (2010) "Witness narratives in seventeenth century trial proceedings: a case study of public discourse". In Nicholas Brownlees, Gabriella Del Lungo and John Denton (eds.). *The language of public and private communication in a historical perspective.* Newcastle upon Tyne: Cambridge Scholars Publishing, 245–262.

Cecconi, Elisabetta (2009) "'Ye Tories round the Nation': an analysis of markers of interactive-involved discourse in 17th century political broadside ballads". *The Nordic Journal of English Studies,* 8 (3): 59–85.

Cecconi, Elisabetta (2008) "Legal discourse and linguistic incongruities in Bardell vs Pickwick: an analysis of address and reference strategies in *The Pickwick Papers* trial scene". *Language and Literature,* 17 (3): 205–219.

Chaemsaithong, Krisda (2009) "Re-visiting Salem: Self-Face and self-Politeness in the Salem Witchcraft Trials". *Journal of Historical Pragmatics* 10(1): 56–83.

Clark, G. Kitson (1967) *The Critical Historian.* London: Heinemann.

Clegg, Stewart R. (1989) *Frameworks of Power.* London: Sage.

Collins, Daniel (2001) *Reanimated Voices. Speech reporting in a historical-pragmatic perspective.* Amsterdam/Philadelphia: John Benjamins.

Conrad, Susan and Biber, Douglas (2001) "Adverbial Marking of Stance in Speech and Writing". In Susan Hunston and Geoff Thompson (eds.). *Evaluation in Text,* Oxford: Oxford University Press, 56–73.

Cressy, David (2006) *England on Edge: Crisis and Revolution 1640–1642.* Oxford: Oxford University Press.

Culpeper, Jonathan (1996) "Towards an anatomy of impoliteness". *Journal of Pragmatics,* 25: 349–367.

Culpeper, Jonathan (1998) "(Im)politeness in drama". In P. Verdonk, M. Short and J. Culpeper (eds.). *Exploring the Language of Drama: From Text to Context,* London: Routledge, 83–95.

Culpeper, Jonathan (2005) "Impoliteness and entertainment in the television quiz show: *The Weakest Link*". *Journal of Politeness Research* 1 (1): 35–72.

Culpeper, Jonathan, Bousfield, Derek and Wichmann, A. (2003) "Impoliteness revisited: with special reference to dynamic and prosodic aspects". *Journal of Pragmatics,* 35: 1545–1579.

Culpeper, Jonathan (2008) "Reflections on impoliteness, relational work and power". In D. Bousfield and M.A. Locher (eds.). *Impoliteness in Language. Studies on its Interplay with Power in Theory and Practice.* Berlin, New York: Mouton de Gruyter, 17–44.

Culpeper, Jonathan and Archer, Dawn E. (2008) "Requests and directness in Early Modern English trial proceedings and play texts, 1640–1760" in A. Jucker, and I. Taavitsainen (eds.). *Speech Acts in the History of English.* [Pragmatics & Beyond New Series 176]. Amsterdam: John Benjamins, 45–84.

Culpeper Jonathan and Kytö, Merja (2000a) "Gender voices in the spoken interaction of the past: A pilot study based on early modern English trial proceedings". In D. Kastovsky and A. Mettinger (eds.). *The History of English in a Social Context.* Berlin: Mouton de Gruyter, 53–98.

Culpeper, Jonathan and Kytö, Merja (2000b) "Spoken interaction (re)cast as writing". *Journal of Historical Pragmatics,* 1(2): 175–199.

Cust, R. (1986) "News and Politics in early 17th century England". *Past and Present,* 112(1): 60–90.

Dandelion, Pink B. (2008) *The Quakers. A very short introduction.* Oxford: Oxford University Press.

Danet, Brenda (1980) "Language in the Legal Process". *Law and Society Review,* 14: 3, 445–565.

Doty, Kathleen and Hiltunen, Risto (2002) "'I will tell, I will tell'. Confession patterns in the Salem witchcraft Trials". *Journal of Historical Pragmatics* 3(2): 299–335.

Doty, Kathleen L. (2007) "Telling tales. The role of scribes in constructing the discourse of the Salem witchcraft Trials". *Journal of Historical Pragmatics* 8(1): 25–41.

Eelen, Gino (2001) *A Critique of Politeness Theories.* Manchester, UK: St. Jerome Publishing.

Fairclough, Norman (1989) *Language and Power.* London: Longman.

Fowler, Roger (1985) "Power". In T.A. van Dijk (ed.). *Handbook of Discourse Analysis vol. 4: Discourse Analysis in Society.* London: Academic Press, 61–82.

Gibbons, J. (2003) *Forensic Linguistics: an introduction to language in the judicial system.* Malden, MA: Blackwell.

Goffman, Erwin (1967) *Interactional Rituals: Essays on Face-to-.face Behaviour.* Garden City, NY: Anchor Books.

Goodrich, P. (1988) "Modalities of annunciation: an introduction to courtroom speech". In R. Levelson (ed.). *Law and Semiotics,* vol. 2. New York: Plenum Press, 143–165.

Grice, H. Paul (1975) "Logic and conversation". In Peter Cole and Jerry L. Morgan (eds.). *Syntax and Semantics, Vol. 3: Speech Acts.* New York: Academic Press, 41–58.

Halliday, M.A.K. [1985] (1994) *Introduction to Functional Grammar.* 2nd Edition. London: Edward Arnold.

Heinemann, Margaret (1982) *Puritanism and Theatre.* Cambridge: Cambridge University Press.

Hiltunen, Risto and Peikola, Matti (2007) "Trial discourse and manuscript context. Scribal profiles in the Salem witchcraft records". *Journal of Historical Pragmatics* 8(1): 43–68.

Holmes, Janet and Stubbe, Maria (2003) *Power and Politeness in the Workplace. A sociolinguistic analysis of talk at work.* London: Longman.

Hostettler, J. (2006) *Fighting for Justice: the history and origins of adversary trial.* Winchester: Waterside Press.

Irvine, Judith T. (1995) "Honorifics". In Jan-Ola Ostman, Jef Verschueren and Jan Blommaert (eds.) *Handbook of Pragmatics.* Amsterdam: John Benjamins.

Jakobs, Andreas and Jucker, Andreas H. (1995) "The historical perspective in pragmatics". In A.H. Jucker (ed.). *Historical Pragmatics. Pragmatic Development in the History of English* (Pragmatics and Beyond New Series 35) Amsterdam/Philadelphia: John Benjamins, 3–36.

Jucker, Andreas H. (2000) "Historical Pragmatics: Problems of Data and Methodology", in Gabriella Di Martino and Maria Lima (eds.). *English Diachronic Pragmatics,* Naples: CUEN, 17–55.

Jucker, Andreas H. and Taavitsainen Irma (2000). "Diachronic speech act analysis. Insults from flyting to flaming". *JHP,* 1(1): 67–92.

Jucker, Andreas and Taavitsainen, Irma (eds.) (2008) *Speech acts in the history of English.* (Pragmatics and Beyond New Series) Amsterdam/Philadelphia. John Benjamins.

Kahlas-Tarkka, Leena and Rissanen, Matti (2007). "The sullen and the talkative: Discourse strategies in the Salem examinations". *Journal of Historical Pragmatics* 8: 1–24.

Kahlas-Tarkka, Leena and Rissanen, Matti (2011) "Attitudes of the accused in the Salem Witchcraft trials". In Patha Päivi and Andreas Jucker (eds.). *Communicating Early English Manuscripts.* Cambridge: Cambridge University Press, 241–258.

Kenyon, John P. (1972) *The Popish Plot.* Harmondsworth: Penguin.

Kilburn, T. and Milton A. (2002) "The public context of the trial and execution of Strafford". In J.F. Merritt (ed.). *The Political World of Thomas Wentworth Earl of Strafford 1621–1641.* Cambridge: Cambridge University Press, 230–251.

Koch, Peter (1999) "Court records and cartoons: reflections of spontaneous dialogue in Early Romance texts". In A.H. Jucker, G. Fritz and F. Lebsanft (eds). *Historical Dialogue Analysis.* Amsterdam/Philadelphia. John Benjamins.

Kohnen, Thomas (2002) "Towards a history of English directives". In Andreas Fischer, Gunnel Tottie and Hans Martin Lehmann (eds.). *Text Types and Corpora. Studies in Honour of Udo Fries.* Tübingen: Gunter Narr, 165–175.

Kohnen, Thomas (2004) "Let me be so bold to request you to tell me:Constructions with 'let me' and the history of English directives". *Journal of Historical Pragmatics* 5 (1): 159–173.

Kryk-Kastovsky, Barbara (2000) "Representations of orality in Early Modern English trial records". *Journal of Historical Pragmatics* 1 (2): 201–230.

Kryk-Kastovsky, Barbara (2006) "Impoliteness in Early Modern Courtroom Discourse". *Journal of Historical Pragmatics,* 7 (2): 213–243.

Kryk-Kastovsky, Barbara (2010) "Power in Early Modern English courtroom discourse". In Sanna-Kaisa Tanskanen, Marija-Liisa Helasvuo, Marjut Johansson. *Discourses in Interaction.* Amsterdam/Philadelphia: John Benjamins, 153–171.

Labov William and Waletzky, Joshua (1967) "Narrative analysis: Oral versions of personal experience". In J. Helms (ed.). *Essays on the verbal and visual arts.* Seattle: University of Washington Press, 12–44.

Lachenicht, Lance G. (1980) "Aggravating language: A study of abusive and insulting language". *International Journal of Human Communication* 13 (4): 607–688.

Langbein, John H. (1978) "The criminal trial before the lawyers". *University of Chicago Law Review,* 45: 263–316.

Langbein, John H. (1999) "The prosecutorial origins of defence counsel in the eighteenth century: the appearance of solicitors". *Cambridge Law Journal,* 58 (2): 314–365.

Langbein, John H. (2003) *The origins of adversary criminal trial,* Oxford: Oxford University Press.

Lakoff, Robin T. (1989) "The limits of politeness: Therapeutic and courtroom discourse", *Multilingua* 8/2–3: 101–129.

Leech, Geoffrey N. (1983) *Principles of Pragmatics,* London: Longman.

Leech, Geoffrey N. and Short, Mick (1981), *Style in Fiction.* London: Longman

Levorato, Alessandra (2009) "'From you, My Lord, Professions are but words – they are so much bait for fools to catch at': Impoliteness strategies in the 1797–1801 Act of Union pamphlet debate". In A. Jucker (ed.). *Early Modern English News Discourse.* Amsterdam/Philadelphia: John Benjamins, 159–185.

Locher, Miriam (2004) *Power and Politeness in Action. Disagreement in Oral Communication.* Berlin, New York: Mouton de Gruyter.

Locher, Miriam A. and Watts, Richard J. (2008) "Relational work and impoliteness. Negotiating norms of linguistic behaviour". In D. Bousfield and M. Locher (eds.). *Impoliteness in Language.* Berlin: Mouton de Gruyter, 77–99.

Lukes, Steven (1974) *Power. A Radical view.* London: Macmillan.

Martinez-Insua, Ana (2010) "'I desire to have more tyme to consider of it'. A pragmaphilolgical approach to refusals and refutation in Modern-English trials". In Sanna-Kaisa Tanskanen, Marija-Liisa Helasvuo, Marjut Johansson *Discourses in Interaction.* Amsterdam/Philadelphia: John Benjamins, 173–192.

Matoesian, Gregory M. (1993) *Reproducing rape. Domination through talk in the courtroom.* Chicago: Chicago University Press.

Merrit, J.F. (ed.) (1996) *The Political World of Thomas Wentworth, earl of Strafford, 1621–1641.* Cambridge: Cambridge University Press.

McHale, Brian (1978) "Free indirect discourse: a survey of recent accounts". *A Journal for Descriptive Poetics and Theory of Literature,* 3: 249–278.

Mills, Sara (2003) *Gender and Politeness.* Cambridge: Cambridge University Press.

Mills, Sara (2005) "Gender and Impoliteness". *Journal of Politeness Research* 1(2): 263–280.

Milton, Anthony (1996) "Thomas Wentoworth and the political thought of the Personal Rule". In J.F. Merritt (ed.). *The Political World of Thomas Wentworth, earl of Strafford, 1621–1641.* Cambridge: Cambridge University Press, 133–156.

Nevelainen, Terttu and Raumolin-Brunberg, Helena (2003) *Historical Sociolinguistics: language change in Tudor and Stuart England.* London: Longman.

Orr, D. Alan, (2002) *Treason and the State. Law, Politics, and Ideology in the English Civil War,* Cambridge: Cambridge University Press.

Peacey, Jason (2004) *Politicians and Pamphleteers. Propaganda during the English Civil War and Interregnum.* Aldershot: Ashgate.

Penman, Robyn (1990) "Facework and politeness: Multiple goals in courtroom discourse". In K. Tracy and N. Coupland (eds.). *Multiple Goals in Discourse.* Clevedon, PA: Multilingual Matters, 15–37.

Plucknett, Theodore Frank Thomas (1983) *Studies in English legal history.* London: Hambledon Press.

Raymond, Joad (1999) *News, Newspapers and Society in Early Modern Britain.* London: Frank Cass.

Raymond, Joad (2003) *Pamphlets and Pamphleteering in early modern Britain.* Cambridge: Cambridge University Press.

Raymond Joad (2005) *The Invention of the Newspaper: English Newsbooks, 1641–1649.* Oxford: Oxford University Press.

Rigney, Azucena C. (1999) "Questioning in interpreted testimony". *Forensic Lingusitics* 6(1): 83–108.

Rubenstein, H.L. (1975) *Captain Luckless-James, First Duke of Hamilton, 1606–1649.* Scottish Academic Press: Edinburgh.

Russell, Conrad (1965) "The Theory of Treason in the Trial of Strafford", *EHR* 80: 30–50.

Sauer, Elizabeth (2005) *'Paper Contestations' and Textual Communities in England, 1640–1675*. Toronto: University of Toronto Press.

Scally, John J. (2004) *James the first duke of Hamilton,* Oxford DNB.

Sharpe, James A. (1985) *"Last Dying Speeches": Religion, Ideology and Public Execution in seventeenth century England.* Oxford: Oxford University Press.

Spencer-Oatey, Helen (2002) "Managing rapport in talk: using rapport sensitive incidents to explore the motivational concerns underlying the management of relations". *Journal of Pragmatics* 34: 529–545.

Spencer-Oatey, Helen (2007) "Theories of identity and the analysis of face". *Journal of Pragmatics* 39: 639–656.

Stacy, W.R. (1985) "Matter of Fact, Matter of Law, and the Attainder of the Earl of Strafford", *AJLH* 29: 323–347.

Stein, Dieter (1985) "Perspectives on historical pragmatics". *Folia lingusitic historica,* 6(2): 347–355.

Stern, Simon (2002) "Between Local Knowledge and National Politics: Debating Rationales for Jury Nullification after Bushell's Case", *Yale Law Journal,* 111: 1815–1848.

Suhr, Carla (2002) "Speaking to the Masses: Orality and Literacy in Six Early Modern Texts on Witchcraft", *Helsinki English Studies* 2. <http://www.eng.helsinki.fi/projects-and-events/hes/Corpora/speaking_to_the_masses2.htm>.

Taavitsainen, Irma (1995) "Interjections in Early Modern English: From Imitation of Spoken to Conventions of Written Language". In A. Jucker (ed.). *Historical Pragmatics: Pragmatic Development in the History of English.* Amsterdam/Philadelphia: John Benjamins, 439–465.

Thompson, G. and Hunston, Susan (2001) "Evaluation: An Introduction", in S. Hunston and G. Thompson (eds.). *Evaluation in Text,* Oxford: Oxford University Press, 1–27.

Timmis III, J.H. (1978) "Evidence and 1 *Eliz. I, Cap. 6:* The Basis of the Lords' Decision in the Trial of Strafford", *HJ,* 21: 677–683.

Trevor-Roper, H.R. (1988) *Archbishop Laud, 1573–1645.* 3rd edition London: Macmillan.

Van Dijk, Teun A. (1988) *News as Discourse.* Hillsdale, NJ: Lawrence Elbaum Associates.

Vuchinich, Samuel (1990) "The sequential organization of closing in verbal family conflict". In Allen D. Grimshaw (ed.). *Conflict Talk: Sociolinguistic investigations of arguments and conversations.* Cambridge: Cambridge University Press, 118–138.

Walker, Anne G. (1987) "Lingusitic manipulation, power and the legal setting". In L. Kedar (ed.). *Power through Discourse.* Norwood, NJ: Ablex, 57–82.

Wartenberg, Thomas E. (1990) *The Forms of Power. From Domination to Transformation.* Philadelphia: Temple University Press.

Watts, Michael R. (1978) *The Dissenters: From the Reformation to the French Revolution.* Oxford: Oxford University Press.

Watts, Richard J. (1991) *Power in Family Discourse.* Berlin, New York: Mouton de Gruyter.

Watts, Richard J. (1992) "Linguistic politeness and politic verbal behaviour: reconsidering claims for universality". In R. J. Watts, Sachiko Idee and Konrad Ehlich (eds.). *Politeness in Language: Studies in its History, Theory and Practice.* Berlin, New York: Mouton de Gruyter, 43–71.

Watts, Richard J. (2003) *Politeness.* Cambridge: Cambridge University Press.

Wedgwood, Cicely V. (1961) *Thomas Wentworth First Earl of Strafford 1593–1641: A Revaluation.* London: Cape.

Weizman, Elda (1989) "Requestive hints". In S. Blum-Kulka, J. House and G. Kasper (eds.). *Interlanguage Pragmatics,* NY: Oxford University Press, 123–138.

Wigmore, John H. (1904) "The history of the hearsay rule". *Harward Law Review,* 17: 437–458.

Wilcher, Robert (2001) *The Writing of Royalism 1628–1660.* Cambridge: Cambridge University Press.

Woodbury, Hanni (1984) "The strategic use of questions in court". *Semiotica,* 48 (3/4): 197–228.

Wright, Laura (2000) "On the construction of some Early Modern English courtroom narratives". In Gabriella Di Martino and Maria Lima (eds.). *English Diachronic Pragmatics,* Naples: Cuen, 79–102.

Zaret, David (2000) *Origins of Democratic Culture: Printing, Petitions and the Public Sphere in Early-Modern England.* Princeton: Princeton University Press.

Index